I0810558

IMAGES
of America

THE VALLEY DALE BALLROOM

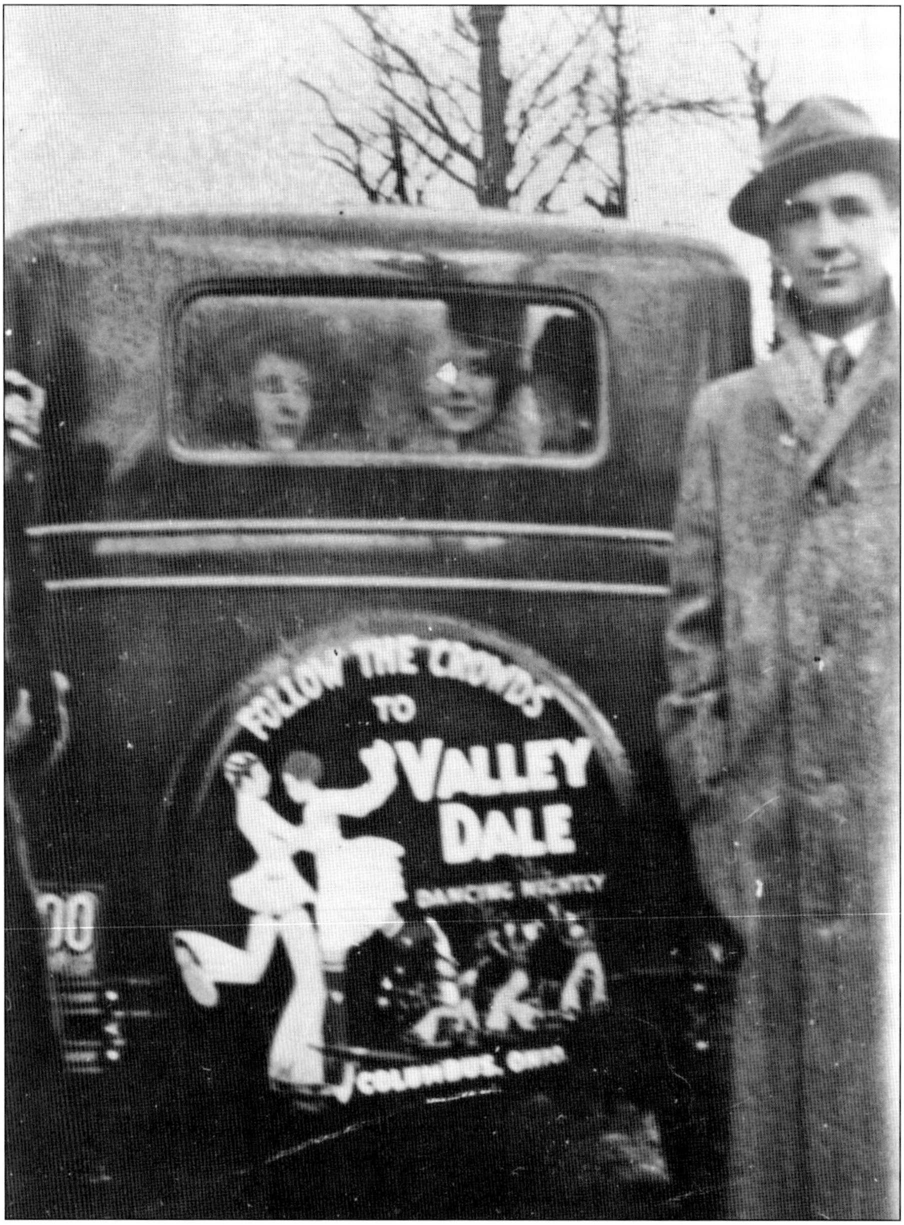

This c. 1935 Valley Dale Ballroom promotional logo invites high school kids to the "spot" to dance. From left to right are Philomena "Phyllis" Priore Davis, Josephine Peppe, and Vincent Priore, cousins and sister of Valley Dale Ballroom owners the Peppe brothers. (Valley Dale Ballroom Peppe Family Archives.)

On the Cover: The Don Crawford Band is pictured with vocalist Margie Alden Coyle in 1944. This was one of a very few 16-piece big bands in Columbus, Ohio, during the 1930s and 1940s, and it played as a favored house band at the Valley Dale Ballroom. Crawford launched the careers of multiple Columbus musicians and vocalists. Flanking the stage are rare twin booths transmitting live simultaneous radio broadcasts from Valley Dale, a keystone of the ballroom. (Valley Dale Ballroom Peppe Family Archives.)

IMAGES
of America

The Valley Dale Ballroom

Landa Masdea Brunetto
Foreword by Deana Martin

ARCADIA
PUBLISHING

ISBN 978-1-4671-2957-2

Published by Arcadia Publishing
Charleston, South Carolina

Printed in the United States of America

Library of Congress Control Number: 2018949200

For all general information, please contact Arcadia Publishing:
Telephone 843-853-2070
Fax 843-853-0044
E-mail sales@arcadiapublishing.com
For customer service and orders:
Toll-Free 1-888-313-2665

Visit us on the Internet at www.arcadiapublishing.com

To the children, grandchildren, and great-grandchildren of the musicians in this book. When I sought information, the children enthusiastically responded. I share their pride and dedication in perpetuating their loved ones' accomplishments.

Contents

Foreword

The first time I stepped onto the Valley Dale Ballroom stage was magical. I wondered what my father, Dean Martin, was feeling when he first performed there in 1936 with the Ernie McKay Band. If he could have only known what life had in store for him.

I know the incredible history of the Valley Dale Ballroom, so when Landa Masdea Brunetto asked me to write the foreword, I was honored and excited to share my memories and recollections.

After a tour of the magnificent structure, it was time for me to rehearse. I climbed the four wooden steps, entered stage left, and approached the piano. As I gazed over the enormous dance floor, a wave of emotion washed over me and took my breath away. I felt a connection to the great female singers who stood there before me, including Peggy Lee, Helen O'Connell, Lena Horn, Nancy Wilson (a Columbus girl), and my dear friend Natalie Cole. I thought about the untold thousands of people who were entertained there by the greatest orchestras and conductors from around the country, like Les Brown, who would one day conduct his Band of Renown orchestra for one of the most successful TV shows of all time, *The Dean Martin Show*.

History shows so many interesting details about the Valley Dale Ballroom, including the fact that my father and I were the only father and daughter entertainers to have performed there.

In 2016, Landa began writing this book with her father, the very talented musician Bruno Masdea. And one of my favorite memories of the Valley Dale Ballroom was singing "What Are You Doing New Year's Eve" for Bruno on that very stage. Fathers and daughters have a very special bond, and I love and respect the way Landa has honored her father.

This is a "go to" book for anyone interested in the music history of big bands and ballrooms. You will love it!

—Deana Martin

Acknowledgments

In deep appreciation to everyone who gave your remarkable support to me and the Valley Dale history project, thank you!

There could be no book without the verbal and documented chronicles from Valley Dale's royalty Mike and Kathy Peppe. This beautiful couple worked tirelessly with me through my visits, phone calls, and e-mails responding to my survey of questions on the prestigious Peppe family's 91 years of VDB history. Cousin Jim Peppe also provided valuable assistance.

With appreciation, to Piqua Public Library, Gary Meek, and Greg Herroon; Ohio History Connection; Ohio State University Library; Columbus Public Library; Wake Forest University; University of North Texas; Meadowbrook Ballroom Collections; University of Colorado, Glenn Miller Orchestra Archives, director Dennis M. Spragg and Brian Lang, GMO; a distinct thank you to Doris Day and her Animal Foundation director, Lea Price. I expressly thank Linda Deitch, archivist for the Columbus Dispatch, for working closely with me to clarify random dates and tales that surfaced while I dug deep through personal papers.

To Deana Martin, for your heartfelt writing, and to John Griffith (Deana's husband) for your support and uncovering the photograph.

Thanking my exceptional musicians: Bobby Everhart, Vaughn Wesiter, John Barnes and Larry Fox, Mark Frye and Tony Alfano, Ray Eubanks, Les Susi, John Vermulen, Chuz Alfred, Lynn Wehr, Peter Noone, Sterling Smith, and Tommy Smith. To the children of musicians: Mary Theresa Latorre Farrand, Rocky Latorre, Mimi Cummins Anderson, Phil Franck, Laurel Franck Brast, Doug Franck, Bill Selby, and Terry Beckman. Filling in the fragmented, Fabulous Forties Fable: my dedicated supporters, brothers Ron and Ken Groves. To my sister, Margi Masdea Baker, although 10 years younger, we shared this journey differently, but together.

Thanking Angel Hisnanick and Arcadia Publishing. Unless otherwise specified, all images are courtesy of VDB Peppe Family Archives.

Humble appreciation to Joe Pishitelli for pushing me to write. Thanks to friends cheering me on: Sharon Dugan, Randy Emrich, WCOL's Mike Adams, Denise Van Balen Adams, and Walter Adamkosky. A nod to my special teams: Kelly Lombardo Matthews, Judy Miller, Michael Young, and Colleen Ishler Soriotis. Photographers Graham Brannon and Larry Pishitelli, thanks for the "extras." Valuing my family's interest, especially Pat Gentile. For 25 years, the Fintas operated VDB. Thank you, Marty, for your input. Dana took Valley Dale to its renaissance.

Thanks to those who lived Valley Dale Ballroom in their youth, especially Gilda Savko, Bob Stoll, Frankie Di Cesare, Lou Nobile, and Lola Mattox. Those cherished Valley Dale Ballroom spirits that have passed on but whose flame eternally burns include Jim Peppe, Dottie and Lou Peppe, Mary Max, Richard Stants, and manager Jim Killilea, a touchstone from the 1920s to his 1970s retirement.

To Rick Brunetto, my husband, for his love, and keeping my precious big bands present in my adult life, even learning to cook after 43 married years during the intensity of this book. For our immense passion in creating unique VDB Garland and Rooney productions.

To my muses: my "Four Notesmen," Glen Gray, Benny Goodman, Tommy Dorsey, and Harry James, who were uncannily with me every step until I turned in the manuscript, then they drifted from my daily life; these real stories are a book unto themselves.

My father, musician Bruno Masdea, is followed in this book by the part his cherished Valley Dale played in his life. My sweet mother, Louise Giantonio Masdea, with her words: "My first date with daddy was at Valley Dale"—at that very moment in time, this seven-year-old miss was first charmed by the idea of Valley Dale Ballroom.

Introduction

Over a century ago, the placeholder for the now-beloved Valley Dale Ballroom started as a necessary stagecoach stop during the 1800s serving routes between Columbus and Sunbury, Ohio. Farmers would stop at the tollgate, positioned at the current gates of Ohio Dominican College, as they entered Columbus to sell their produce, primarily at Central Market on Rich and Fourth Streets.

Down the path from the tollgate, a tavern was built as a respite for a lengthy journey. An overnight lodge was attached to the tavern some while later for exhausted farmers hauling their produce, mostly by wagon, to sell all day at market. The inn attracted travelers for a 50-mile radius arriving in Columbus to sell or purchase provisions. Later still, a dance hall was erected, providing entertainment for commuters and locals.

Articles in the *Columbus Dispatch* from 1930 to 1933 state concise information for the birth of the Valley Dale Ballroom (VDB). Initially named Natchez Under the Hill, a roadhouse was built on the VDB location in 1883, with the first land title recorded in 1879. The first orchestra consisted of a banjo, a fiddle, and a guitar simply playing country and bluegrass music for its imbibing patrons. Just think the first music on the site of VDB was for square dancing. The Natchez saloon is believed to have stood since the mid-1800s, and it was demolished in 1895. A more massive dance hall stood between 1895 and 1918. Jules and Marie Melancon and Clem and Grace Melancon were back to back owners of the Valley Dale Company from 1919 to 1927. The entertainment lodge now revamped with a massive dance hall added sometime between 1919 and 1921. Harold Elford of Valley Dale Company assisted in building and running the new structure. The Peppe family's written archives present the opening year as 1918. According to an article about the 1923 New Year's Eve blaze, the fire happened "on a five-year-old building," which presents the opening date as possibly 1919. Harkening, an official opening date for "Valley Dale Hall" was published as October 21, 1922; that *Columbus Dispatch* article is the first time the Valley Dale name is presented.

According to this timeline, its second New Year's Eve witnessed an unusual firework display. Employee and later manager James Killilea lived only three miles away from Valley Dale from 1925 until his 1980 retirement. Killilea was the eyes, ears, and heartbeat of Valley Dale during that time, and his collected interviews provide a history of VDB.

On December 31, 1923, members of VDB's first house band, Robert Royce's Collegians, set up their band fronts, music, and instruments in preparation for a grand evening. Clement Alspach, a trombonist in the band, came in early to practice alone before the jubilant crowd arrived. Folktales relate how James Killilea's older brother attempted to warm the habitually chilly building by overstocking the wood-burning furnace. As instrumentalist Alspach steered into the parking lot at 8:00 p.m. on New Year's Eve, he was stunned to see the five-year-old building in flames—the overloaded furnace raged into an inferno. With the VDB being, at that time, out in the country, the only thing to do was to watch the wooden edifice dissolve into a pile of smoldering embers as it burned to the ground. The only possessions found in the New Year's Day light were the liquefied metals of trumpets and trombones. This spellbinding retelling has survived nine decades.

Reading the actual written accounts from musician Clement Alspach, oral history passed down over four generations, and the writings of VDB caretaker Jim Killilea left this author yearning for clarification. The January 6, 1924, Sunday edition of the *Columbus Dispatch* headlined this tragedy, stating that the so-called New Year's Eve Fire actually took place on Saturday night, January 5. The spectacular blaze also resulted in the greatest amount of damage on the night, occurring shortly after 6:00 p.m. With temperatures below 12 degrees, the Columbus Fire Department was powerless due to 23 other calls within the city limits, hindering a run to the outskirts of Sunbury Pike, where there was no water supply in reach of the blazing structure. The Saturday event could have been considered a New Year's Eve dance, since the holiday was on Monday that week, but no one will ever know for sure why this was labeled the New Year's Eve Fire.

On the day of the fire, Jules Melancon was looking over his accounts in the front office. Charles Gordon, a youth working in the building, became startled, believing the fire was chasing him. Gordon managed to scramble up the cellar stairs with flames leaping at his heels; he escaped slightly before Melancon. Later, it was understood that Gordon had over-stoked the furnace to make sure the pipes would not freeze. The hot furnace pipes next to pinewood caused sap to seep out of the wood and thus started the fire.

Melancon found himself completely hemmed in by disaster, nearly risking his life to escape the doomed building: "I was surrounded by fire, in making my way to the door I was nearly overcome by the dense smoke. The only thing that saved me, I knew the exact position of the nearest exit."

Melancon placed the destruction at $32,000, including updates finished the week before. Less than 50 percent of the loss was covered by insurance. This fire swept the dance hall, leveling it to the ground within 30 minutes. The orchestra's instruments and the brand-new grand piano were also destroyed in the fire.

According to the written journal Jim Killilea kept between 1930 and 1980, his older brother was responsible for the fire; the presence of a person named Charlie Gordon identified in the 1924 newspaper did not tally, so the author casually asked the Peppe family if they knew anything about a Charlie Gordon or if they knew Killilea's brother's first name. They responded "It was Charlie!"—the author suspects that Charlie Gordon chose his middle name as his last name to save embarrassment for his family.

Valley Dale Company was sold out to The Metro Amusement Company in 1927. Southern Ohio coal miner Tom Lawson was Metro's structural engineer enhancing and enlarging the Valley Dale from 1927 through 1934 bringing it to what we know as VDB today. During his employment, Lawson also hired local bands to play VDB on weekends. Jim Peppe was employed by Valley Dale beginning in 1925 first as a band leader.

The Metro Amusement Company feted a riveting eighth Valley Dale anniversary in 1933. It also named employee Jim Peppe manager. A one-week-long anniversary celebration welcomed permanent changes, including an increase from three nights a week to nightly dancing with notable musicians. Dick Fiedler's NBC band was the first orchestra to play an anniversary, an upgrade from past local groups. Jim Peppe promised that "The policy of bringing the best orchestras to the city will continue." The Casa Loma band was next in line. Valley Dale admitted only couples, stating that it was a dancing pavilion, and someone without a partner need not be present. Peppe refused to introduce the latest beer, observing that alcohol also was not needed at "VDHall." Peppe's motto was "No beer, but better bands."

There are so many articles during this decade about Jim Peppe, it was surprising to this author how an employee could garner so much publicity. During one of many sporadic 2018 questioning sessions of Jim Peppe's son, it emerged that the Metro Amusement owner was actually Jim Peppe. It would not be surprising that at that time in our history an Italian would not use their name on a business front, but would develop a commerce name and put that forth for the public recognition. It has never been verified if Jim Peppe started Metro in 1927, or if he purchased the business sometime before 1933 when he became the VDB manager, then bringing in his brothers. In 1938, Jim's brother Lou Peppe purchased the VDB.

The roaring 1920s, with its fringed flapper and her boyfriend sporting knickerbocker pants, were dwindling, Prohibition was repealed, and hot jazz ensembles were dissolving into elegant orchestras coupled with passionate melodic writings. Unheard of innovative music and its instrumentalists emerged as a force that revolutionized generations of music to follow. A startling poised fresh musical onset crushed the singsong tunes of the past and flourished the musicality and its newly recognized phrase, "Follow the Crowds to Valley Dale."

After World War II, the Valley Dale was transformed. It was no longer the nightly spot for music and dancing it once was. Those high schoolers of the 1940s grew up, attending college, getting married, and working or joining the service. When they returned to their world on Sunbury Road, they found that it too had matured. Where once seven evenings a week saw two to three big bands a night, there were now merely two nights with barely two bands each month. The big band era had waned: the cost to take bands on the road—musicians, hotel, and food—soared, and gasoline rationing and the destructive musicians' strike of 1942 to 1944 contributed to the greatest music decline in history. But the Valley Dale had to survive, and local musicians did keep "the Dale" alive as they created new bands to resuscitate a newer era of music.

As a little girl during the 1950s, on most weekends, the author unknowingly glimpsed that fabulous big band era: after his workday at Livingston Avenue's Seymour Bakery, her father immersed himself into preparation for the weekend band performances. Practicing his trumpet was a daily occurrence. He would select the numbers (bands numbered their instrumental charts when calling a tune). Gig day brought trumpet preparation and packing the music charts and carbon-paper, hand-typed setlists. Then he trimmed his shirt with a unique tie worn only with his band jacket or a bow tie with his tuxedo. Lastly, he fastidiously folded his jacket—he never wore his band jacket anywhere but onstage, keeping it pristine for the performance.

That was the author's commencement in music—other fathers played golf on the weekends, hers had a band. Music was as much part of her home as a Georgian coffee table was in another's. Her mother played albums all day while the author used to curl up to read every album cover; her favorite was Julie London's. The author was subtly schooled about the musicians: Harry James, Glenn Miller; the bands: Les Brown, Kenton, and Herman; the tunes: "Moonlight Serenade;" the lyrics: "Boogie Blues;" and the vocalists: Sinatra, Martin, and her mom's favorite, Eydie Gormé. In the 1960s, as she got a little older, her father would point out phrasings for her to listen to, always asking "How could you like those ugly Beatle-heads, you know better." True, she was plagued by Beatlemania growing up, but overall, the author cherished those big bands, their leaders, and their sidemen as if they were family residing in different states.

The British Invasion dismantled the mainstream easy-listening genre, further pushing the big bands to become enveloped by the personas of vocalists. Eighteen-piece-plus big bands evolved to smaller rock groups. Valley Dale turned from Saturday evening nostalgic dancing to Sunday afternoon sock-hops. And Valley Dale's teenagers returned, now with silky straight haircuts, foreheads covered with bangs, bell-bottoms, and brashness; 1960s rock found its home.

While melodies and harmonies were transforming, the ballroom was less for dancing and more for weddings, charities, pageants, and trade shows. In the 1950s and 1960s, the Chuck Selby Orchestra was the keeper of the passage of time at VDB. In 1970, a new band refreshed VDB: 18 musicians with a male and female vocalist and also a quartet, the Fabulous Forties was the original new big band in Columbus. The Dale was swinging again. Valley Dale suffered through its ups and downs, and it was condemned by the City of Columbus, but its seasoned teenagers marched in to "Save Valley Dale." By the early 1980s, the bands of the 1930s and 1940s—James, Miller, Kenton, Ellington, Basie, Lombardo, Herman, and others—returned to VDB, several with their iconic leaders. When asked if the swing era would ever return, Artie Shaw responded, "Will the 1938 Ford ever come back?" Respectfully, Mr. Shaw, there is a 1938 Ford sitting in the parking lot of the 2018 Valley Dale.

With additional exciting presentations such as Alice Cooper, Peter Noone, Natalie Cole, Buster Douglas, the 2011 beginning of the Holiday Show Series, the Deana Martin Christmas Shows, Lucinda Williams, and the Ballroom Breakout Concert Series, the Valley Dale found its place in the modern age.

There are forever teenagers woven through these pages. Promotions director Mary Max Stants and her husband, Richard, both North High School alumni, presented a timeless quote for the Clintonville *Booster* on March 22, 1982: "Valley Dale is truly a Columbus heritage. I am thrilled that it will continue to be there for future generations of dancers."

One

Once upon a Stagecoach

Where the Valley Dale stands today, Natchez under the Hill was a tavern named after a questionable Mississippi port that once welcomed steamboats, paddleboats, rough sea captains, and ghosts had an earthquake altering the mighty Mississippi River configuration. Possibly because of the continual flooding of nearby Alum Creek and the area being a toll road, the owners may have found it interesting to select such a dubious name for the tavern. This chapter presents events and artists appearing at Valley Dale Hall before the Peppe family took over operations in the late 1920s.

Rebuilt, restructured, and redesigned after its January 5, 1924, fire, VDB blossomed for its inaugural summer season opening on Saturday, June 7, 1924. An outdoor dancefloor was uncommon at the time as indoor plumbing. With layered geometric fencing and lattice work and an incredible handcrafted band shell displaying the fresh design style of Art Deco. The Valley Dale took on enterprising panache that was remarked and marveled over throughout Columbus. It became a must-see wonder, having carloads of dancers flocking to VDB to spend the evening dancing on the dual option of indoor and outdoor dance floors.

The question is always asked, "Where did the name Valley Dale come from?" In the 1920s, the Valley Dale had its own section within the regular *Columbus Citizen Journal*. The section would give highlights about the building, its entertainers, its management, and later the Peppe family happenings. In one such section, Jules Melancon, the owner before the Peppes (1919–1927) described how he heard of a first-born daughter given the glorious name Valley Dale, and he decided to borrow her name and christen the dance palace Valley Dale Hall.

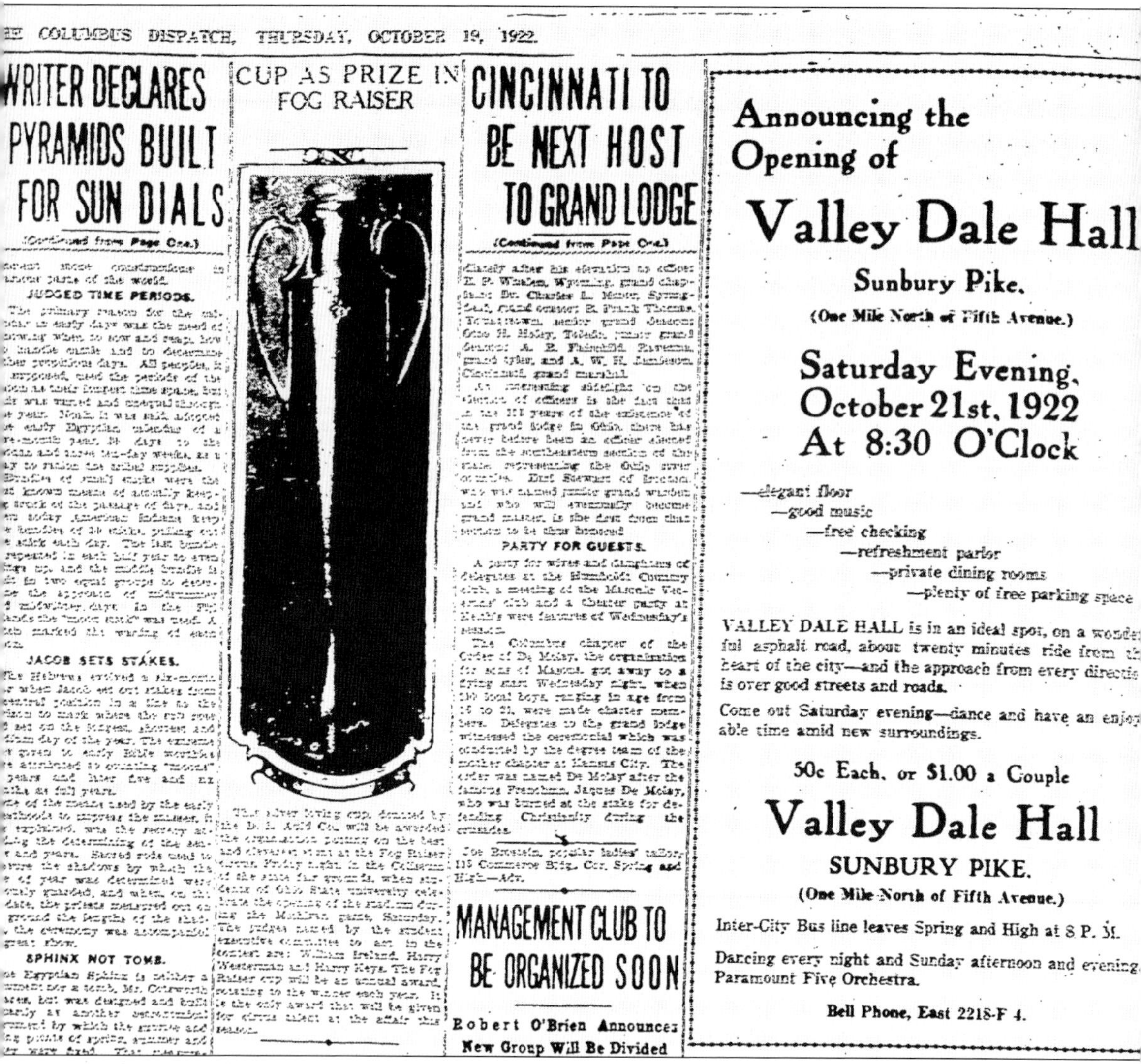
THE COLUMBUS DISPATCH, THURSDAY, OCTOBER 19, 1922.

WRITER DECLARES PYRAMIDS BUILT FOR SUN DIALS

(Continued from Page One.)

JUDGED TIME PERIODS.

JACOB SETS STAKES.

SPHINX NOT TOMB.

CUP AS PRIZE IN FOG RAISER

CINCINNATI TO BE NEXT HOST TO GRAND LODGE

(Continued from Page One.)

PARTY FOR GUESTS.

MANAGEMENT CLUB TO BE ORGANIZED SOON

Robert O'Brien Announces New Group Will Be Divided

Announcing the Opening of

Valley Dale Hall

Sunbury Pike.

(One Mile North of Fifth Avenue.)

Saturday Evening,
October 21st, 1922
At 8:30 O'Clock

—elegant floor
—good music
—free checking
—refreshment parlor
—private dining rooms
—plenty of free parking space

VALLEY DALE HALL is in an ideal spot, on a wonderful asphalt road, about twenty minutes ride from the heart of the city—and the approach from every direction is over good streets and roads.

Come out Saturday evening—dance and have an enjoyable time amid new surroundings.

50c Each, or $1.00 a Couple

Valley Dale Hall

SUNBURY PIKE.

(One Mile North of Fifth Avenue.)

Inter-City Bus line leaves Spring and High at 8 P. M.

Dancing every night and Sunday afternoon and evening. Paramount Five Orchestra.

Bell Phone, East 2218-F 4.

This 1922 advertisement carries the most power to sway the argument of the actual opening date of VDB. Most communication indicating the opening date has been verbally passed down or handwritten from individuals employed at VDB. A print ad shows the first evidence of an actual opening date of what was first labeled Valley Dale Hall under the ownership of Jules Melancon and Valley Dale Company. Other articles about the fire of 1924 state that the building was five years old when the fire occurred, bringing VDB's beginning date to 1919, not 1918 as has been reported for several decades.

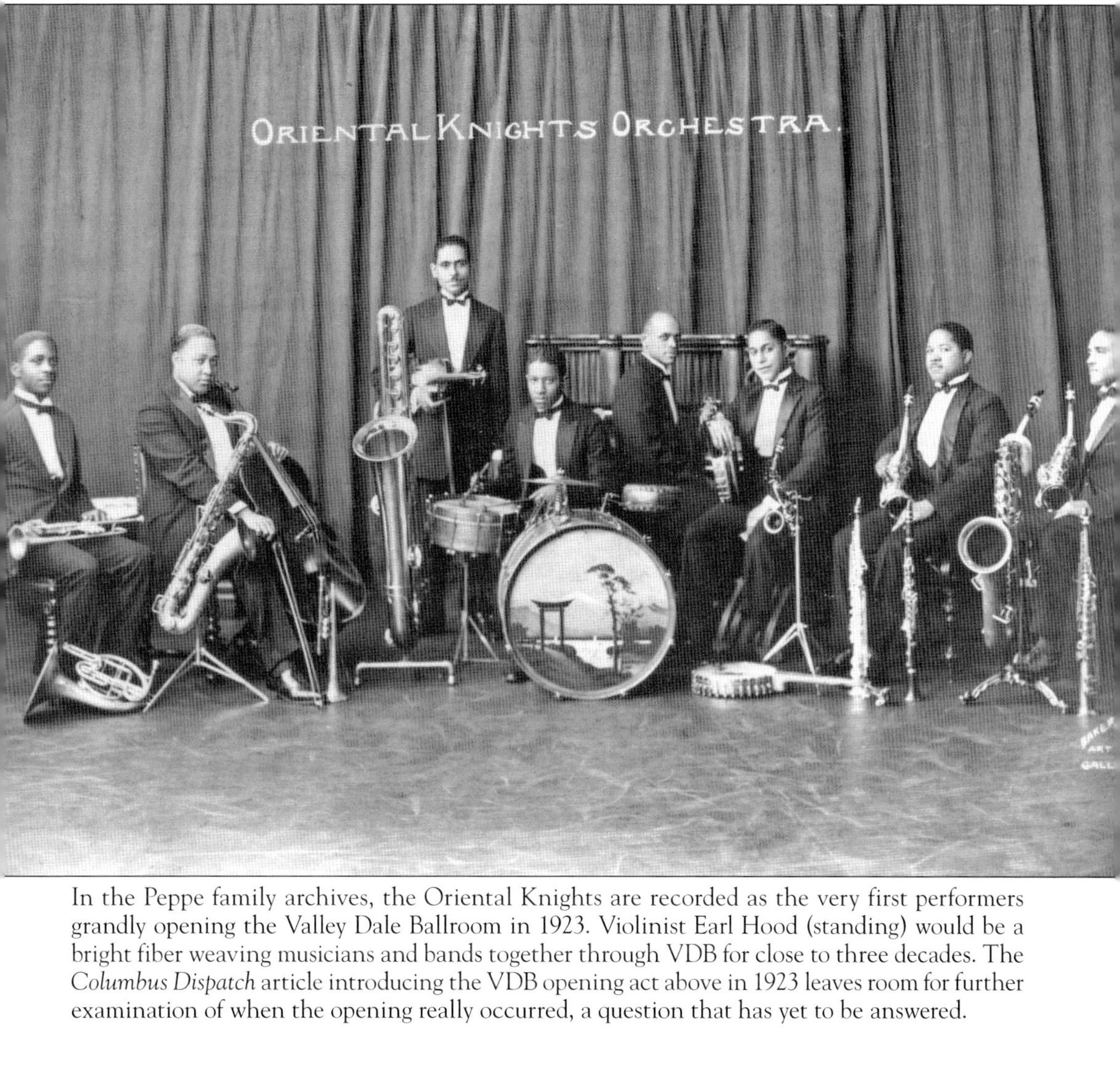

In the Peppe family archives, the Oriental Knights are recorded as the very first performers grandly opening the Valley Dale Ballroom in 1923. Violinist Earl Hood (standing) would be a bright fiber weaving musicians and bands together through VDB for close to three decades. The *Columbus Dispatch* article introducing the VDB opening act above in 1923 leaves room for further examination of when the opening really occurred, a question that has yet to be answered.

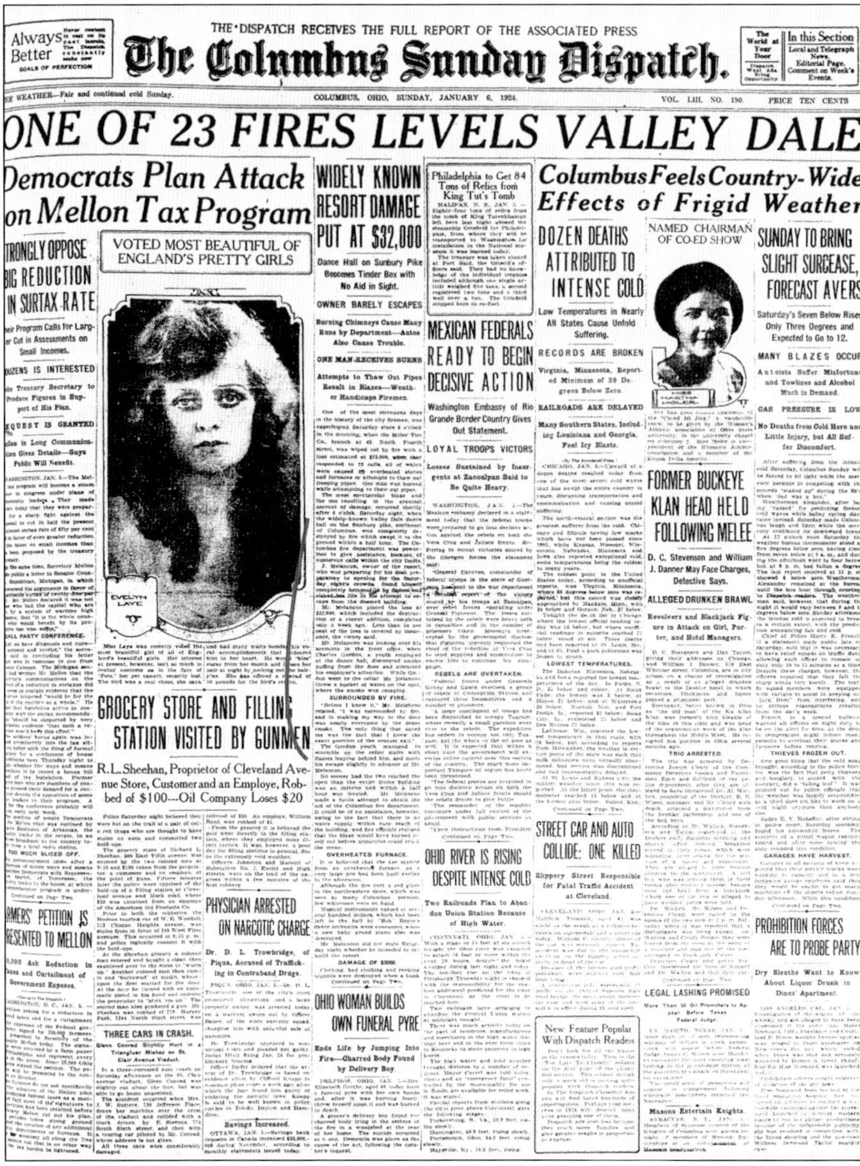
THE·DISPATCH RECEIVES THE FULL REPORT OF THE ASSOCIATED PRESS

The Columbus Sunday Dispatch.

COLUMBUS, OHIO, SUNDAY, JANUARY 6, 1924. VOL. LIII. NO. 190. PRICE TEN CENTS

ONE OF 23 FIRES LEVELS VALLEY DALE

Democrats Plan Attack on Mellon Tax Program

STRONGLY OPPOSE BIG REDUCTION IN SURTAX RATE

VOTED MOST BEAUTIFUL OF ENGLAND'S PRETTY GIRLS

WIDELY KNOWN RESORT DAMAGE PUT AT $32,000

Dance Hall on Sunbury Pike Becomes Tinder Box with No Aid in Sight.

OWNER BARELY ESCAPES

Philadelphia to Get 84 Tons of Relics from King Tut's Tomb

MEXICAN FEDERALS READY TO BEGIN DECISIVE ACTION

Columbus Feels Country-Wide Effects of Frigid Weather

DOZEN DEATHS ATTRIBUTED TO INTENSE COLD

NAMED CHAIRMAN OF CO-ED SHOW

SUNDAY TO BRING SLIGHT SURCEASE, FORECAST AVERS

FORMER BUCKEYE KLAN HEAD HELD FOLLOWING MELEE

GROCERY STORE AND FILLING STATION VISITED BY GUNMEN

R.L. Sheehan, Proprietor of Cleveland Avenue Store, Customer and an Employe, Robbed of $100---Oil Company Loses $20

FARMERS' PETITION IS PRESENTED TO MELLON

THREE CARS IN CRASH.

PHYSICIAN ARRESTED ON NARCOTIC CHARGE

OHIO WOMAN BUILDS OWN FUNERAL PYRE

OHIO RIVER IS RISING DESPITE INTENSE COLD

STREET CAR AND AUTO COLLIDE; ONE KILLED

PROHIBITION FORCES ARE TO PROBE PARTY

LEGAL LASHING PROMISED

New Feature Popular With Dispatch Readers

The most spectacular blaze of the evening of Saturday, January 5, 1924, also resulted in the greatest amount of damage that night, occurring shortly after 6:00 p.m. With temperatures below 12 degrees, the Columbus Fire Department was powerless due to 23 other calls within the city limits, hindering a run to the outskirts of Sunbury Pike, where there was no water supply in reach of the blazing structure. It is rumored this could have been a New Year's Eve dance, because the holiday was on Monday that week, but no one will ever know for sure why this fire was labeled the New Year's Eve Fire. Rebuilt, restructured, and redesigned after the January 5, 1924 fire, VDB blossomed for its summer opening on Saturday, June 7, 1924. After a construction investment of more than $18,000, VDB was enhanced with two dance pavilions, one outside and one inside, and a dramatic observation balcony of 2,000 square feet overlooking the interior dancefloor. The balcony required a 10¢ admission, while the areas for dancing inside and outside charged 35¢. In the reporting, it is casually mentioned that a war tax was included in each ticket price. A 600-table seating capacity was also developed.

Not every big band was a smash success when playing the Valley Dale: "Guy Lombardo and his band of Royal Canadians were a bad drawing card first time they played Valley Dale," recalled Tom Lawson, the builder of VDB in 1925, at 91 years of age in a 1967 *Columbus Dispatch* article written by Johnny Jones. "Second time I played Guy, I had to pay him $5000.00. He certainly was a draw in the 1920's." The Lombardo band began in 1924; it appears that Guy played for the first time after the 1925 expansion and restructuring of the VDB, then played for the second time at a much greater fee around 1927. Today's equivalent for that second gig would be $71,942.53.

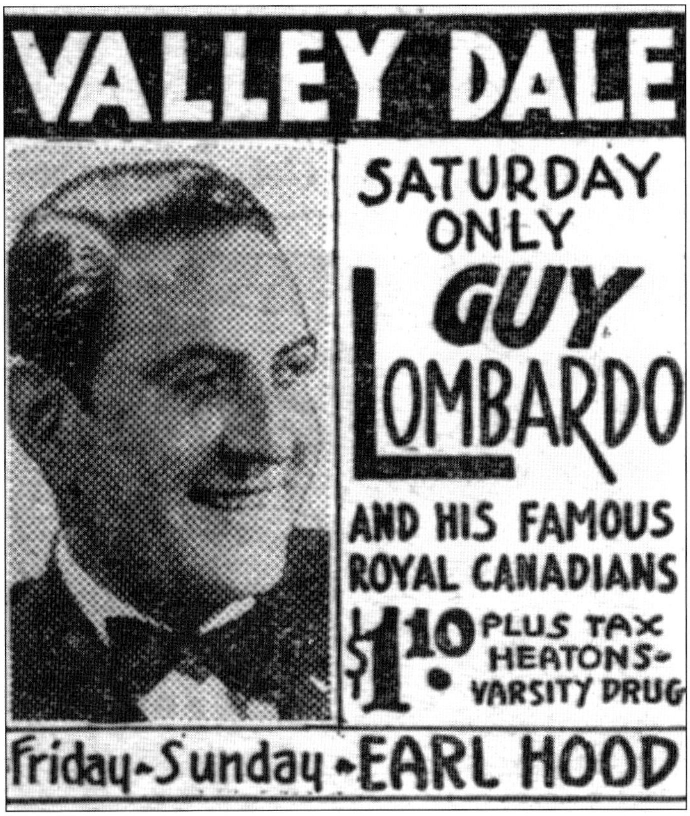

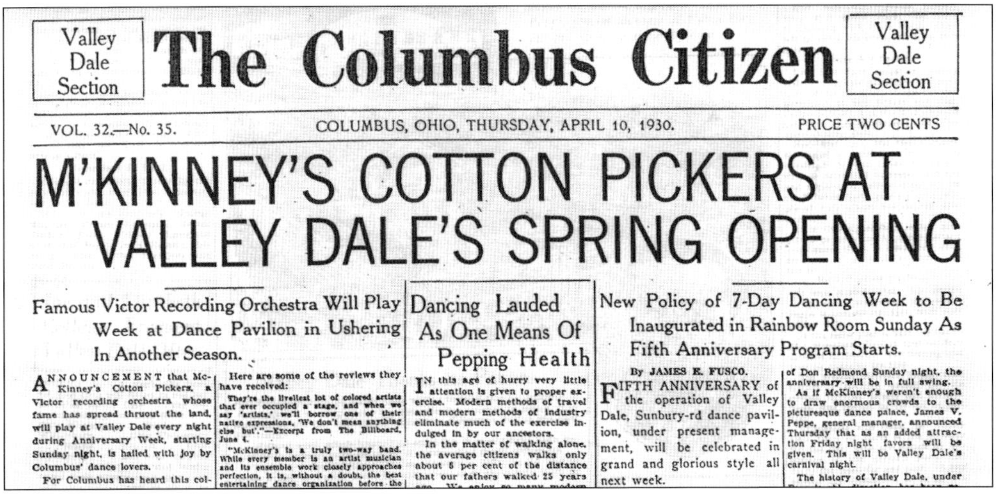

Valley Dale Section | **The Columbus Citizen** | Valley Dale Section

VOL. 32.—No. 35. COLUMBUS, OHIO, THURSDAY, APRIL 10, 1930. PRICE TWO CENTS

M'KINNEY'S COTTON PICKERS AT VALLEY DALE'S SPRING OPENING

Famous Victor Recording Orchestra Will Play Week at Dance Pavilion in Ushering In Another Season.

ANNOUNCEMENT that McKinney's Cotton Pickers, a Victor recording orchestra whose fame has spread thruout the land, will play at Valley Dale every night during Anniversary Week, starting Sunday night, is hailed with joy by Columbus' dance lovers.

For Columbus has heard this col-

Here are some of the reviews they have received:

They're the liveliest lot of colored artists that ever occupied a stage, and when we say 'artists,' we'll borrow one of their native expressions, 'We don't mean anything else but'."—Excerpt from The Billboard, June 4.

"McKinney's is a truly two-way band. While every member is an artist musician and its ensemble work closely approaches perfection, it is, without a doubt, the best entertaining dance organization before the

Dancing Lauded As One Means Of Pepping Health

IN this age of hurry very little attention is given to proper exercise. Modern methods of travel and modern methods of industry eliminate much of the exercise indulged in by our ancestors.

In the matter of walking alone, the average citizens walks only about 5 per cent of the distance that our fathers walked 25 years

New Policy of 7-Day Dancing Week to Be Inaugurated in Rainbow Room Sunday As Fifth Anniversary Program Starts.

By JAMES E. FUSCO.

FIFTH ANNIVERSARY of the operation of Valley Dale, Sunbury-rd dance pavilion, under present management, will be celebrated in grand and glorious style all next week.

of Don Redmond Sunday night, the anniversary will be in full swing.

As if McKinney's weren't enough to draw enormous crowds to the picturesque dance palace, James V. Peppe, general manager, announced Thursday that as an added attraction Friday night favors will be given. This will be Valley Dale's carnival night.

The history of Valley Dale, under

McKinney's Cotton Pickers played Valley Dale continually between 1925 and 1934. France native Jean Goldkette adopted Detroit as his home, where he put together an ensemble for the Graystone Ballroom. Goldkette also added musicians from Springfield, Ohio, making up an ensemble of soon-to-be-distinct powerhouse founders of jazz, bebop, and beyond, including Benny Carter, Coleman Hawkins, Rex Stewart, Fats Waller, Claude Jones, Quentin Jackson, Hilton Jefferson, and Don Redman. Redman was the group's front man, while Bill McKinney was the business manager and lent his name to the group for a twist of alliteration. McKinney's Cotton Pickers return to VDB multiple times through the 1980s under the direction of local musician Chuz Alfred.

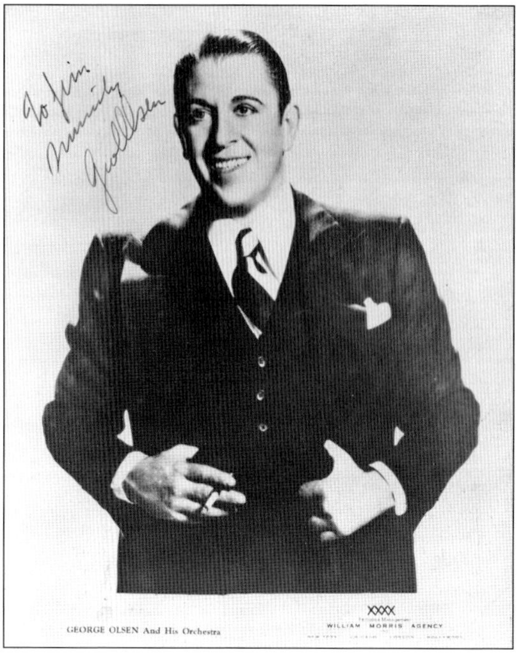

George Olsen's band, considered number one in 1926, exuded joy and entertainment. Olsen handled his band similar to a marching band director, adding abundant choreographed moves for every song. As the band played, he had them sit, stand, spin, and march in place with startling gyrations aimed to wow the crowd. He autographed this photograph to Jim Peppe.

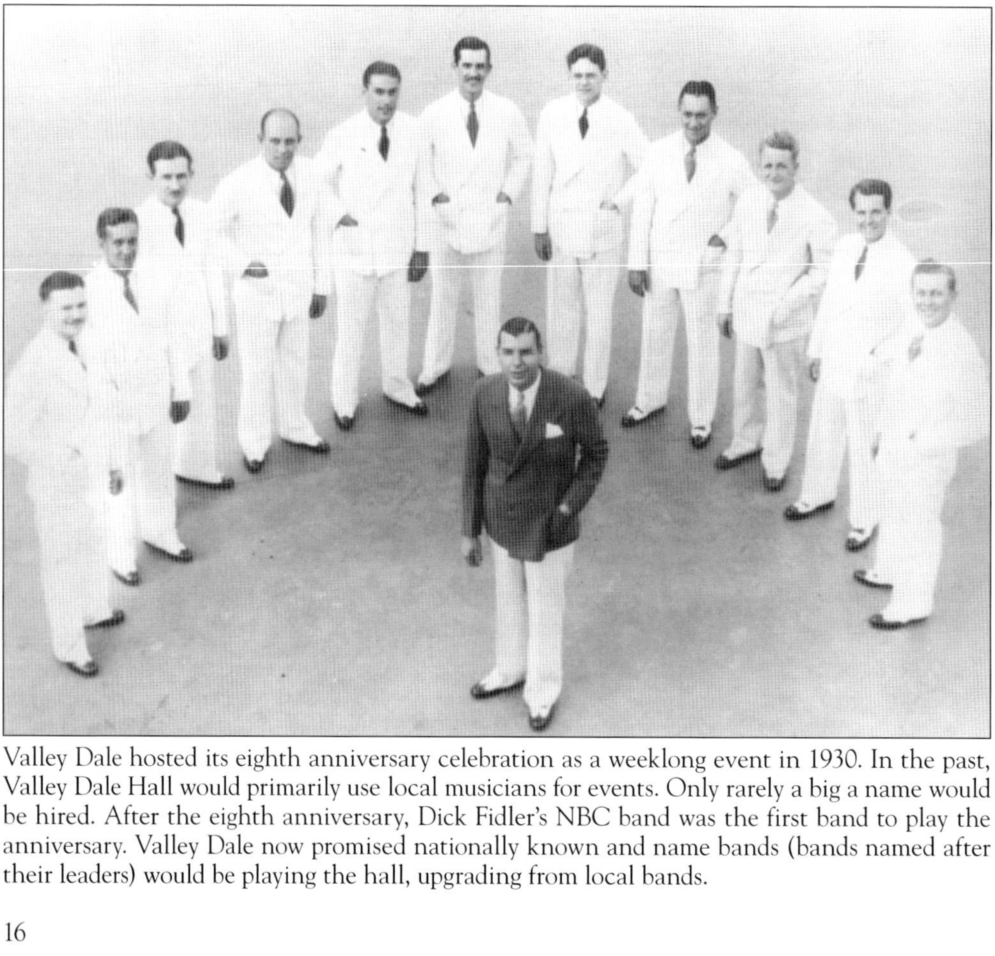

Valley Dale hosted its eighth anniversary celebration as a weeklong event in 1930. In the past, Valley Dale Hall would primarily use local musicians for events. Only rarely a big a name would be hired. After the eighth anniversary, Dick Fidler's NBC band was the first band to play the anniversary. Valley Dale now promised nationally known and name bands (bands named after their leaders) would be playing the hall, upgrading from local bands.

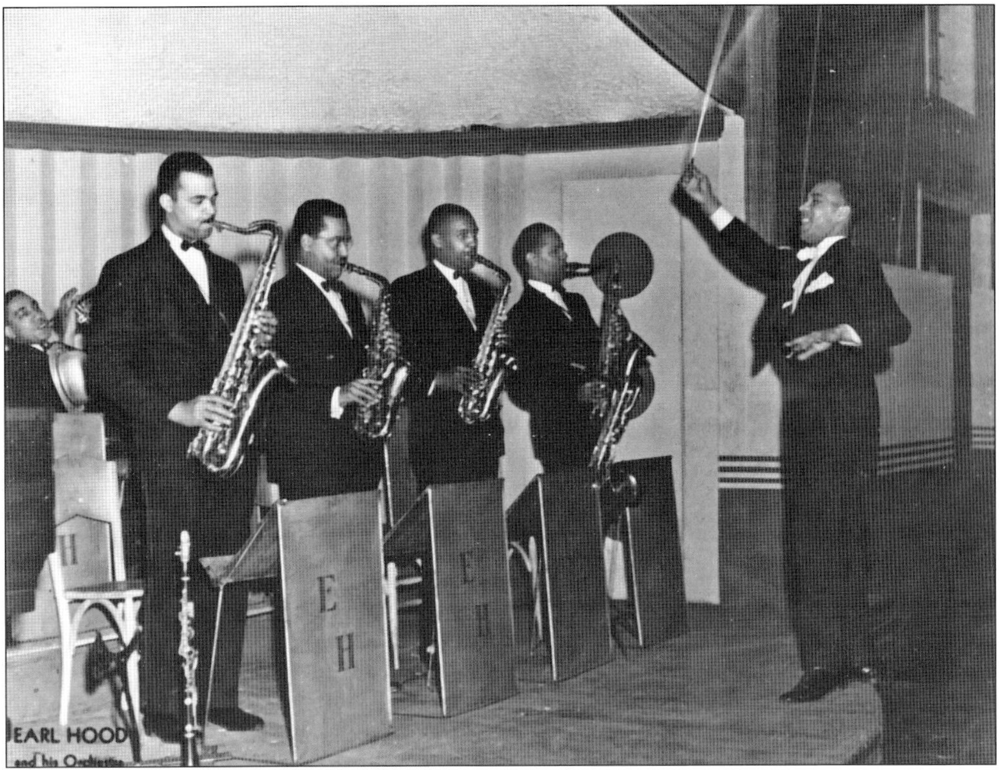

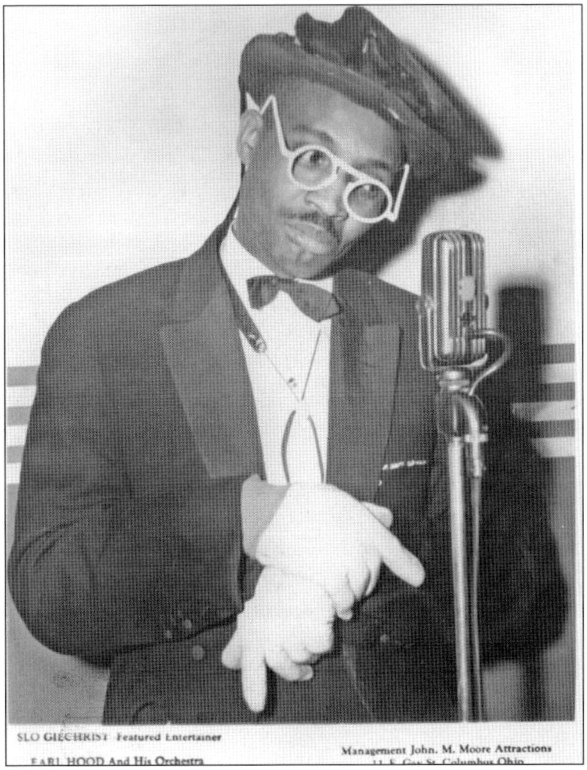

Before the Peppes owned VDB, Earl Hood was a local musician playing in the first band to ever play the VDB (The Oriental Knights). His first instrument was a violin. He was the first to bring The McKinney's Cotton Pickers to VDB in the 1930s. Hood's ensemble was the first house band at Valley Dale from 1938 to 1951. Discovering iconic trumpeter Harry "Sweets" Edison and insuring his ability to read music was also among Hood's firsts. In this photograph, talented Hood is playing his second instrument, the baritone saxophone.

Slo Gilchrist played a smooth saxophone in Earl Hood's Orchestra, but while the band was on breaks, he became a zany wisecracking solo comedian, entertaining the dance crowd from on stage.

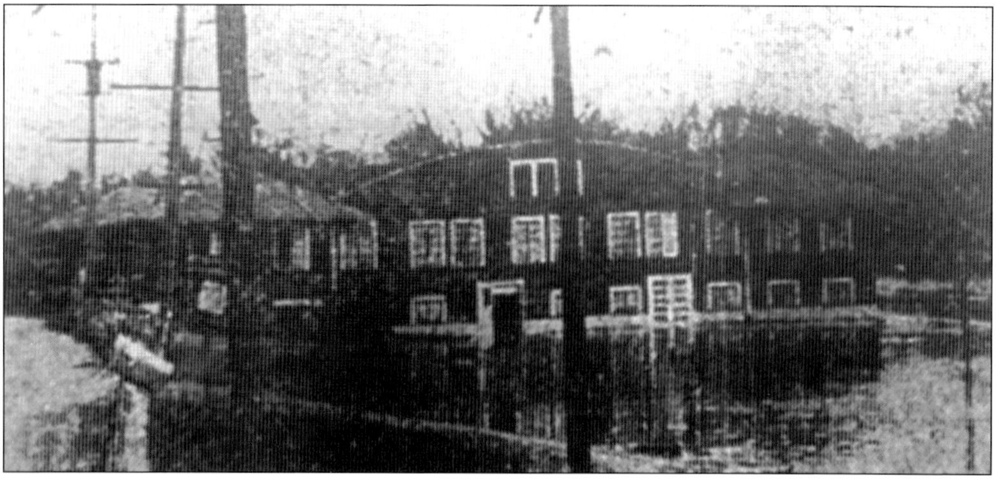

When the nearby creek flooded in 1927, it devastated the Valley Dale. There would be one additional destructive flood in Valley Dale history. There are ample windows in this photograph, not present in later years. For a short time, the front of the building was its main entrance. Later, the main entry would be at the side of the building. Patrons ascended 30 steps to reach the grand covered entryway. The flood occurred on December 2, 1927, and VDB reopened with a splashy ad for December 9, 1927. (*Ohio State Journal.*)

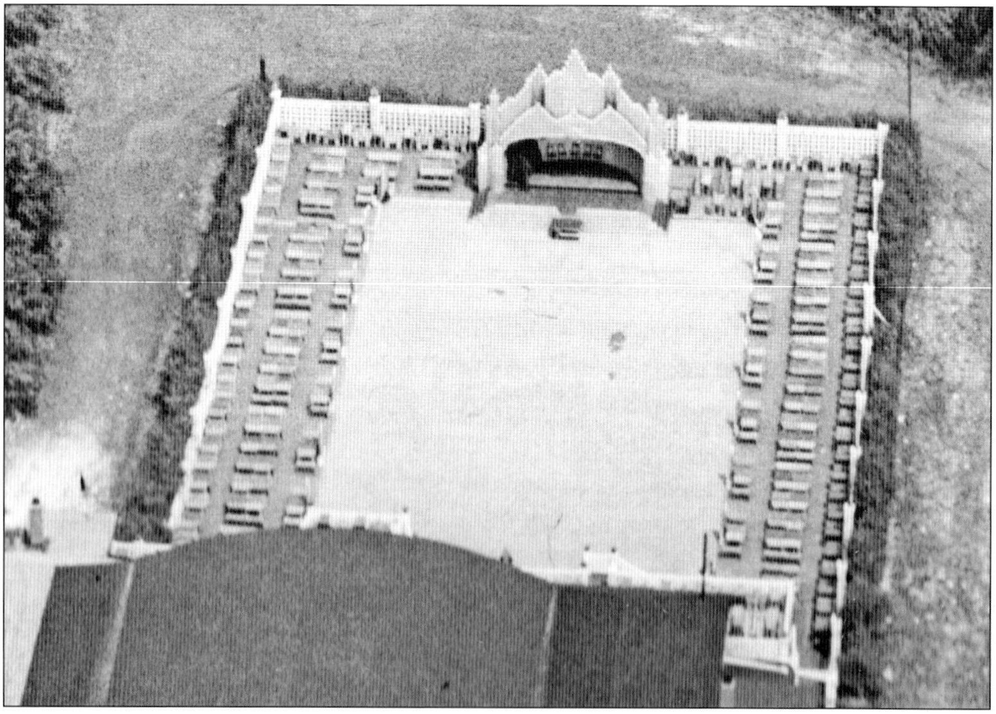

In 1929, Rudy Vallee broke the admission record at Valley Dale. He was the first performer needing a police escort at VDB; as the *Citizen Journal* reported, "The girls tore the buttons right off his coat, (like they might have done for Elvis, the Beatles, or Michael Jackson)." This is the space Rudy and the Lombardo Band played in the early days at VDB. The *Citizen Journal* noted that "Rudy, thought it was the finest crowd he had ever performed to, playing until almost dawn." (*Columbus Citizen Journal.*)

The ad from the *Citizen Journal* in 1930 features Paul Whiteman. Whiteman was also a powerhouse as a musician, braiding symphonic overtures with jazz, such has George Gershwin's "Rhapsody in Blue." Whiteman understood jazz; in the 1920s, he was writing books on the topic. When Ed McMahon passed, the author purchased a collection of his books, many of those books were on big bands, one such title was Whiteman's introductory book on jazz studies. Whiteman played VDB, but there has been no proof to date that Gershwin was with him.

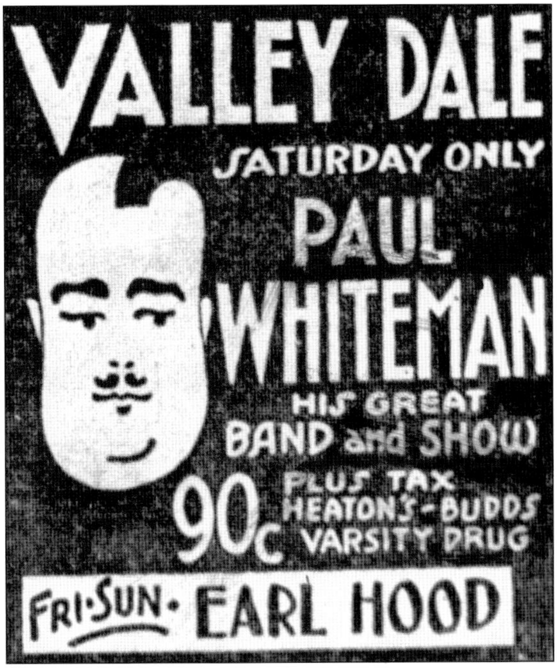

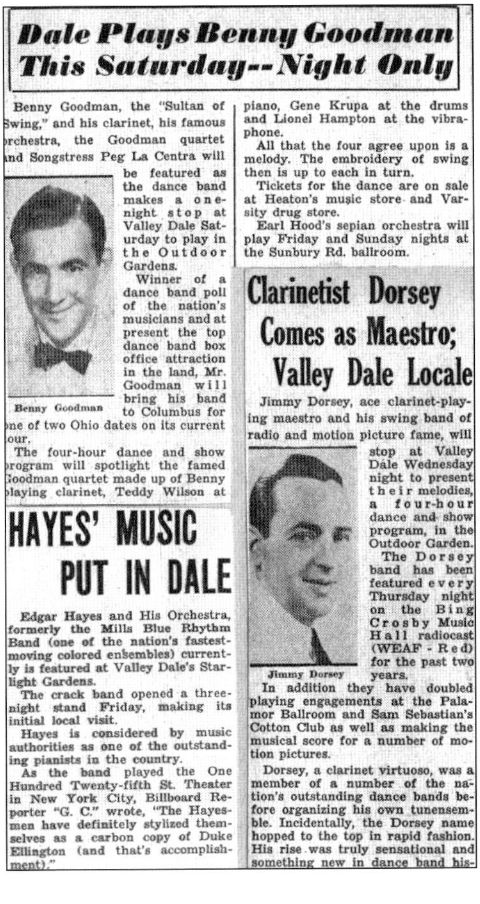

Dale Plays Benny Goodman This Saturday--Night Only

Benny Goodman, the "Sultan of Swing," and his clarinet, his famous orchestra, the Goodman quartet and Songstress Peg La Centra will be featured as the dance band makes a one-night stop at Valley Dale Saturday to play in the Outdoor Gardens.

Benny Goodman

Winner of a dance band poll of the nation's musicians and at present the top dance band box office attraction in the land, Mr. Goodman will bring his band to Columbus for one of two Ohio dates on its current tour.

The four-hour dance and show program will spotlight the famed Goodman quartet made up of Benny playing clarinet, Teddy Wilson at piano, Gene Krupa at the drums and Lionel Hampton at the vibraphone.

All that the four agree upon is a melody. The embroidery of swing then is up to each in turn.

Tickets for the dance are on sale at Heaton's music store and Varsity drug store.

Earl Hood's sepian orchestra will play Friday and Sunday nights at the Sunbury Rd. ballroom.

HAYES' MUSIC PUT IN DALE

Edgar Hayes and His Orchestra, formerly the Mills Blue Rhythm Band (one of the nation's fastest-moving colored ensembles) currently is featured at Valley Dale's Starlight Gardens.

The crack band opened a three-night stand Friday, making its initial local visit.

Hayes is considered by music authorities as one of the outstanding pianists in the country.

As the band played the One Hundred Twenty-fifth St. Theater in New York City, Billboard Reporter "G. C." wrote, "The Hayesmen have definitely stylized themselves as a carbon copy of Duke Ellington (and that's accomplishment)."

Clarinetist Dorsey Comes as Maestro; Valley Dale Locale

Jimmy Dorsey, ace clarinet-playing maestro and his swing band of radio and motion picture fame, will stop at Valley Dale Wednesday night to present their melodies, a four-hour dance and show program, in the Outdoor Garden.

Jimmy Dorsey

The Dorsey band has been featured every Thursday night on the Bing Crosby Music Hall radiocast (WEAF - Red) for the past two years.

In addition they have doubled playing engagements at the Palamor Ballroom and Sam Sebastian's Cotton Club as well as making the musical score for a number of motion pictures.

Dorsey, a clarinet virtuoso, was a member of a number of the nation's outstanding dance bands before organizing his own tunensemble. Incidentally, the Dorsey name hopped to the top in rapid fashion. His rise was truly sensational and something new in dance band his-

Benny Goodman brought his dance band to VDB one July night, only weeks before his August 1935 destiny date at the Los Angeles Palomar Ballroom. Unlike most audiences, which left in the middle of his performances, VDB was a huge supporter of Goodman's latest charts. Benny believed VDB fans really understood his music, as no other spot on tour responded so enthusiastically, as cited in a *Citizen-Journal* review. Possibly due to the VDB success, drummer Gene Krupa encouraged Goodman: "If we're gonna die, Benny, let's die playing our own thing." Possibly due to the VDB success, drummer Gene Krupa strongly encouraged Goodman to give the audience all they had on August 21, 1935, the evening at the Palomar when the Era of Swing was born. Sadly for history, the Palomar Ballroom was lost to fire only four short years later on October 2, 1939.

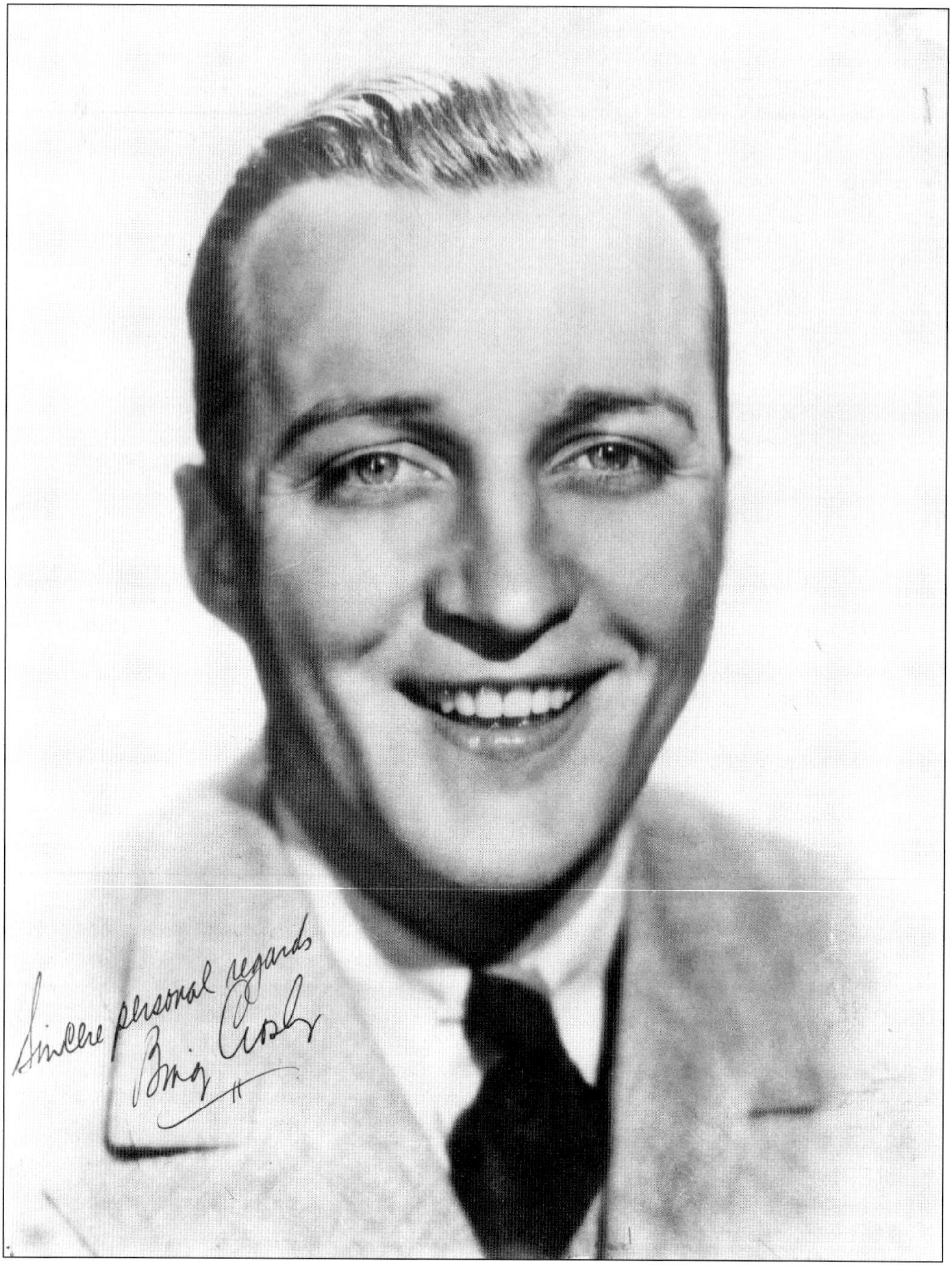

Paul Whiteman's unknown singer Bing Crosby appeared at the Valley Dale only once, in 1926 or 1927. Bing's first ever recording, in 1929, was "Old Man River" with Paul Whiteman's Orchestra. Crosby became dedicated to his solo singing career in 1931, after his 1930 marriage to Dixie Lee. Bing's brother, Bob Crosby, had a thriving big band that became a favorite playing at Valley Dale.

Two

The Peppe Family Scrapbook

A composition of life displays a score of movements between three brothers accompanied by a wife, a daughter-in-law, and a son. There was ad-libbing and improvisation since early 1925 by Jim Peppe as he worked for Valley Dale Hall, owned by the Melancon family since 1919. Beginning as a band leader, then becoming its manager, Jim insisted his brothers join him between classes at Ohio State to become a trio of workers for Valley Dale Hall. Brothers Mike and Lou studied athletics at Ohio State. In 3/4-time, Jim became the next owner of VDB possibly in 1927 under the heading of his new company, Metro Amusements. This was a huge deal for the children of Italian immigrants, to purchase an edifice such as the Valley Dale Hall so early in the 20th century. Lou, like Jim, became equally passionate with the bands, the music and the hall ownership. Jim is nationally recognized in 1935, which creates the opportunity for brother Lou Peppe's 1938 purchase of the Valley Dale Hall. The family affair continued through the third Peppe purchase by Lou's son Mike in 1980. This chapter presents the parts each member played in the legend that is Valley Dale.

Lou Peppe had a great friendship with Les Brown (Band of Renown). Brown played VDB beginning in 1937, and at his last VDB performance he was strolling the balcony gazing at the Wall of Fame, where Brown's portrait is also hung. Coming around a corner was Lou Peppe, briskly walking toward his lifetime friend; by the time the two reached one another, they were consumed with sentiment. Grasping this might be a last visit for both, neither man could contain their emotions.

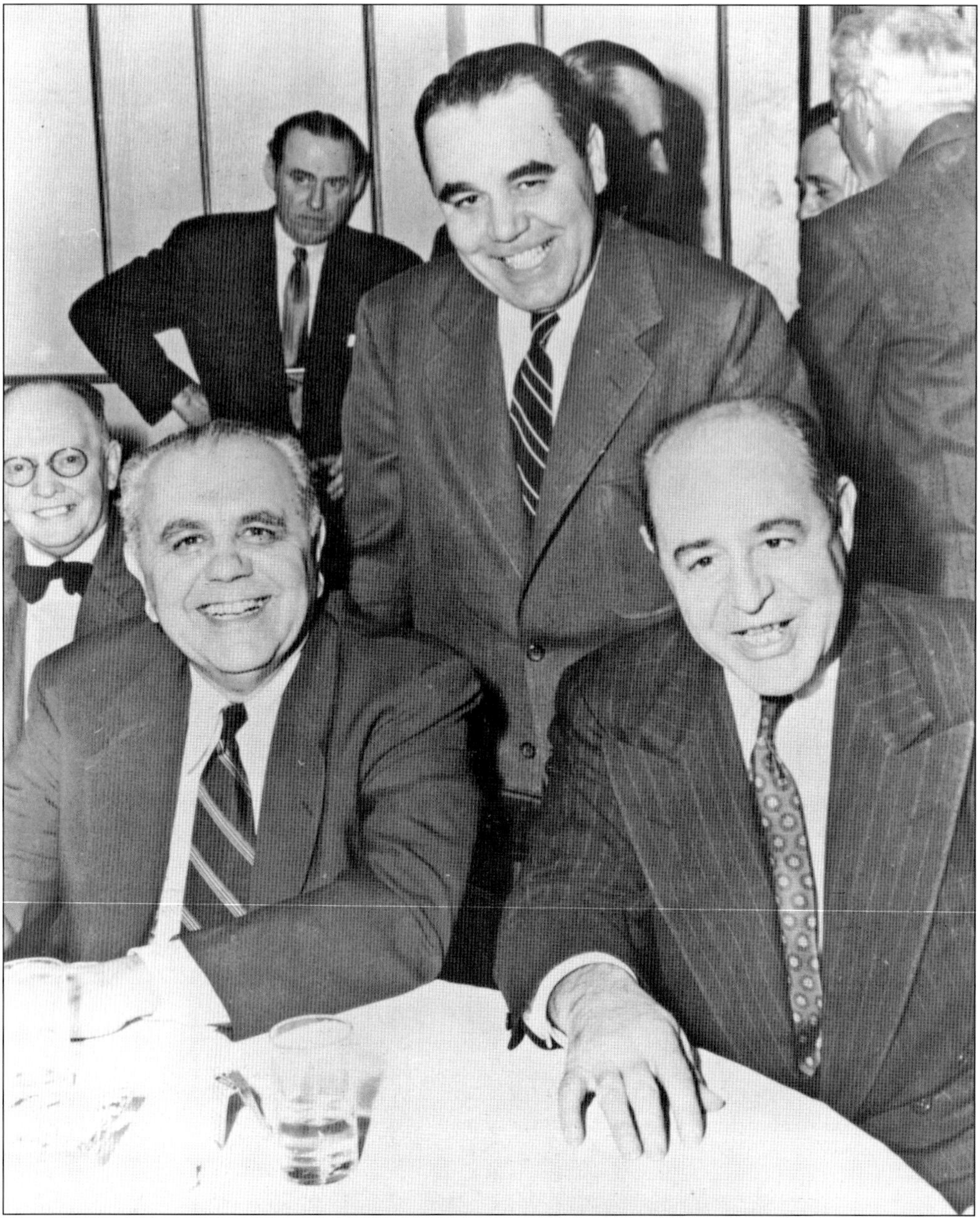

There would be no Valley Dale mystique without the Peppe brothers, Jim (left), Lou (center), and Mike. The Depression hit everything hard in the United States, but in the 1930s, the Peppe brothers saw their future as opposite to most Americans. They would go on to create a Columbus monument.

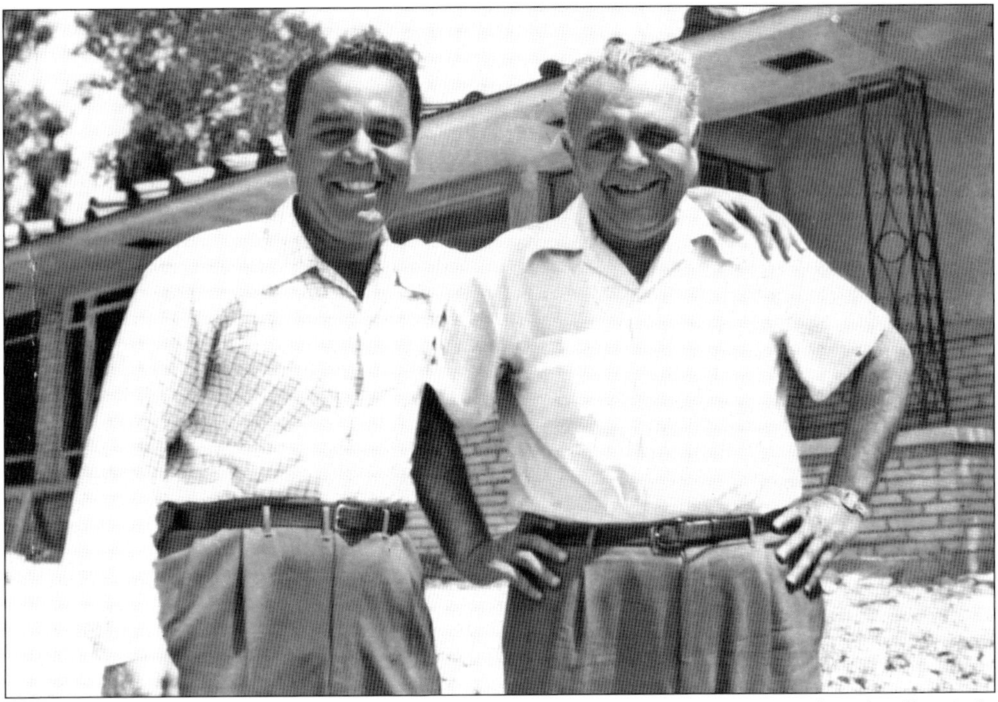

Lou (left) and Jim (right) Peppe created a mansion of memories for nine decades of Valley Dale devotees. Jim worked VDB from 1925, owned VDB from 1927 to 1938, followed by Lou from 1938 to 1980. Lou's Ohio State University major was physical education. Upon graduation, he coached Ohio State freshman football. Jim encouraged Lou to manage his Dayton, Ohio, ballroom. In mid-1930s, Lou left Ohio State. Jim strengthened the VDB name with his strategic placement of bands traveling through Ohio from Buckeye Lakes' Pier and Crystal Ballrooms to Green Mill Ballroom on Fishinger Road in Columbus and then over to Sunbury Road's VDB.

The writing of this book would not have the personal insights of its first decade without the thick scrapbook begun by Jim Peppe in 1932. Pages of tea-toned clippings from the *Columbus Dispatch* and *Citizen Journal* are fascinating reads charting the visits of the major and minor "chords" of arguably the greatest generation of artists and fans this country has ever witnessed. The uninterrupted compilation of records and articles, tracked further still by Lou Peppe, keeps pristine visuals of the VDB wonder years while recording the hundreds of bands that passed through this stage door.

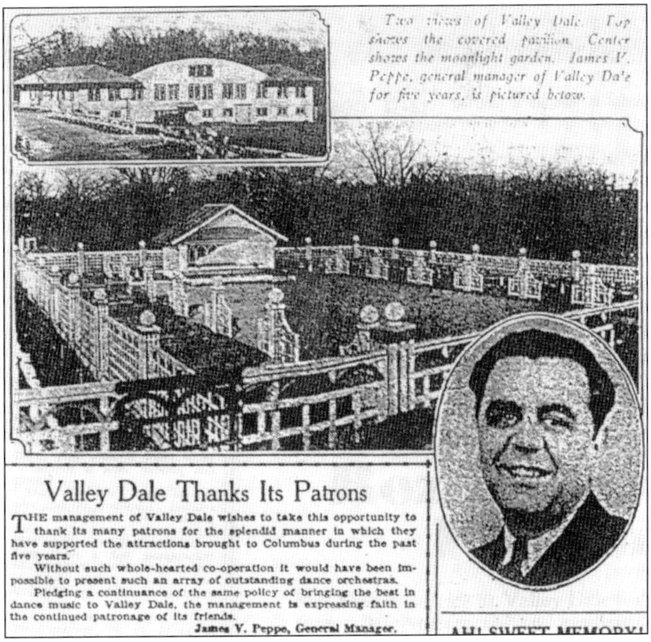

Two views of Valley Dale. Top shows the covered pavilion. Center shows the moonlight garden. James V. Peppe, general manager of Valley Dale for five years, is pictured below.

Valley Dale Thanks Its Patrons

THE management of Valley Dale wishes to take this opportunity to thank its many patrons for the splendid manner in which they have supported the attractions brought to Columbus during the past five years.

Without such whole-hearted co-operation it would have been impossible to present such an array of outstanding dance orchestras.

Pledging a continuance of the same policy of bringing the best in dance music to Valley Dale, the management is expressing faith in the continued patronage of its friends.

James V. Peppe, General Manager.

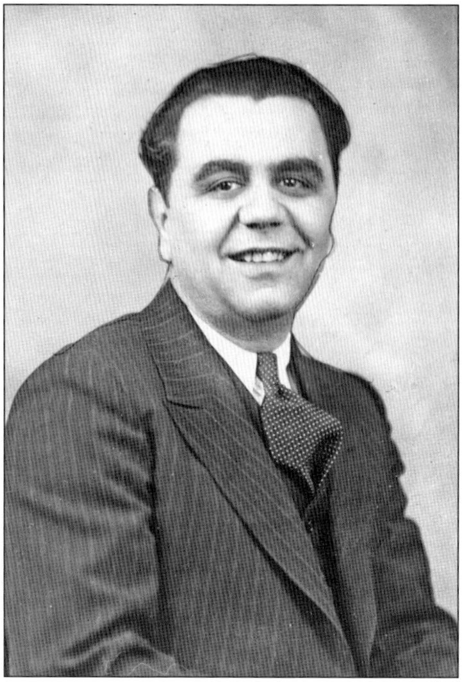

In 1927, the oldest Peppe brother, Jim, born in 1896, bought the VDB. In the seventh year of his ownership, CBS became extremely impressed with his dedication in developing the ballroom. Jim was offered a position with the CBS radio network in New York as president of the band department, handling over 52 traveling dance bands. When Jim took the CBS job, his brother Lou moved back to Columbus to manage VDB. Jim's new position gave VDB a natural booking pipeline for all the national big bands. (April 13, 1930, *Columbus Dispatch*.)

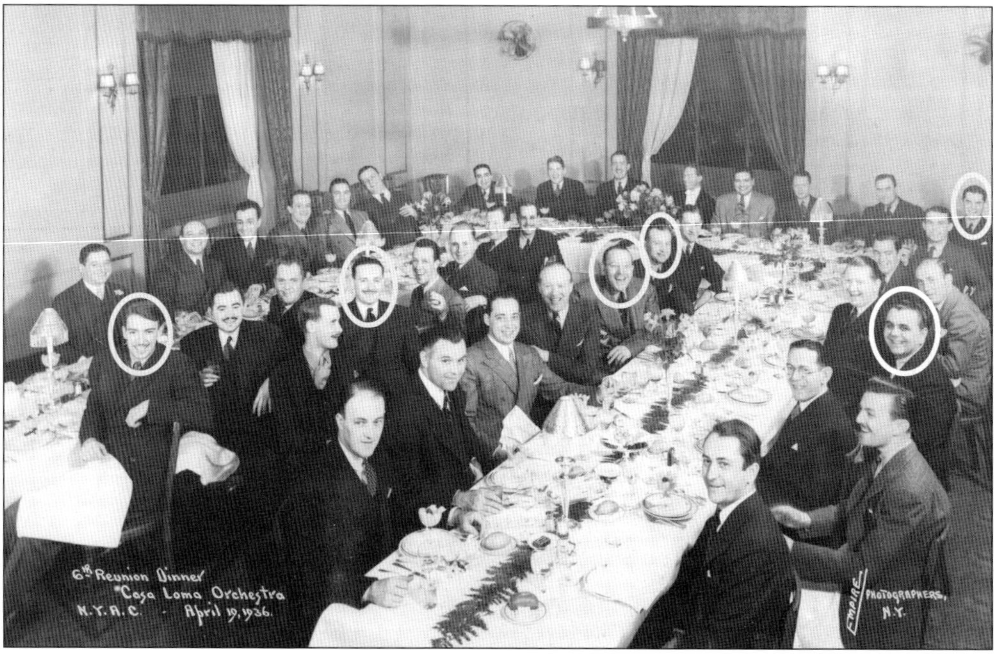

Jim Peppe became lifelong friends with an early group to play the VDB, the Casa Loma Orchestra. Unlike other bands, whose leader started the band, Casa Loma musicians voted on which band member would become their leader. After Henry Biagini, the first leader, left to start his own band, Glen Gray was voted in. This striking image is a band reunion photograph from 1936 depicting then CBS director of national bands Jim Peppe at dinner with the musicians. Circled here are, from left to right, Glen Gray, Henry Biagini, Pee Wee Hunt, Fritz Hummel, Jim Peppe, and Kenny August.

Another band Jim Peppe would manage for CBS was his dear VDB friend Sammy Kaye's. While at CBS together, they invented the moniker "Swing and Sway with Sammy Kaye." After two years in New York City, Kaye encouraged Peppe to become his orchestra manager and agent. After deliberating, Jim accepted the offer in 1938. Kaye later sweetened the deal by offering equal ownership of the band, which Jim accepted.

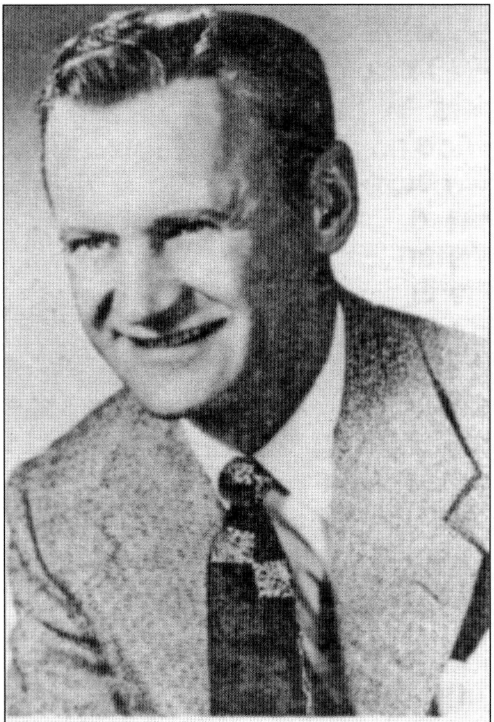

Sammy Kaye

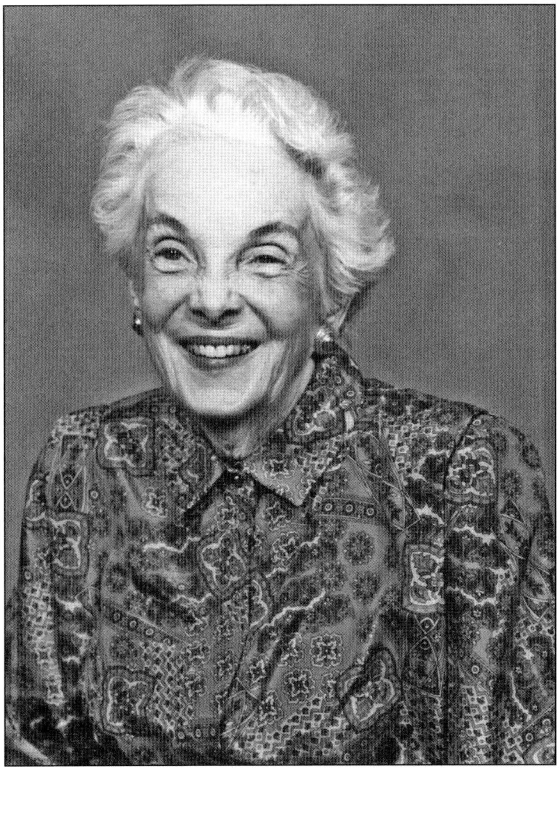

After Lou and Dottie Peppe had their first date at VDB, she spent 43 years as the first lady of Valley Dale. When Lou introduced Dottie to bandleader Sammy Kaye, she was miffed that Sammy did not tip his hat to her. Later in the day, Lou noted that Kaye was missing his toupee. In between VDB duties, she was a volunteer giving hope to many after surviving cancer. Dottie remained ageless to all who knew her.

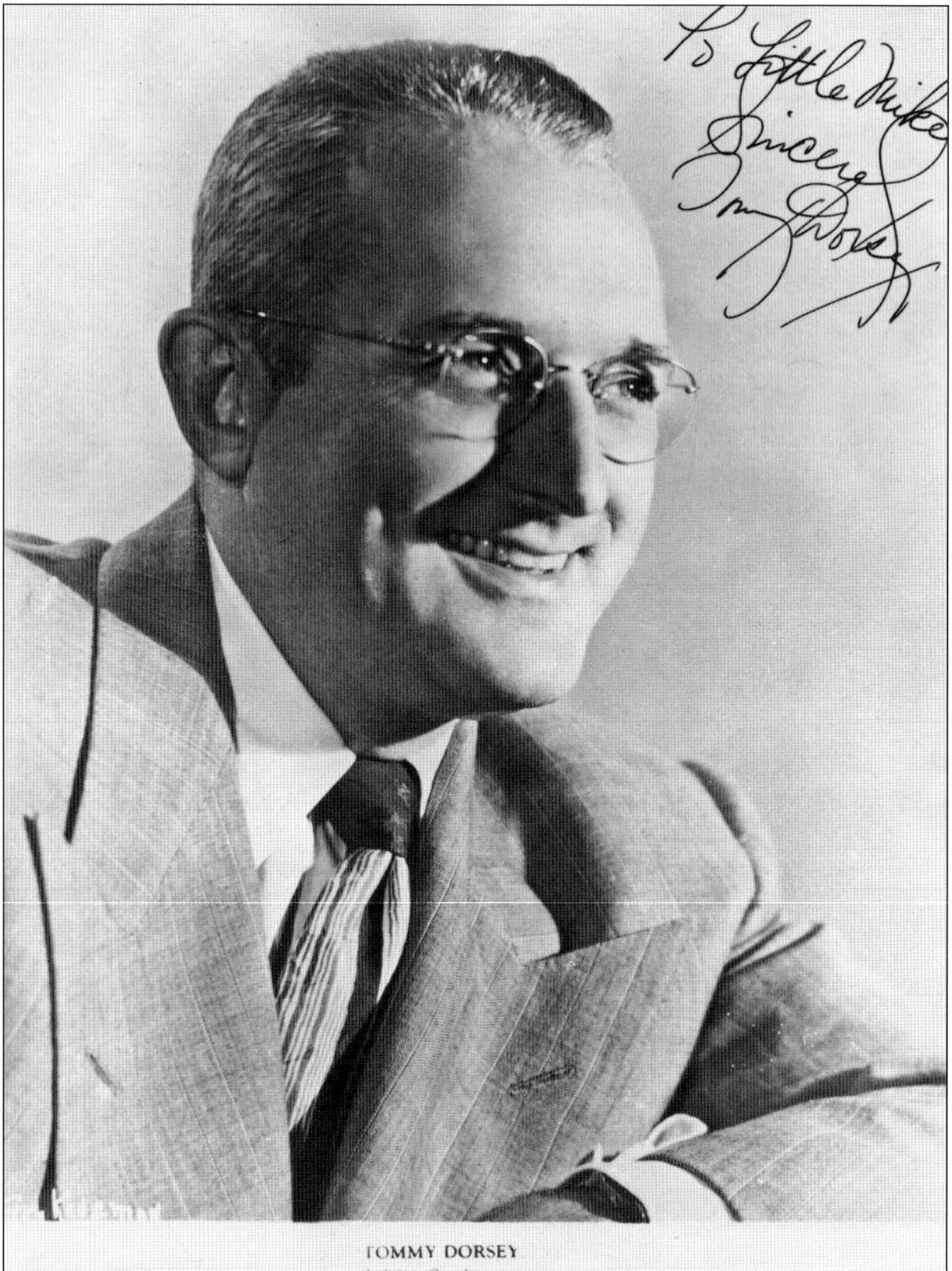

Lou Peppe's son "Little Mike" Peppe told the author this fish story, which took place at the vacation home of his uncle Jim: "Tommy Dorsey and Buddy Rich were invited to dinner at Uncle Jim's Sarasota home in 1950. While the adults talked on the porch overlooking Sarasota Bay, I mentioned that I was going to check my 'string of cane fishing poles.' Tommy Dorsey asked me if he could come along. After I showed him how to hold a pole and cast into the water, he remarked that this was his first fishing experience. He really enjoyed fishing, as my mom had to walk to the pond to get us when the homemade spaghetti dinner was ready." "Little Mike" became the owner of the Valley Dale in 1980 when he purchased it from his father, Lou.

Since 1980, the VDB has been owned by Mike Peppe, the son of Lou (owner from 1938 to 1980) and the nephew of Jim (owner from the late 1920s to 1938). Mike remembered that "as a kid in the 1950s I used to fall asleep across a couple tables in the balcony." Mike Peppe had every job from cleaning toilets to waiting on outdoor tables. On warm summer nights, the bands would play out of doors. In the early fall, Mike would wipe down the outdoor seats and tables as the nightfall became dewy. Later in the evening, he was in charge of overseeing the movement of the bands and guests inside.

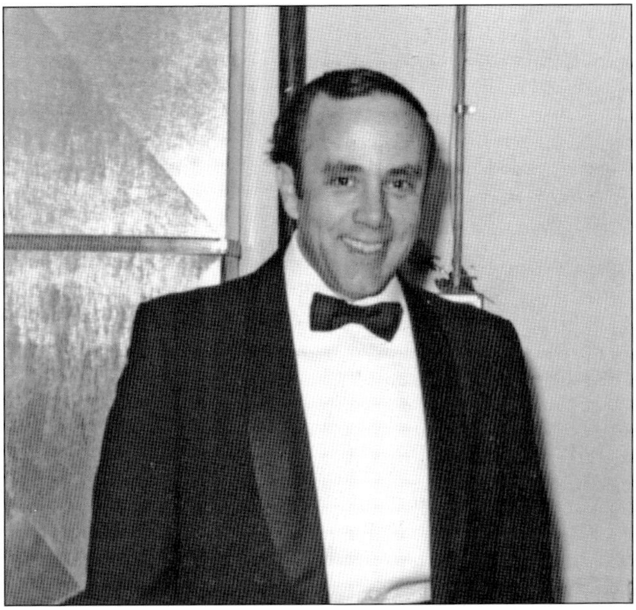

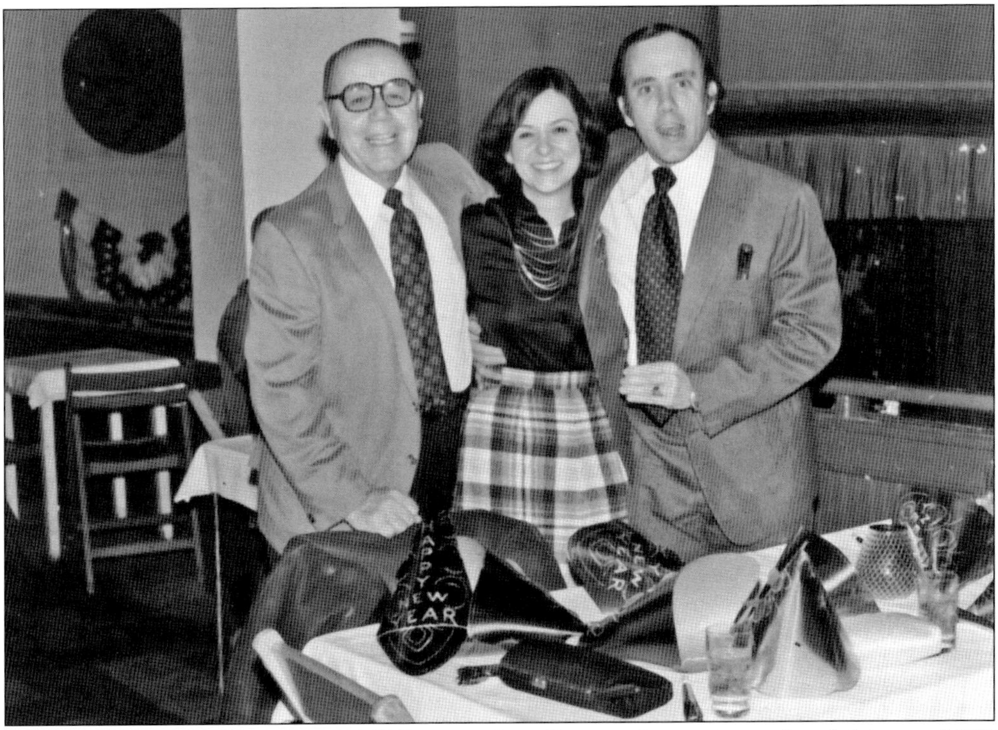

An eve of excitement for former VDB owner Lou Peppe, who is pictured with his son, VDB owner Mike, and Mike's wife, Kathy, in the balcony overlooking the bandstand as they celebrate New Year's Eve, 1982. The band that year was Bruno Masdea's. Kathy Peppe took care of VDB bookkeeping and payroll, alternating at the ticket booth or as a bartender. She was employed as a staff nurse at Ohio State's hospital and later as a nurse instructor at the OSU Nisonger Center for Mental Retardation and Developmental Disabilities. She coedited a textbook for nurses that won three national awards.

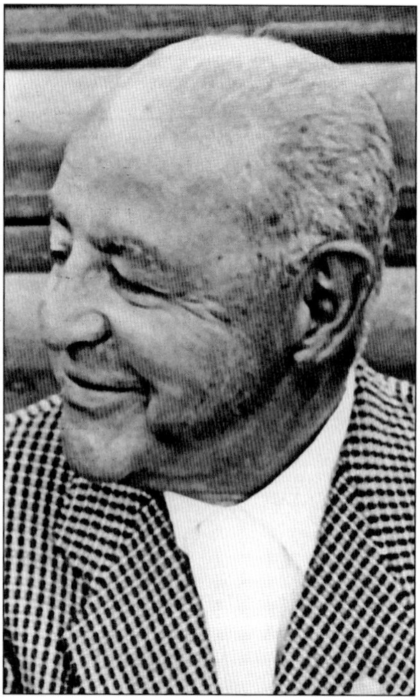

"Mike Peppe meant more to the world of water than chlorine, mermaids, or a good scotch," stated a eulogy line from the *Columbus Dispatch*. The elder Mike Peppe was an Ohio State swimming and diving coach from 1931 to 1962. He received his physical education degree from Ohio State and his master's from Columbia. Peppe served as a US Olympic diving coach for 1948 and 1952 and was also the head swimming and diving coach of the US team at the first Pan American Games of 1951. Mike worked at VDB while attending Ohio State in the late 1920s. OSU honored Mike's accomplishments by naming its natatorium the Mike Peppe Aquatic Center upon his 1963 retirement. The pool was recognized as the first deep-water pool in America, with a seven-foot shallow end and a 12-foot diving end. The natatorium was razed in 2005 to make way for a new campus swimming facility, The McCorkle Pavilion, it's pool also housing his medals is named in his honor. His bronze bust and oil painting are prominently displayed at The Swimming and Diving Hall of Fame in Ft. Lauderdale, Florida. (Kathy Peppe.)

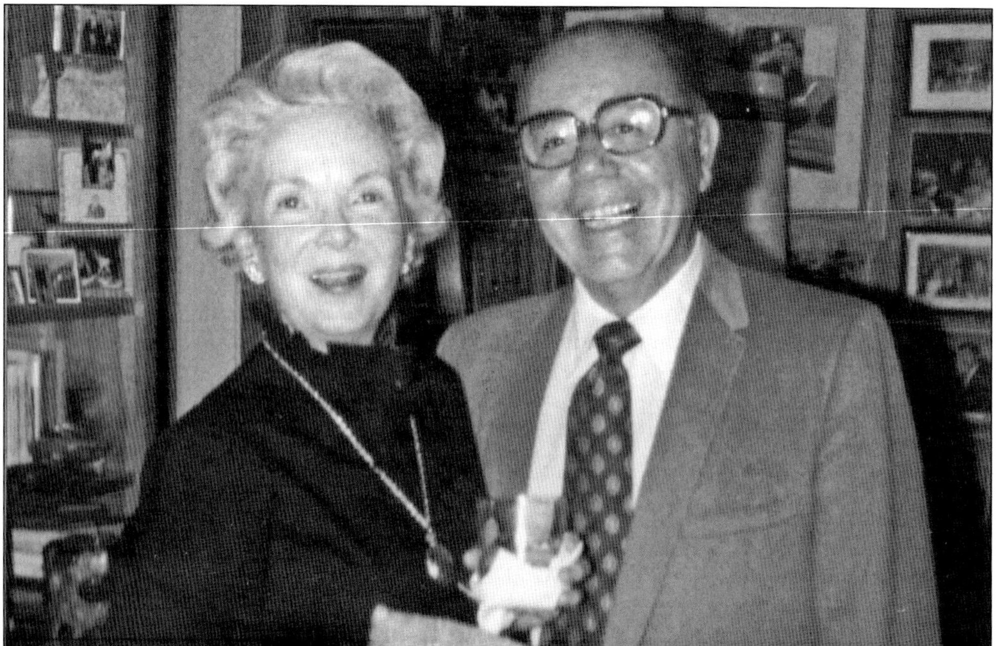

"A song ended softly and a piece of Columbus passed into memory with the death of a man who for 48 years owned VDB," the *Columbus Dispatch* commented on the 1983 passing of Lou Peppe. The father of current VDB owner Mike, Lou Peppe booked bands for other Ohio ballrooms, and getting to know the bands helped him when he returned to run VDB. He played a significant role in launching the careers of Sammy Kaye and Les Brown. Lou is pictured with his wife, Dottie.

Three

Sunbury Road Is Swing Street

Anyone who was remotely anyone played VDB. Many times it was a first gig, as for Bing Crosby; Doris Day before she was known for her golden voice and hair; or Ozzie Nelson, who was just getting to know his girl singer Harriet. The legends of today were barely kids while playing that VDB stage. Rudy Valle's sidemen begged him not to sing while on stage, believing his voice would be unappealing to audiences. Ben Pollack, considered the "Father of Swing" in the 1920s, was overtaken by his sidemen, like Miller, Goodman, and Teagarden. The stylings Fletcher Henderson wrote charts around made Benny Goodman the breakthrough artist of his generation. Many geniuses played VDB, like Charlie Barnet, Art Kassel, Isham Jones, Benny Moten, Hank Biagini leading the Casa Loma band and later his own group. Female bandleader Ina Ray Hutton (who notably had an all-female band, however, at VDB, she brought an all-male band for a rare appearance), the Louisville Ladies dance orchestra, Jimmie Lunceford, Fats Waller, the Hot Chocolates of 1934, Bunny Berrigan, and Freddy Carlone with Perry Como. Columbus's Earl Hood opened for almost every band to play VDB. As the leader of the house band, his name is bannered on all ads, including those with Ellington and Miller. This is only a small sampling of the bands that played VDB, some of which may not be addressed further in this book.

The Valley Dale prided itself after the takeover of the Peppes as a racially diverse club; musicians and couples alike were not prohibited from VDB. During the 1920s and 1930s, when articles were written about bands containing men of color, they used the term "sepia bands" to describe Duke Ellington, Count Basie, the Ink Spots, Fletcher Henderson, and others, including house band Earl Hood. The Valley Dale was recognized as a location where the prejudices of the color barrier were unheard of. Whether black or white, everyone was paid equally, and for black, white, or mixed couples, dancing at VDB was never a problem. The Peppes did not support any prejudices toward their guests or their entertainers. VDB was tagged through Columbus as a color-free zone.

From the 1920s through the 1950s, beginning as unknowns, "journey bands" traveled six nights a week to dance halls, lodges and backwoods VFW, Elks, or Lions Clubs. These journey bands are praised for weaving swing and jazz music throughout America, directly beginning the ballroom rage.

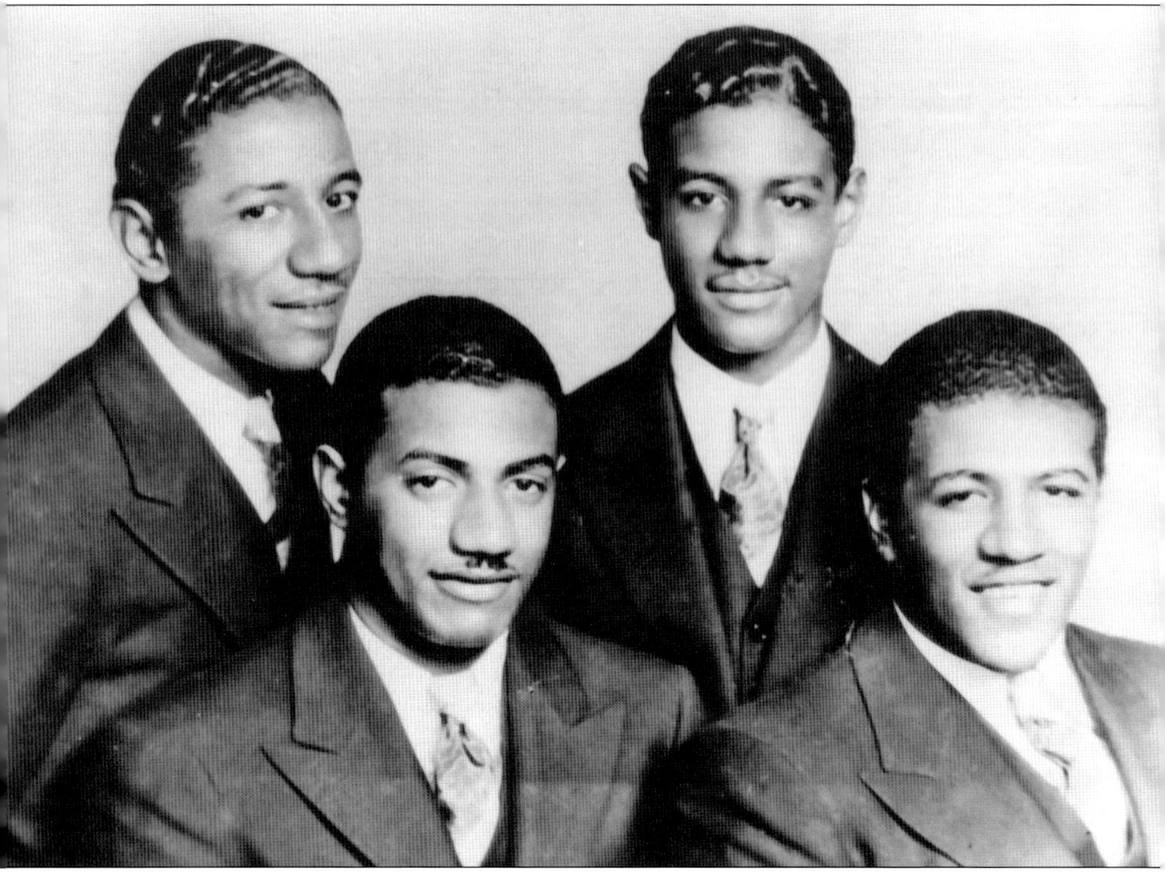

The Mills Brothers, soon to be legends, pulled up in their red truck at VDB in 1930 for their first public appearance outside their home town of Piqua, Ohio. The Piqua big band of Harold Greenamyer played regularly at VDB in the 1920s and 1930s; this could be how the Mills Brothers became familiar with the venue. It is not known if the Mills Brothers were backed by their hometown friends for that performance. Soon after that 1930 VDB show, their major break came in Cincinnati, when Duke Ellington auditioned them. Within two days, they were signed with CBS. A jazz and pop vocal quartet garnering three dozen gold records, they were the first African American act to have a network radio show. Queen Mary and King George V of England requested the quartet for a 1934 command performance. The Mills Brothers' world fame at their height has been likened to the Beatles. (Piqua Public Library.)

Kaye Kyser's orchestra first performed on the stage of VDB in 1931. That one wildly successful evening flowed into three consecutive months of nightly engagements. Kyser's orchestra added a novelty game, quizzing patrons on musical topics. "Kay Kyser's Kollege of Musical Knowledge" became a musical game show that ran from 1938 to 1944, broadcast live from the ballroom on Mutual Broadcast Radio. Mike Peppe said, "My dad told me Kay Kyser would fall backwards off the stage as part of his act. One night at the Dale, the guys who were supposed to catch him either missed or just failed to do the job and Kay Kyser broke his ankle in the fall." Multiple articles on Kyser mention that he fell off a stage one night, ending his falling gimmick, but they never mention that it happened at VDB.

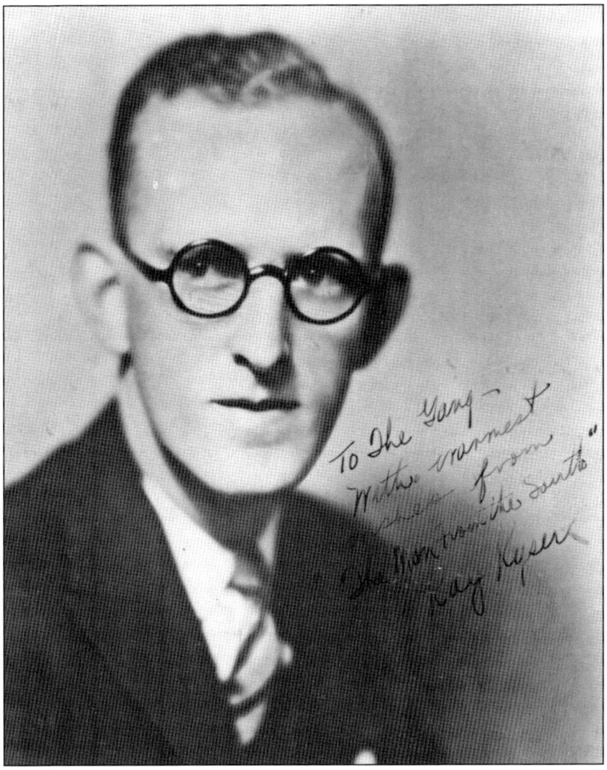

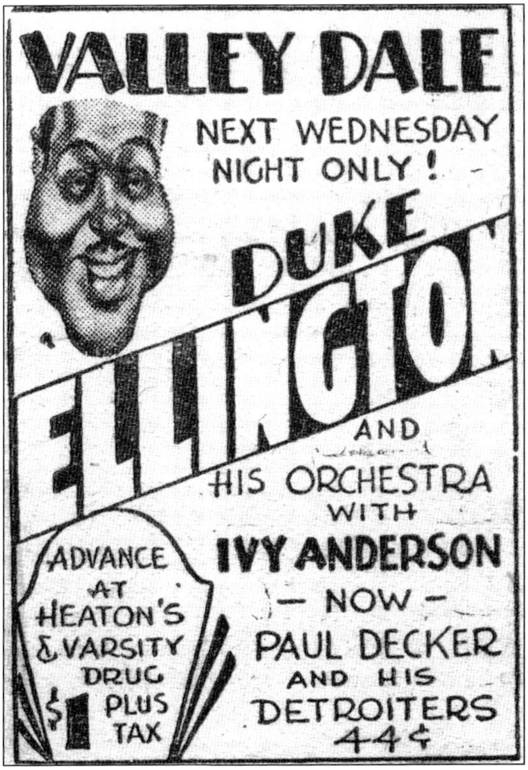

The Duke Ellington Orchestra headlined VDB on December 28, 1932; admission was $2.50 a couple. An ad also boasts a 1932 New Year's Eve party, with dancing from 9:00 p.m. to 4:00 a.m. at just $3.50 a couple.

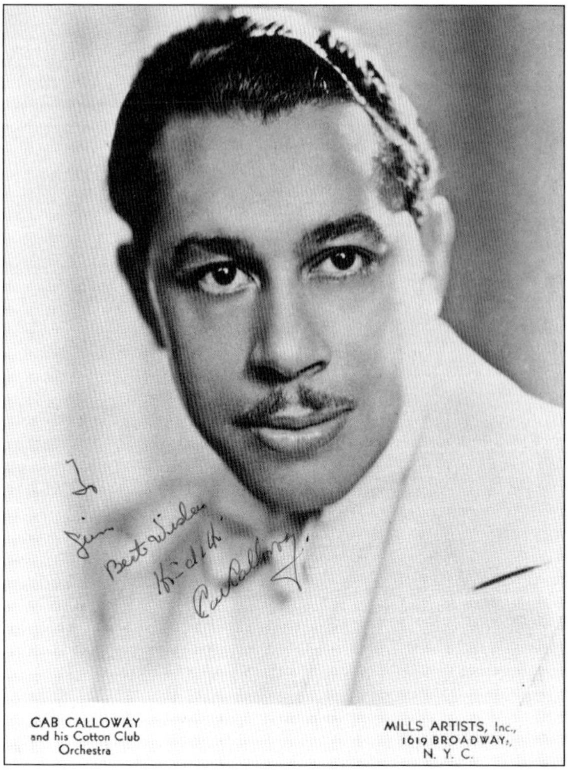

In this portrait, Cab Calloway, notably dressed in his signature ivory tones, has used a lyric from his song "Minnie the Moocher" ("Hi-dee-hi-dee-ho") as his salutation to Jim (Peppe) above his autograph. This print hangs on the VDB Wall of Fame. Calloway was an animated performer direct from Harlem's Cotton Club. He appeared at the VDB to present his unusual and intoxicating numbers.

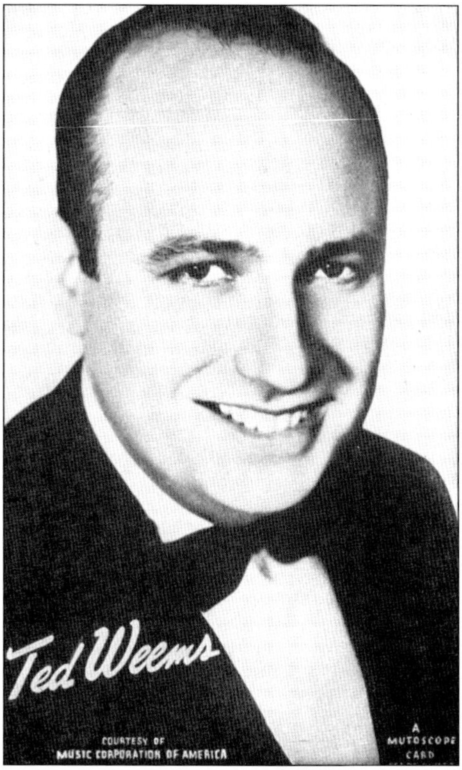

One could purchase a ticket at Columbus's Heaton's music store or Varsity Drug for admission to VDB's Sunday night show featuring the Weems Orchestra on April 25, 1937. Chicagoan Ted Weems and his band, Victor recording artists, played crowds where ladies would swoon for the male singer, the suave but then unknown Perry Como. Sinatra respected Como's work ethic and talent, having Perry fill in when he needed time off for other opportunities. Perry hosted his own television shows for CBS and NBC.

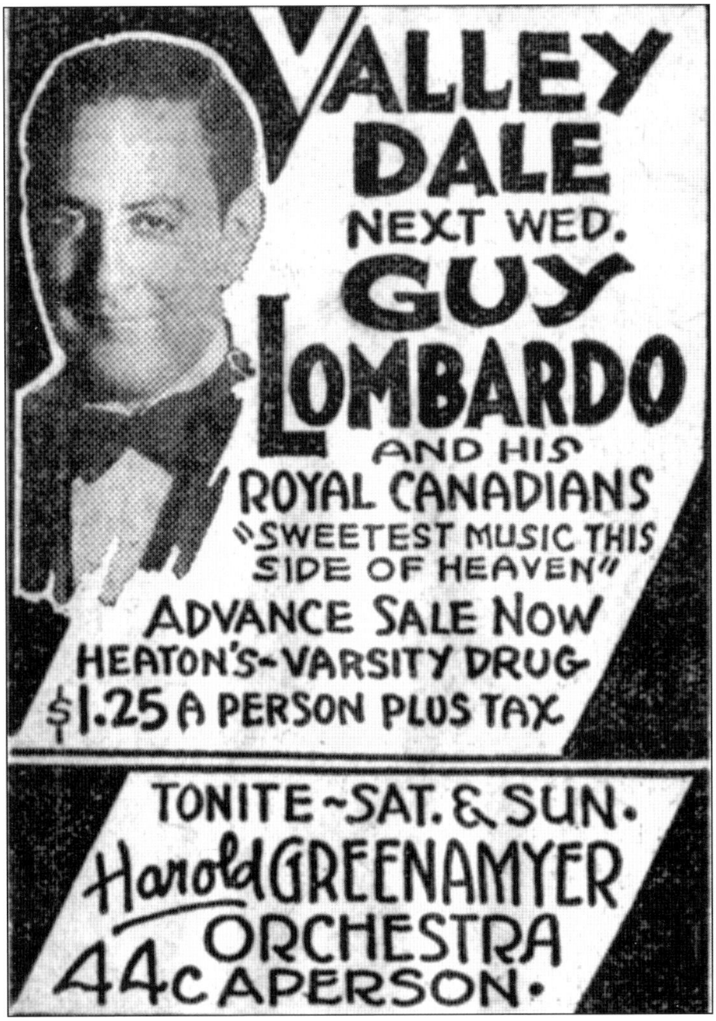

The most significant evening crowd in VDB history began its morning with a horrendous event occurring across the country: Just before dawn on May 23, 1934, on a dirt road in Louisiana, notorious bank robbers Bonnie and Clyde were gunned down in a police ambush. By nightfall in Columbus, Ohio, Bonnie and Clyde were all but forgotten with the single most crowded evening in Valley Dale history. Under Jim Peppe's management, the season-opening of VDB's outdoor *Starlight Gardens* returned *Guy Lombardo and his Royal Canadians.* This high expectation for Columbus brought 5,000 people in house by 7:30 p.m. for the 9:30 p.m. show. The *Columbus Dispatch* described a snapshot image of that Wednesday evening. Guests passed time playing bridge while waiting for Guy Lombardo; others stepped to the opening orchestra of Bobby Blue. Off in the distance, sounds of sirens intensified as they closed in on the ballroom, countless police motorcycles escorted the Lombardians through the city, ushering the musicians to VDB, and within moments of arrival, the band struck its opening chord. It appears a packed house of fans wedged into every corner; guests cramped on the rim of the too-full dance floor, patrons resorted to climbing behind the bandshell, piling upon stacked instrument cases to glimpse the band. With the sardine effect in total play, people dancing, chatting, and drifting, the evening was almost "disturbing" cited a reporter. The newspaper article ends as printed—"A LAST-MINUTE FLASH: According to a phone call from VDB, a reported 5,389 persons attended. That dear readers is what's known as a gang."

The local Ernie McKay Orchestra traveled six nights a week to halls, lodges, and VFW, Elks, and Lions Clubs. After one gig, Ernie stopped at a Youngstown club, where he met Dino Corcetti. McKay offered Dino $40 a week to sing with him; Corcetti claimed he made more working a Steubenville gambling spot. Dino's pals, believing he was star-bound, offered to make up the difference until his career soared. Ernie assumed an Italian singer could be his ticket: Ted Weems had Como, and Harry James had Sinatra. But he thought Corcetti's given name would not do, so he suggested Martini in honor of opera sensation Nino Martini. The first time Dino Martini's name appeared in print was in a 1936 *Columbus Dispatch*. Dino performed with McKay at the Valley Dale. Cleveland bandleader Sammy Watkins polished Dino's name to Dean Martin. (John Griffith, Dean Martin's son-in-law.)

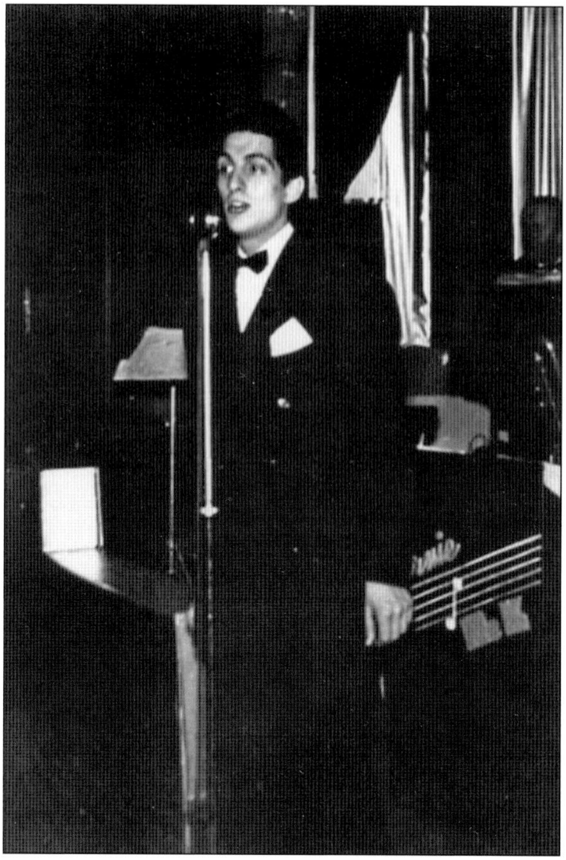

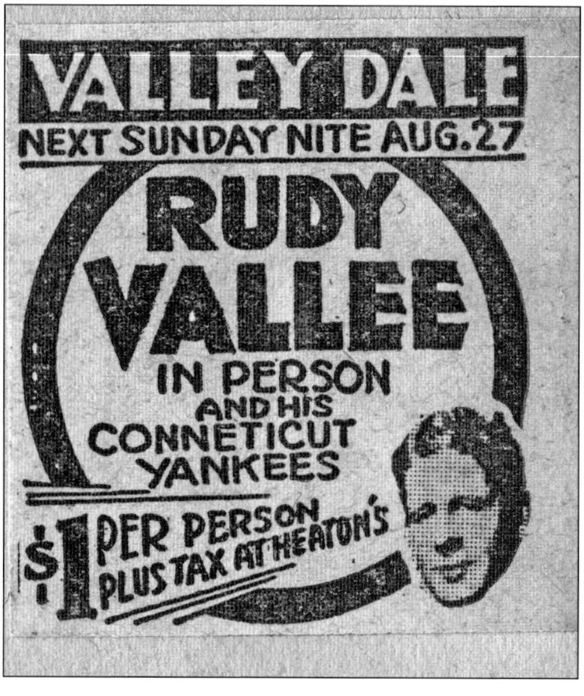

Rudy Vallee played VDB's open-air Starlight Gardens pavilion on his 36th birthday, July 28, 1937. His tour ran from Little Rock to the Indian Lake Ballroom at Russel's Point, Ohio, then to Columbus; Chautauqua, New York; and Manhattan, where he hosted the radio show *The Fleishman's Yeast Hour* (later *The Royal Gelatin Hour*). Arriving at VDB in striped flannels and a white coat, Rudy enthralled his swooners by crooning "Where or When" and "Mad Dogs and Englishmen," posed during his clarinet solo, then stepped it up by syncopating "The Shag." The crowd, in excess of 4,000, was enthralled. Only a few short months later, he was known as "the crooner." Vallee was the very first, before Bing, Frank, Dean, and Como. (*Columbus Citizen Journal.*)

A single night in 1940 brought about one of the favorite stories in the Valley Dale's history. Female vocalist Connie Haines of the Tommy Dorsey band was already spoken for by the band's drummer, Buddy Rich. The group's boy singer believed he could get any girl and began flirting with her. Buddy Rich planned to get even. As the boy singer sang, Rich changed tempos and at times even drowned out the male vocalist, totally ruining his vocal number. After the tune, the lanky singer got even by sneaking up behind Rich; as the drummer struck his solo, the crooner dumped a freezing pitcher of ice water right on the drummer's head. Immediately after the tune, Buddy Rich chased the vocalist, Frank Sinatra, to the knotty pine bar backstage, where an all-out wrestling match occurred. Planks in the bar wall were split, which can still be seen today.

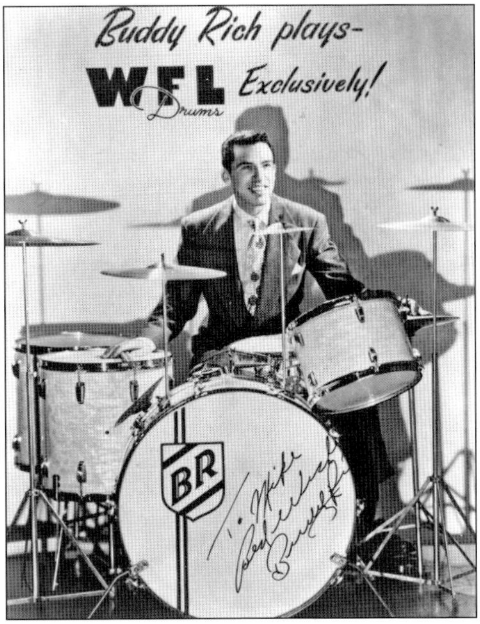

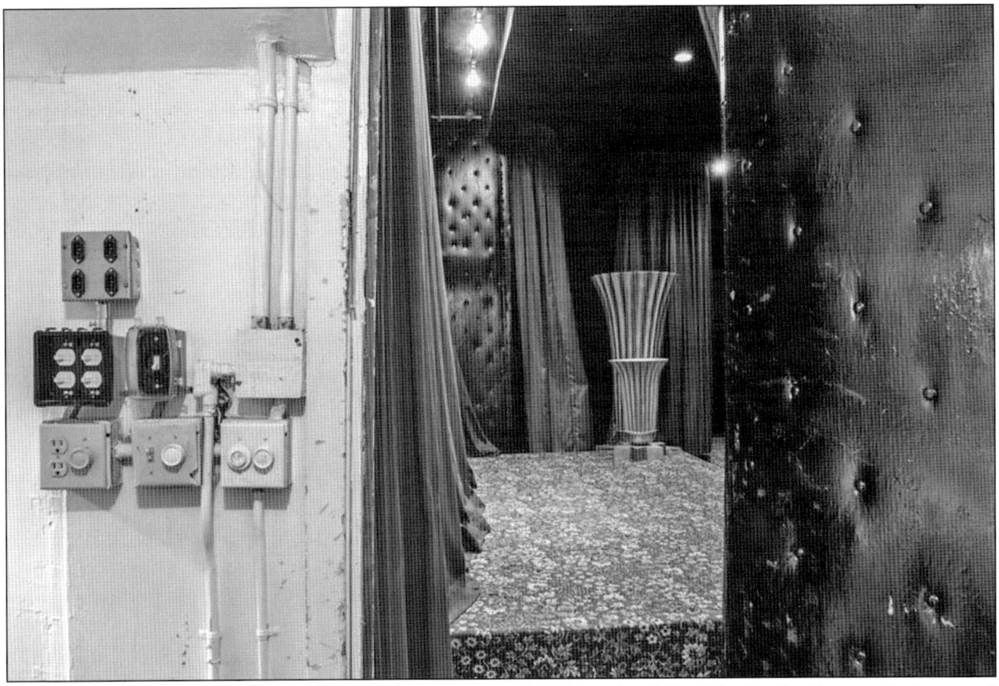

Frank Sinatra strutted through this door when he drenched Buddy Rich. Sinatra's first real hit with Tommy Dorsey was "I'll Never Smile Again" in May 1940, about the time of one of Tommy's VDB dates. During these years, Sinatra made roughly $400 a week. Sinatra credited his vocal success to the bandleader: he would watch Tommy's breathing technique as he played his trombone, and Sinatra later copied the technique. He claimed, "My greatest teacher was not a vocal coach, not the work of other singers, but the way Tommy Dorsey breathed and phrased on the trombone." While Sinatra was on stage at VDB, he studied Tommy, ultimately creating his voice. (Landa Masdea Brunetto.)

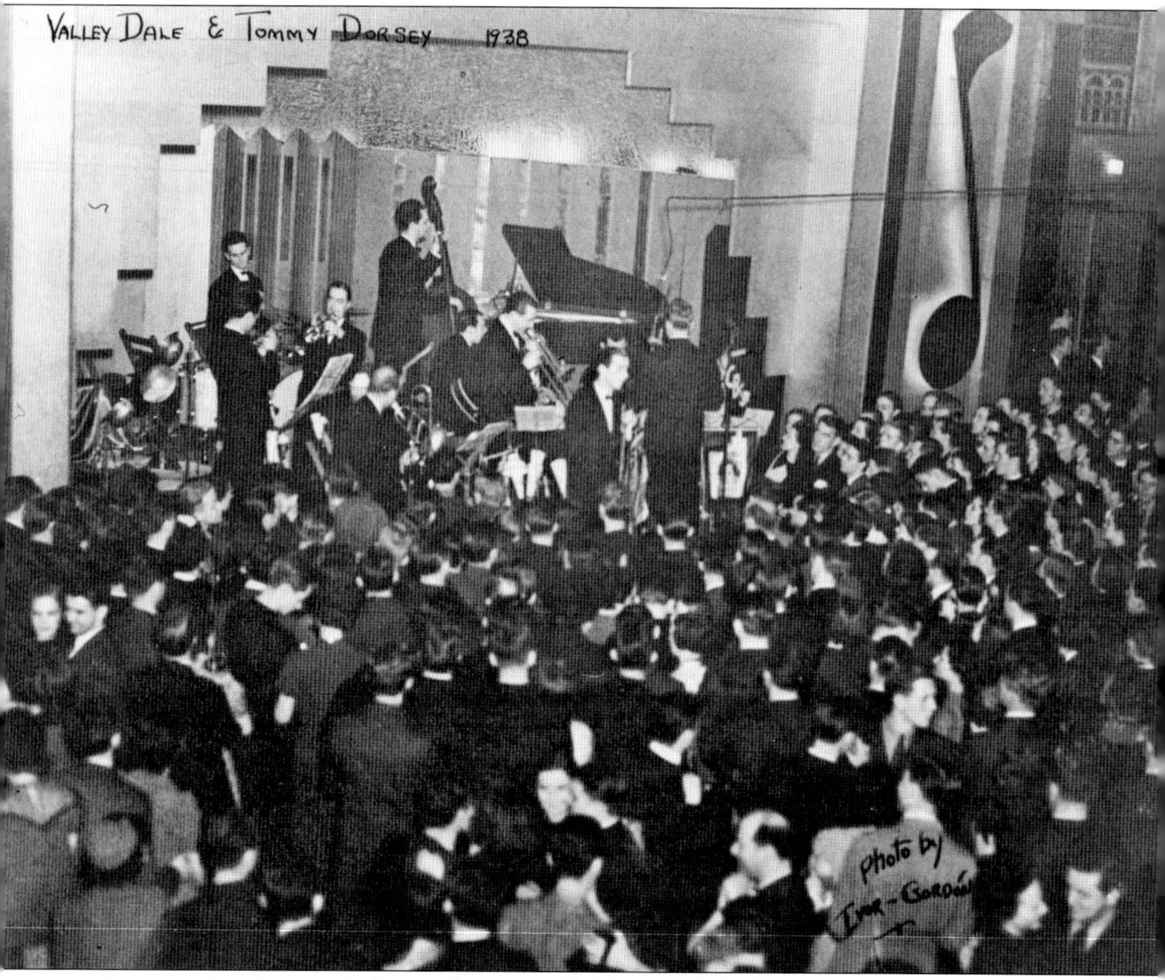

A spectacular photograph depicts the outstanding impact the Tommy Dorsey Orchestra had one evening in 1938, Columbus. Downstage is vocalist Jack Leonard, second only to Bing Crosby at that time and Tommy's favorite until Leonard left for the service in 1939 and before the ultimate singer of all time, Sinatra, joined his band. Notice Tommy poised at a slight angle center-stage, serenading with his trombone. This is an incredibly interesting photograph to study—they could be returning from break with the juxtaposition of the musicians on stage. There is a dueling of horn players, and the drummer himself is hard to locate. They could perhaps be performing "Marie," Leonard's biggest hit. The enthusiast would swarm the stage, barely a sheet of paper could fit between each follower. Another marveling detail—there are primarily male guests mobbing the orchestra. Dancing was nearly impossible for the night of 4,000 fans.

On September 9, 1940, following the VDB gig (the night of the Sinatra and Buddy Rich conflict), WCOL radio recorded a one-hour NBC broadcast of Tommy Dorsey's Orchestra featuring Connie Haines, Pied Pipers, Ziggy Elfman, Buddy Rich, and Frank Sinatra. The recording with an audience and vast sounding background space seems to be at VDB. This precious archive sold for $1,300 in 2013. This story was shared by Collen Sariotis, of Collen's Collectables. (Larry Pishitelli Photography.)

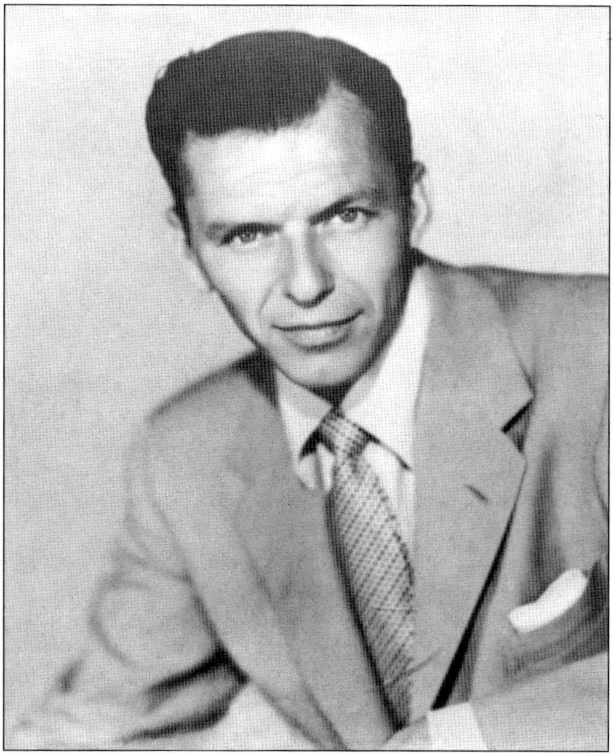

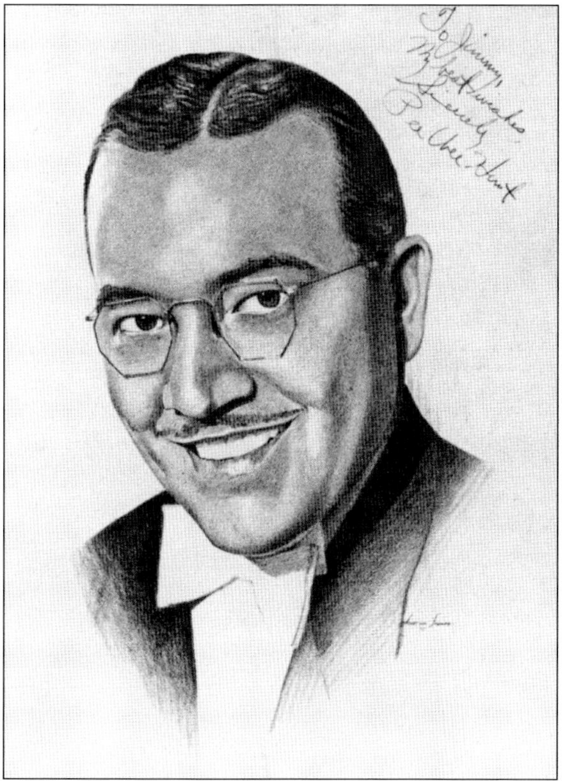

An Ohioan and cofounder of the Casa Loma Orchestra, Pee Wee Hunt, attended Ohio State, then graduated from Cincinnati Conservatory of Music in the mid-1920s. He was also the featured trombonist. During World War II, this band, like many big bands, began to wane; Hunt left the group to become a disc jockey, a similar path taken by Casa Loma's vocalist Kenny August. Another Casa Loma instrumentalist, Fritz Hummel (see page 24), became a trombone teacher to future VDB bandleader Dale Groves of the 1971 Fabulous Forties. See page 24 for photographs of all Casa Loma members.

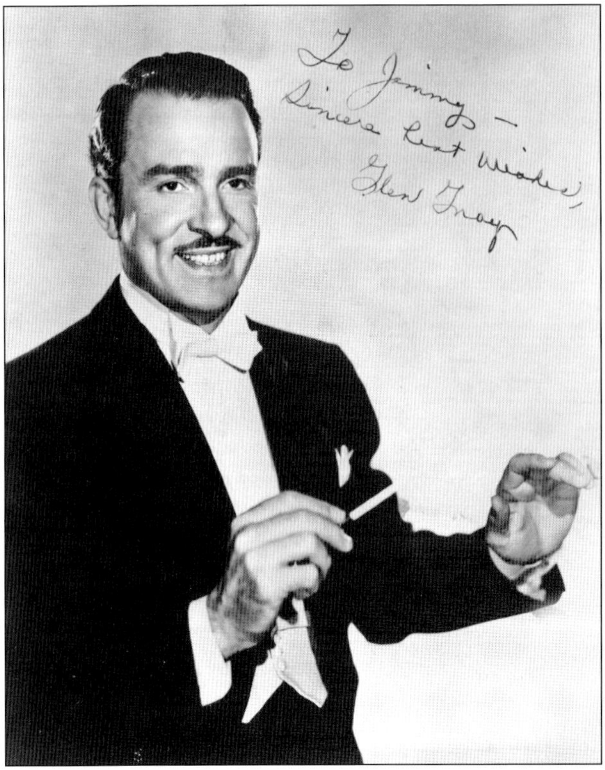

Benny Goodman debatably set off the Big Band era in August 1935. Casa Loma band arguably conceived that era before 1935. Considered to be the first white band with a measured jazz strategy, they intoxicated college kids, unaware of the great black bands on the horizon. Gray's Casa Loma pioneered a craze across the country beginning Christmas week 1935 at the one time most famous theatre in America, The Paramount at the corner of Times Square and Broadway in New York City. Movie houses hosting big bands on stage was unprecedented at the time. The poignant lyric in Barry Manilow's tune, "Singin' with the Big Band"—"At the Paramount in 1943," depicts the start of "Frankie" Sinatra. Autographed photograph to Jim Peppe.

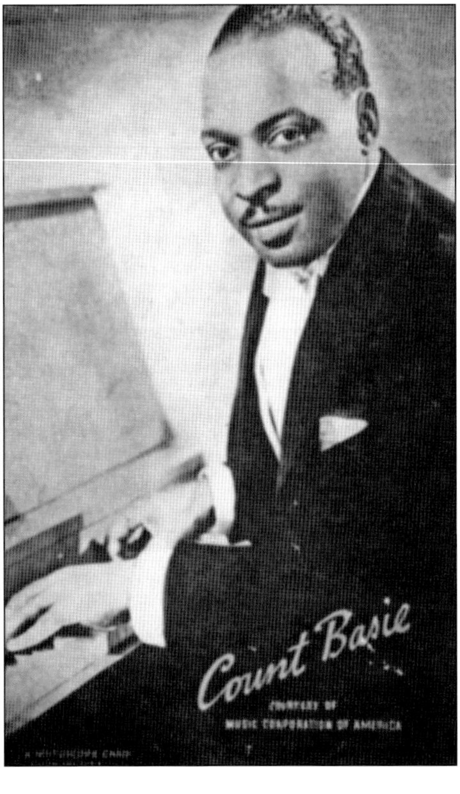

The Count Basie Orchestra was a cheered-for favorite at the Dale. The Basie band's cool and easy swing style appealed to both jazz musicians and dancers. To this day, Count Basie remains one of the most influential and defining bandleaders of the era.

Metronome magazine honored Helen O'Connell as "1940's quintessential big band singer." She was born in Lima, Ohio, and played VDB as the female idol with the Jimmy Dorsey Orchestra. "Those cool and limpid green eyes" was a lyric from her knock-out hit "Green Eyes." Generations later, this song is still studied, because O'Connell's delivery is like no other. Because of her cuteness, Jimmy labeled her "the girl next door." In later years, she became the host of Miss America pageants. This image from July 30, 1939, is preserved from Jim Peppe's scrapbook of newspaper ads and articles.

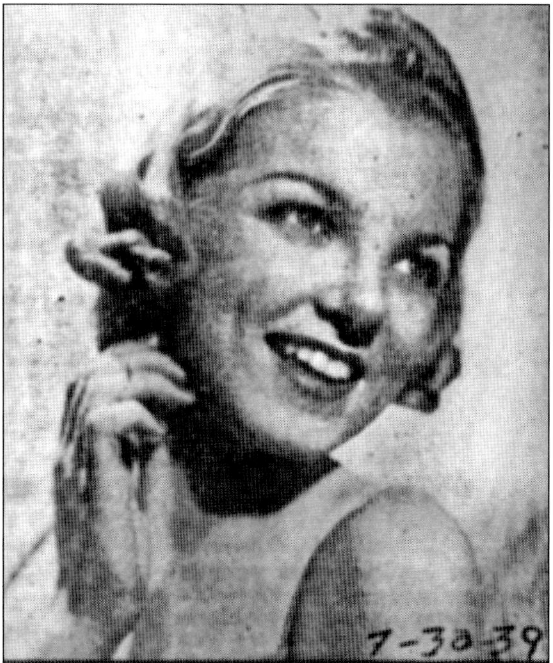

***SONGSTRESS* Helen O'Connell is the attractive dish who will sell songs for Jimmy Dorsey's dance-date at Valley Dale unday night. Advance ticket sale attests band's popularity.**

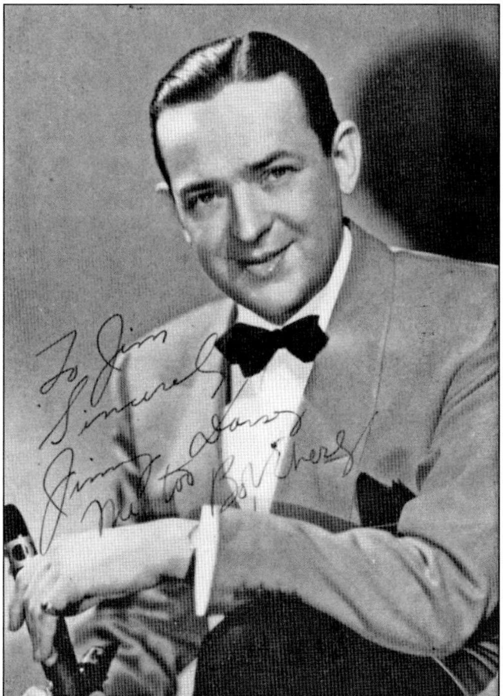

JIMMY DORSEY
and his Orchestra

Once a member of the Dorsey Brothers Orchestra, Jimmy split from his brother Tommy to create his own band. A silver-screen movie was created presenting a "fictional" portrayal of the twists and turns of the turbulent brotherhood of Tommy and Jimmy. Jimmy performed continually at VDB. His music was flavored with Dixieland, unlike most big bands at the time. Jimmy Dorsey autographed this photograph to Jim Peppe.

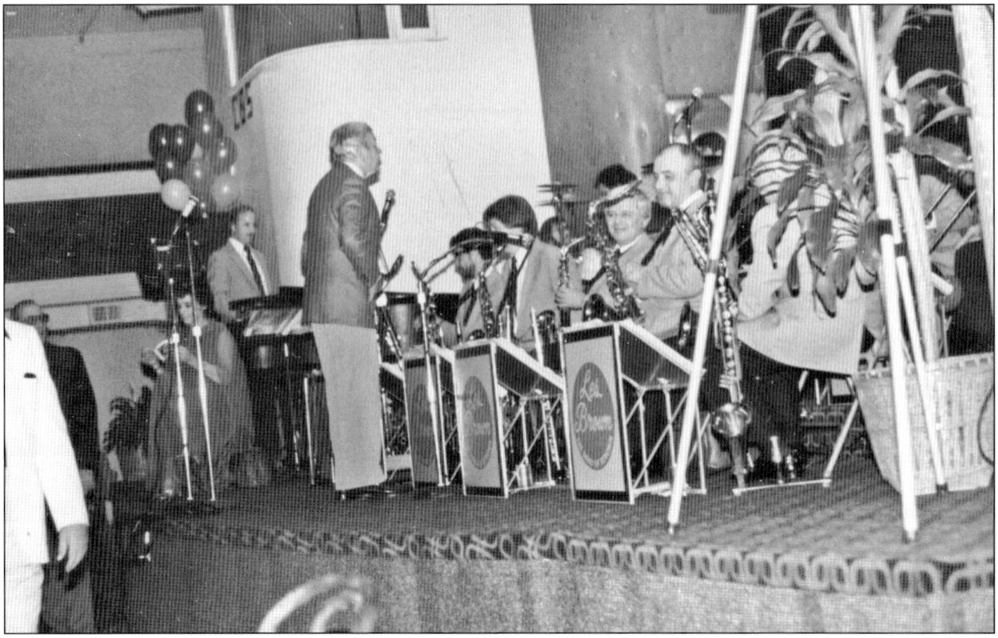

Bandleader Dale Groves, a close acquaintance of Les Brown, passes down an insightful anecdote. Les Brown, pictured here during his last VDB appearance, and His Band of Renown became a favored VDB band. Brown's brother, dumbstruck by a Cincinnati singer's looks and talent, got his brother extremely intoxicated and convinced Les to hire the pretty blonde. Brown did, handing her $200 and requesting she purchase gowns for two Columbus performances, which she did at the F&R Lazarus department store. The girl was Doris Day. Lea Price, a board member for the Doris Day Animal Foundation, stated how much Doris Day enjoyed her days singing with Les Brown, but as it was almost 79 years ago, after so many performances, Day did not exactly remember playing VDB.

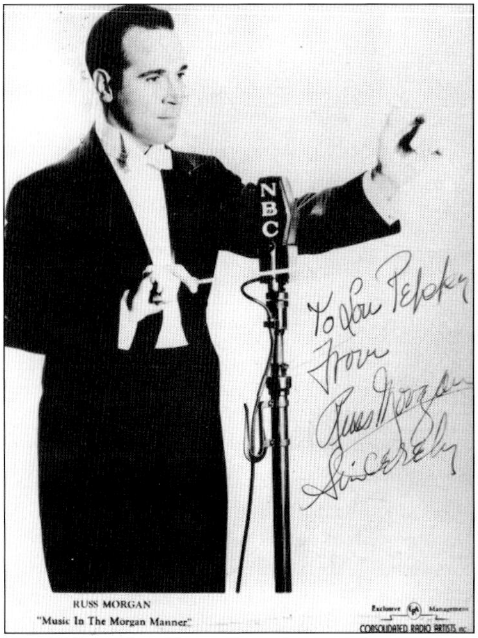

An arranger for John Philip Sousa, Victor Herbert, and VDB guest performer Fletcher Henderson, Russ Morgan was pushed by Rudy Vallee to start an orchestra to perform his own compositions. Morgan played VDB in the mid- to late 1930s and broadcast *In the Morgan Manner* from the ballroom in 1949 for the Mutual Broadcasting System. Considered a "sweet band" (meaning void of jazz), Morgan's orchestra played delicate music with his signature lyrical harmonies. Morgan collaborated on a song that is still well-known 70 years after its 1944 introduction: "You're Nobody Till Somebody Loves You." The song was successful for two other Valley Dale acts, the Mills Brothers and Dean Martin, who in 1964 took the tune to number one on Billboard's Middle-Road Singles (now known as the Adult Contemporary Chart). VDB performer Deana Martin recorded the tune in 2006.

On October 22, 1941, Tommy Tucker opened Frank Dailey's Dale, as it would be known for less than one year. Tucker was hot on radio at that time. His band featured several famous alumni, including saxophonist Gerry Milligan, clarinetist "Buster" Brown, and singer Eydie Gormé. If there is any question whether or not Frank Dailey had managerial duties at VDB, this photograph is proof. In an array of photographs, Dailey printed artist headshots for fans to purchase, enabling admirers to collect autographs for their personal souvenir booklets, with Dailey's printed marketing caption underneath the head shots.

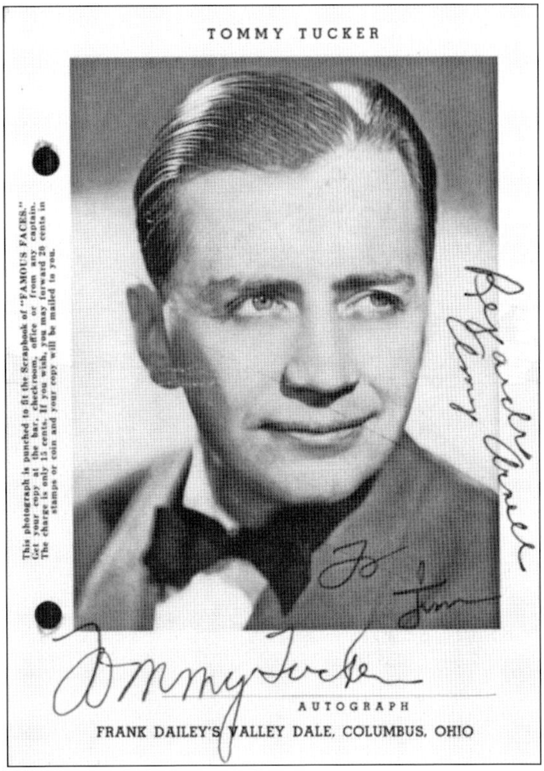

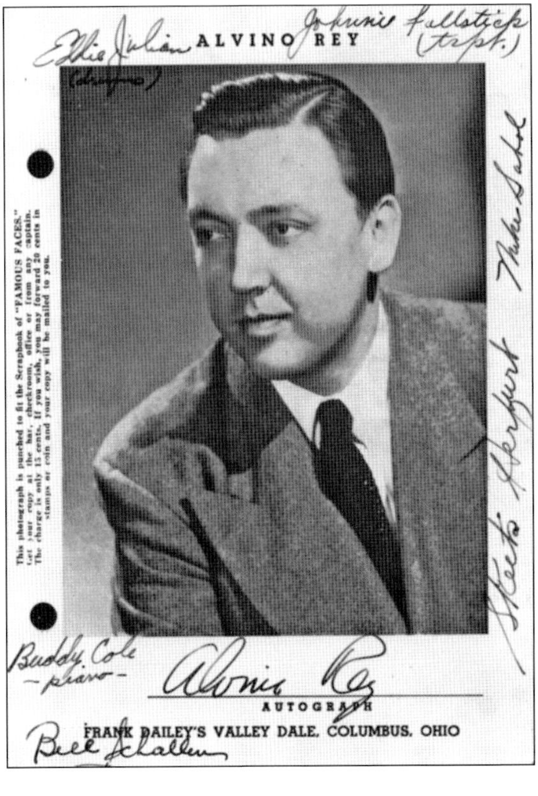

Alvino Rey broke records at Dailey's VDB when he was hired for a two-week engagement beginning December 16, 1941 (nine days after the bombing of Pearl Harbor). Alvino's songstress team was the in-demand King Sisters. Rey married Luise King in 1937. In a VDB interview, he stated that he very much enjoyed the room but lamented that he had little time to fly his plane with his current musical success, so he picked up photography instead.

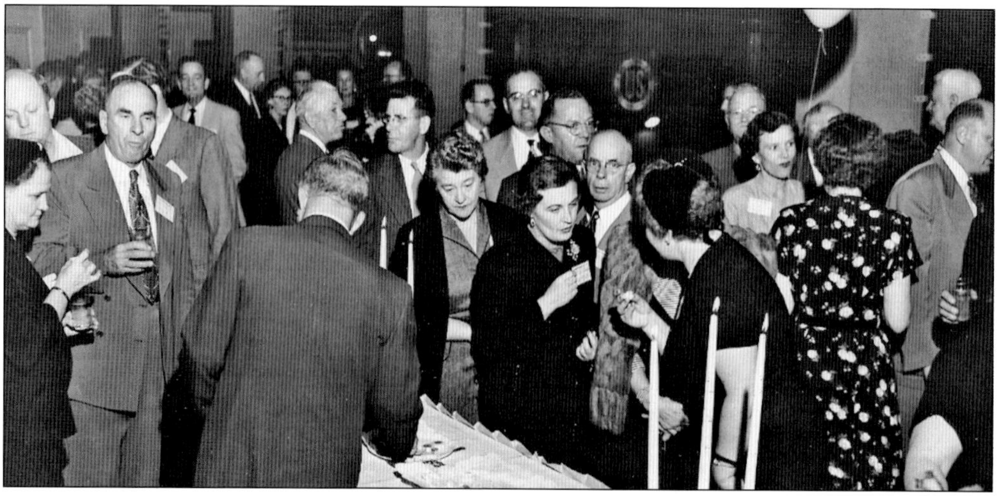

Musicians always cherish their gigs, but when accompanied with food, the experience is transcendent. As bandleader Rick Brunetto quipped, "When food is promised on a gig, it's like the band gets to go to the party, too." The promise of a home cooked dinner was alluring to any road musician who was traveling with 18 or so others on a bouncy, un–air-conditioned, smoke- and gas-fume-filled band bus, weaving through graveled roadways in the 1930s and 1940s. Ham sandwiches on day-old rye bread or ketchup-smothered meatloaf dinners at roadside diners was standard fare. (Bob Stoll.)

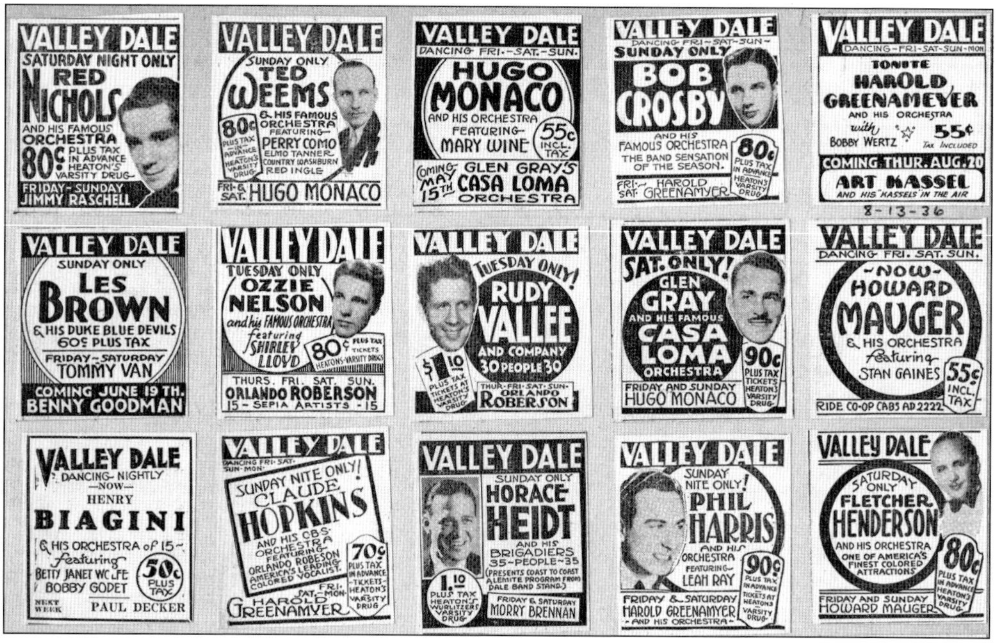

This is an assortment of ads depicting various VDB artists of the 1930s and 1940s. One was Ozzie Nelson, accompanied by his vocalist (and soon-to-be-wife) Harriet. The couple were parents to David and Ricky Nelson, grandparents to actress Tracy Nelson and duo The Nelsons. The famed 1950s sitcom *Adventures of Ozzie and Harriet* was wrapped around this family. Before all of the family blossoming, Ozzy's band gained more popularity due to Harriet's "perky " vocals. Oz starred in his radio shows, television programs, and movies produced by Ozzie. It's worth commenting how Ozzie has such a striking resemblance to his son Ricky in the advertisement.

Stan Kenton played the VDB beginning in 1943 and continuing through four decades. Valley Dale had been broadcasting live for quite a few years at this time, and due to the radio, Kenton became a huge celebrity in Ohio. Kenton stated that at other venues, his audiences were receptive but only marginally aware of his band, but when he hit VDB, he was a star; the crowds were wildly welcoming and larger than most. Kenton was known for progressive jazz. Lifetime VDB fan Wezi Masdea said her favorite band during high school was "Stan Kenton, Hands down! I played his records, dancing till my mother would yell, 'Turn it down and go to bed.'" (University of North Texas.)

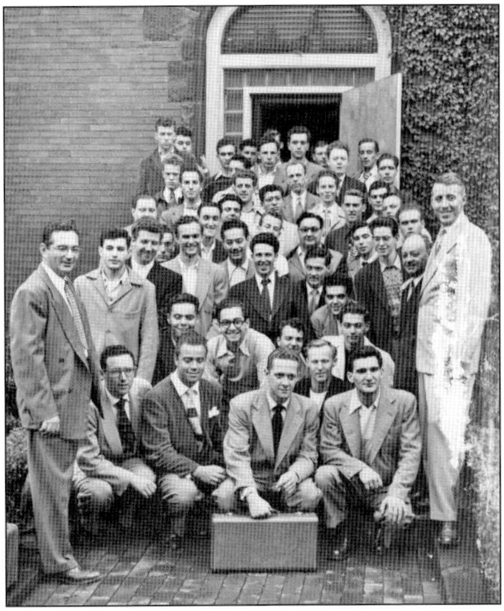

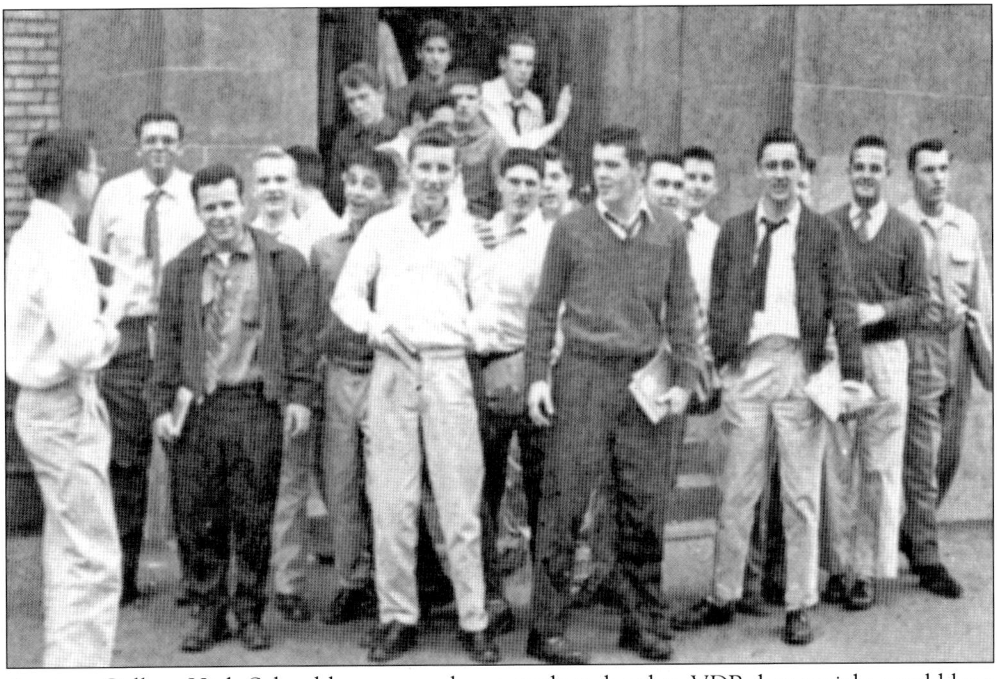

Aquinas College High School boys were always ready to head to VDB, but tonight would be a little bit different for these boys from Central High and Aquinas. About 1:20 a.m., after a 1946 VDB gig, nine cars careened into the VDB parking lot: future Columbus musician and noted high school band director Les Susi, then a 16 year old from Central, was in the middle of what would become an unforgettable evening. Stan Kenton's band was scooped up by the boys for an excursion to St. Lucia Recreation Center on St. Clair Avenue in the nearby Italian neighborhood. Aromas of oregano and garlic greeted them. Ladies carried antipasto and steaming platters of sausage, meatballs, and braciole dripping in Bolognese sauce. The small community's telephone party line broadcast the goings on, and within minutes, nearly 400 neighbors converged on the makeshift eatery. The band and party-crashers stuffed themselves until after 4:00 a.m. (Lou Nobile.)

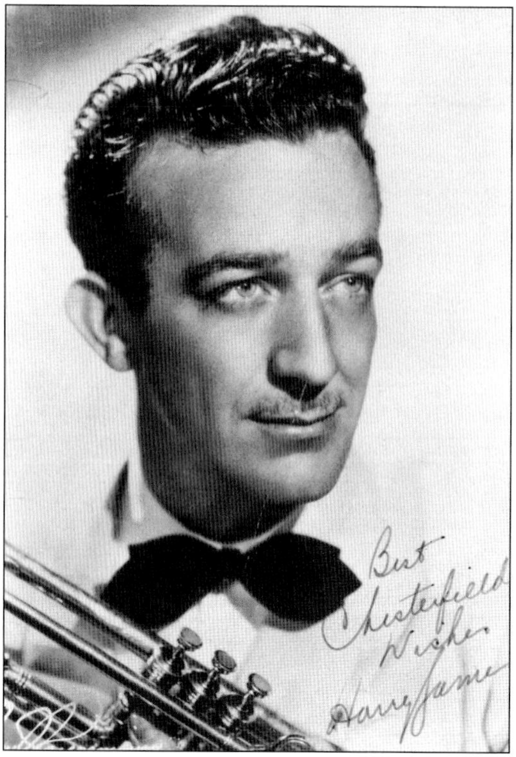

Sultry sweet trumpeter and bandleader—and first to hire Frank Sinatra in 1939—Harry James was a darling of the VDB fans. Like so many top names then and now, he became a spokesperson for market products. In noting his salutation, he slides in a subtle acknowledgment to his advertiser, Chesterfield cigarettes. This autographed picture is hung at VDB.

Glenn Miller and his orchestra traveled from Chicago to Columbus for a one-night engagement beginning at 9:00 p.m. on Saturday, July 13, 1941. Miller's crowd was over VDB capacity, numbering 3,000 pairs of dancing shoes. This image is dated December 1939, when Miller visited Columbus for an Ohio State University Kappa Theta sorority dance; proceeds funded a new sorority house. (University of Colorado Glenn Miller Archive.)

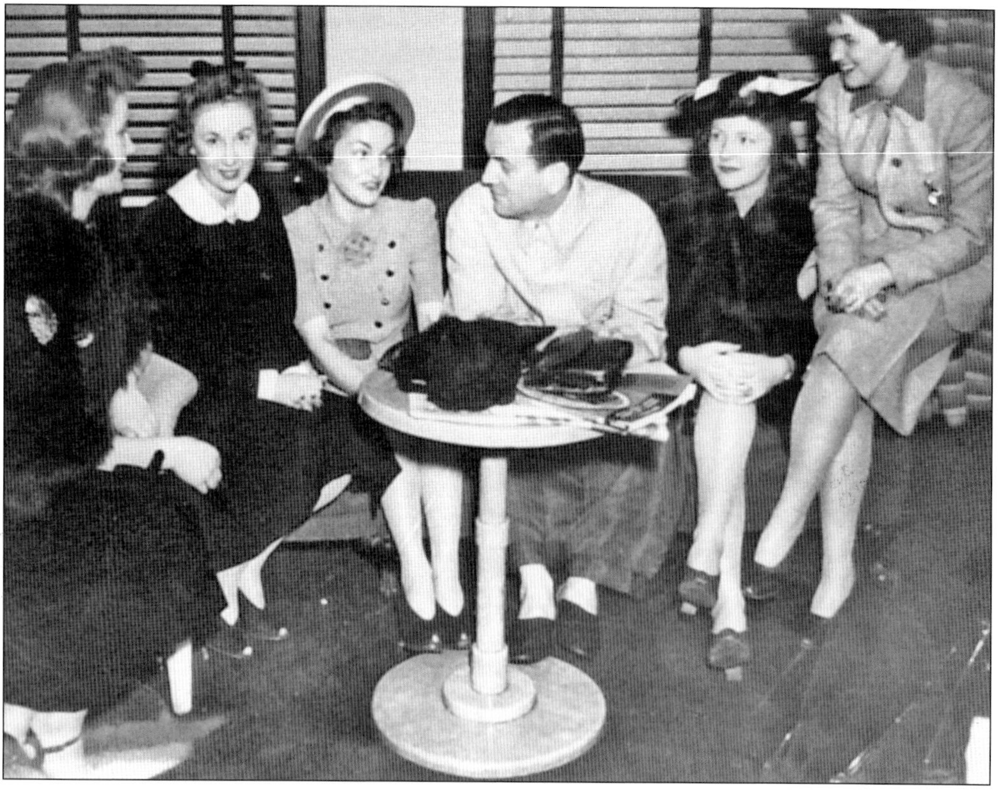

Four

Big Band Mania: The Original Teenage Music

The Charleston age was dying, a new music genre was dawning, and the kids of the 1930s and 1940s were thirsting to see, hear and dance to "that sound"—the sound Glenn Miller gave up almost everything to develop. "That sound"—Tommy Dorsey captured with a smooth-toned elegance as he breathed stunning notes through his trombone for all to idolize. Big bands, orchestras, and soon-to-be-legendary vocalists and instrumentalists left their mark on the vaulted Sunbury Road hall.

"In the warm months on Saturday nights we could hear the music from our front yard"... As a little child living on Cassady Avenue, close to VDB from 1925 to 1930, Gilda Savko a young 95, tenderly shares with me, her childhood remembrance. "The Gibboney's lived across from us having a handful of kids, they would come over to enjoy each other's company, while we kids would run and dance in the yard to the band music until we became so sleepy we would go to the porch swing and fall asleep and awake the next morning in our beds, never knowing how we got there. Of course, I don't remember the names of the songs, just enjoying the music every Saturday night."

Reminiscences such as this is exactly what the Valley Dale means to its lifelong devotee. This chapter focuses on VDB's first teenagers the "Valley Dale Girl" and her Valley Dale and boyfriends. VDB became a dating mecca. During interviews the recollection with so many married couples no matter the generation, I chronicled. "Our first date was at Valley Dale . . . then we got married." This was the "Greatest Generation" as teenagers. Corporate America had only programmed for thirty to fifty-year old's until they saw how the bobby-soxer, the teen girls of the day, spent their coinage on Sinatra, EVERYTHING! This was the first time corporate America started to notice the buying power of its teenagers and young adults. This was the arrival of the big band era, deified by its teenagers, and its reign in Columbus was at the Valley Dale Ballroom.

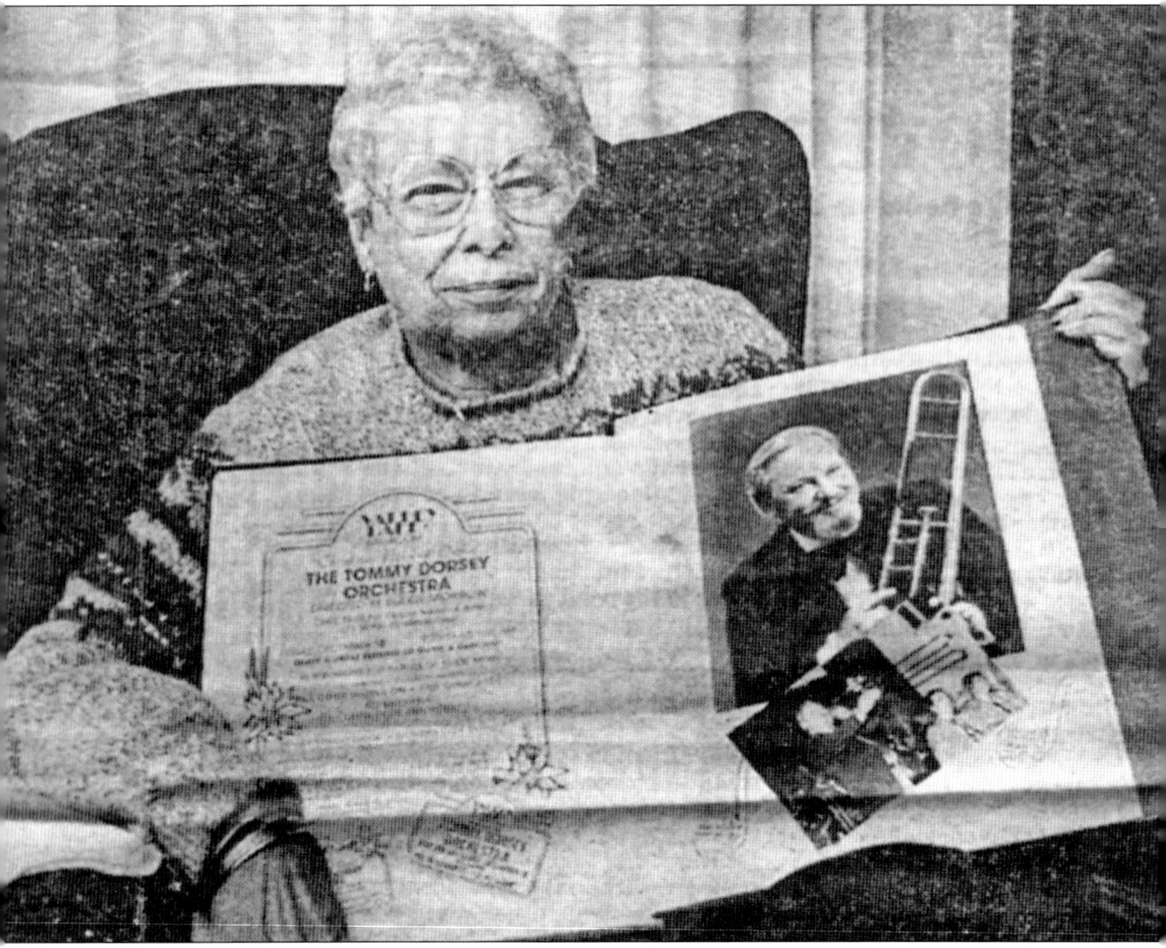

Many girls were invited on their first date to VDB. Including former owners Lou and Dottie Peppe, current owners Mike and Kathy Peppe, and countless others, it is startling how many of these couples wedded. Another teenager was mesmerized by VDB as a junior high girl attending her first dance in 1936, escorted by her boyfriend, Richard Stants. At 14, she learned to jitterbug on that magical dancefloor. This girl would later make her place in VDB history. After graduating from North High in 1940, marrying Richard, and teaching in Columbus schools, Mary Max Stants became the promotional director for VDB in the 1970s and 1980s. She recalled for the October 26, 1988, *NeighborNews*, "Friday nights, kids danced in the school gym, readying for Saturday evenings at THE DALE. It was kind of a Country Club to North High. . . . You were nobody if you didn't go to The Dale." Over the decades, the Stants were glimpsed bopping within the crushing VDB dance throng until the frantic "One O'Clock Jump" sliced through the evening air and the awestruck crowd parted, encircling the couple. Even as septuagenarians, their crowd fascination never wavered—it was always the couple's dance moment, which Fred and Ginger too would have marveled over. (*Clintonville Booster.*)

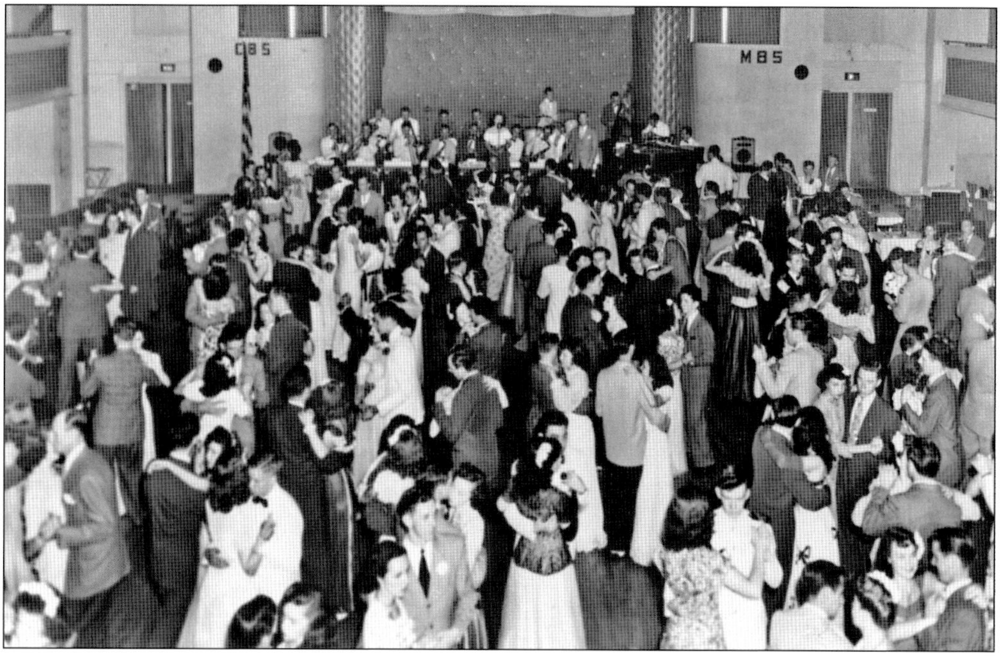

When a teenage girl came home from twirling at the VDB, she would excitedly chat about details from the evening with her mother, who added her own memories of gliding over the immense magical wooden dancefloor. This rite of passage was repeated after Valley Dale dates as the decades marched from the 1920s through the next century of the Valley Dale's existence. (Don Crawford Band, Marilyn Day vocalist.)

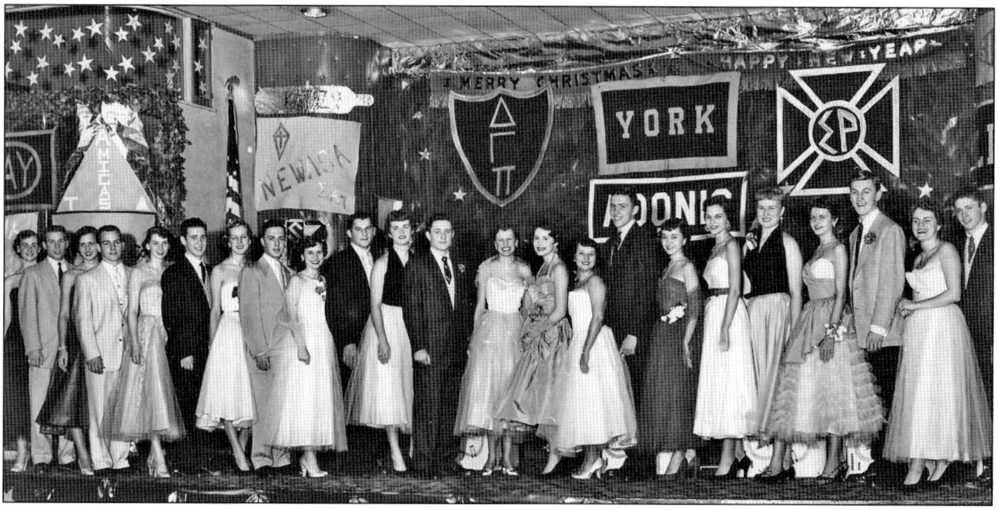

Before October 22, 1941, alcoholic drinks were never tolerated at VDB. Even after Prohibition days, no one was permitted in the hall with a flask. In the 1930s and early 1940s, girls were never permitted to sit or be alone in the building, VDB hired young men to serve as protectors to single women. Even if a girl's date momentarily excused himself, the polite guardsmen would be at her side until her date returned. College sorority house mothers would accompany the girls to Valley Dale and walk the floor keeping the girls in sight at all times. There was a time when society blanketing many cultures would never permit an unmarried girl to be in public unaccompanied. Pictured here is an Ohio State University Agonis Club dance. (Bob Stoll.)

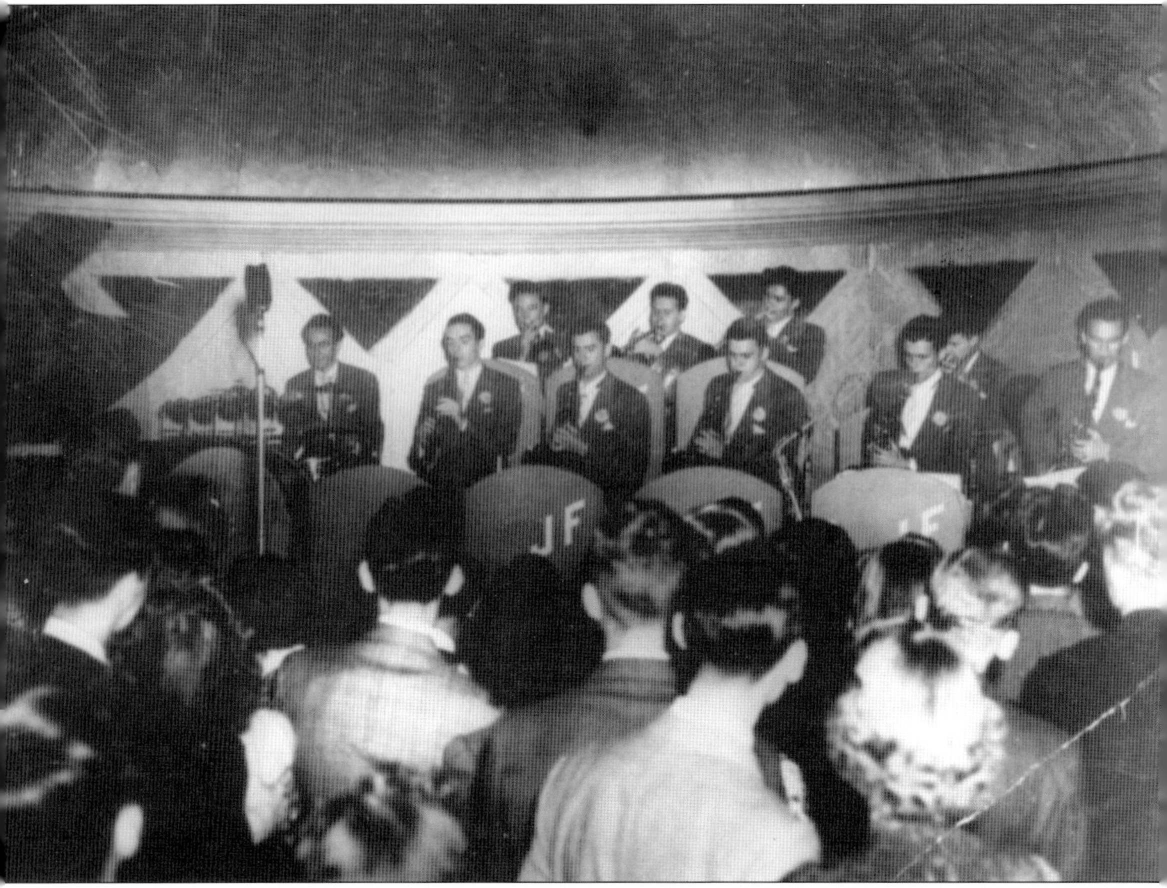

Bands zigzagged the nation creating fans in every town and burg. The local groups were just as cheered as the illustrious big-name bands. According to his children, Jimmy Franck left Oak Harbor, Ohio, as a dedicated 17-year-old trombonist in 1934 to achieve his musical aspirations at Ohio State University. Jimmy Franck created growing recognition, first becoming a member of the OSU marching band, then starting a college swing band. The Jimmy Franck Philharmonics Dance Band was sought after for sorority and fraternity events at Pomerene Hall, OSU's one-time women's student union. Franck won an audition with the Columbus Philharmonic (later the Columbus Symphony), and he also won the heart of symphony bassist Roses Barrett, whom he married. Franck set his Philharmonics up on stage, inviting audiences to dance after each symphonic program. By the late 1930s, Franck appeared at VDB. A newspaper article gained Franck further attention, promoting his New Year's Eve, 1939, VDB performance. While in the service, he played in Nelson Riddle's US Army band. Franck's national recognition grew with his endorsement of Old Bass Trombones, and his poster was hung in Heaton's music store in downtown Columbus. Franck's older brother, Ken, is the trumpeter to the left of trombonist Jimmy.

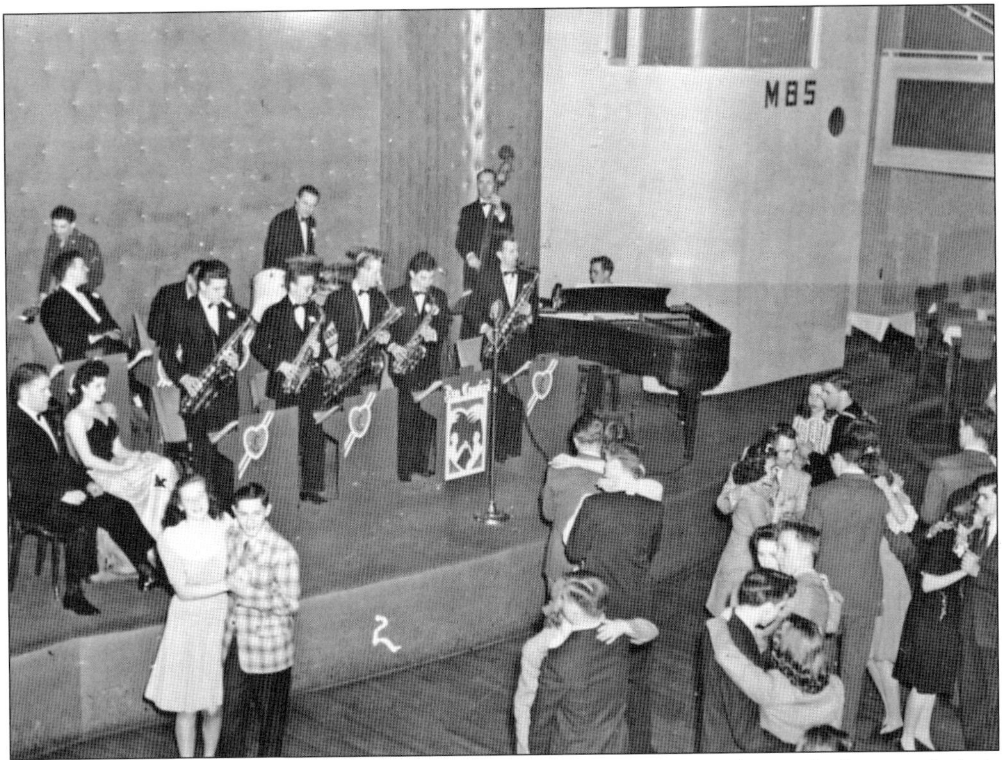

VDB offered an open invitation to parents for a free evening anytime they wished to watch their daughter and boyfriend dance. The regular VDB snack menu consisted of popcorn, cheese cubes, and Cokes. In the 1960s, RC Cola was the beverage. The Don Crawford Band featured high school vocalist Margie Alden (Coyle).

A 1957 prom photograph from the Aquinas High yearbook depicts shy couples posing in front of the Art Deco Bar by New Jersey's Meadowbrook Ballroom's Frank Dailey designed for VDB in 1941. VDB served as one of the few locations for high school events during the 1940s and 1950s. Appreciate the graduated light fixture, which is mounted on the circular mirror. Ornamental iron work at the bar top softens and heightens the look of the radius shaped bar, notice the plaid wall covering above the bar, an exceptional sample of the bygone look for this bar area. (Lou Nobile.)

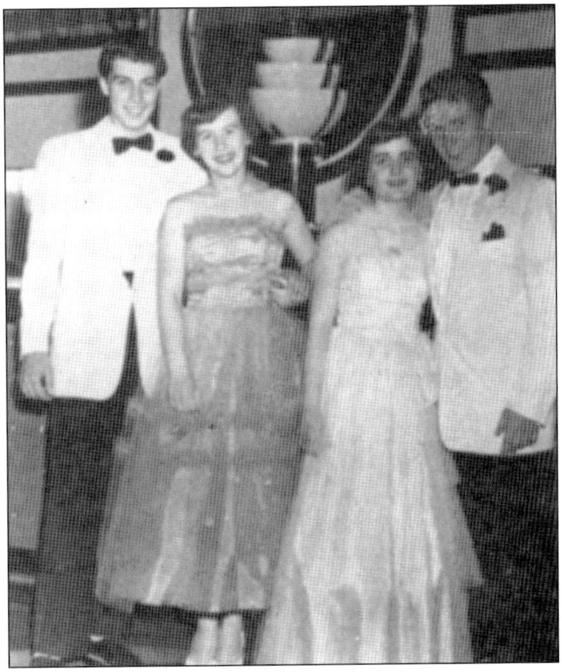

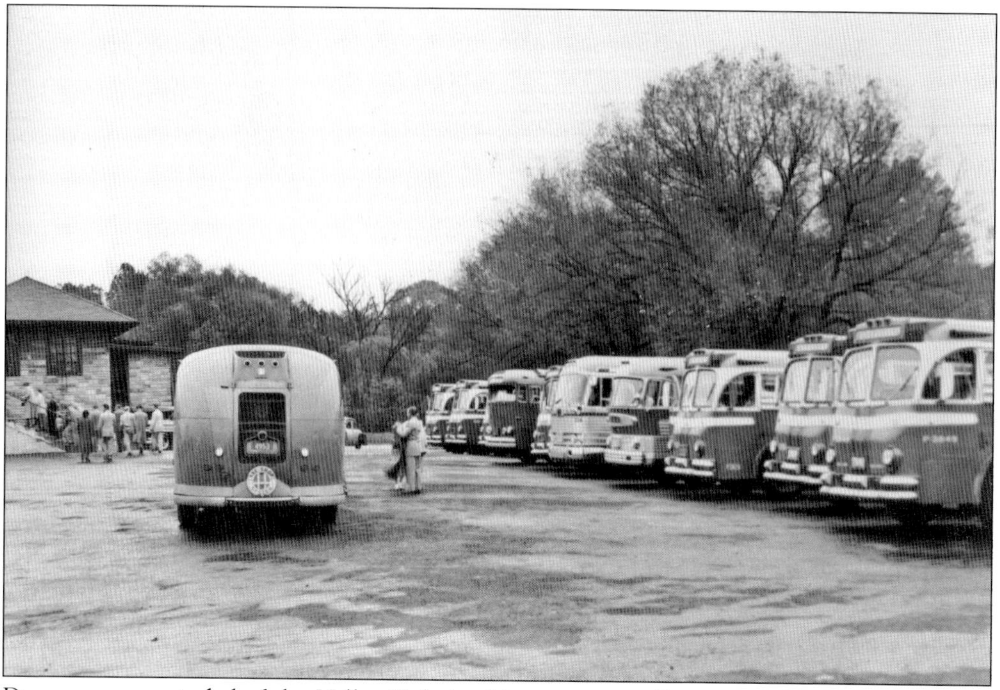

Dancers are reminded of the Valley Dale in this promotion. During World War II, the daily schedule of two to four bands playing until 4:00 a.m. had ceased. Gas was rationed, making it difficult to drive out to the ballroom. Lou Peppe created a novel promotion in which buses picked up fans around the city and at high schools to bring them to and from VDB.

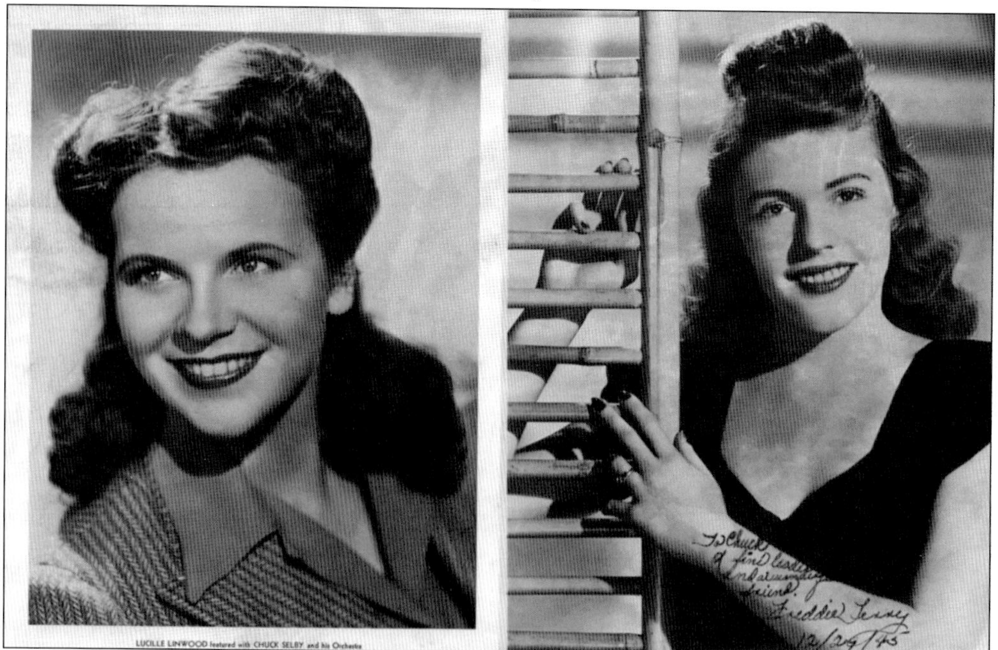

Displaying the hair styles of the decade are Lucille Linwood (left) and Freddie Tenny (right), who were both VDB vocalists with Chuck Selby during the 1940s. Oddly, research uncovered Linwood was related to this author.

A graduate of Columbus Central High School, Margie Alden's (Coyle) first musical notes slipped through her lips at age three. In 1943, she began a singing career with Don Crawford's band, a favorite at VDB. She is pictured here in the 1940s. "Gypsy," as she was nicknamed, appeared with Lawrence Welk in Hollywood at the Aragon Ballroom in 1963. She also sang live on the *Spook Beckman Show* on WLWC and with Doc Everhart during his VDB performances. Until her death in June 2013, at 87 years old, Margie was a welcome guest vocalist for homegrown American Songbook bands led by Vaughn Wesiter and Rick Brunetto. (Doc James Loeffler.)

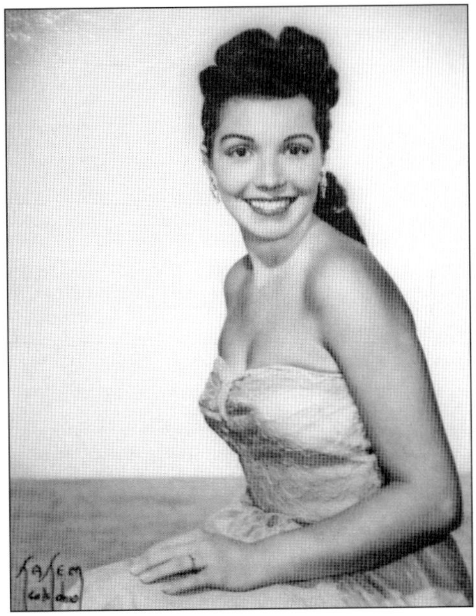

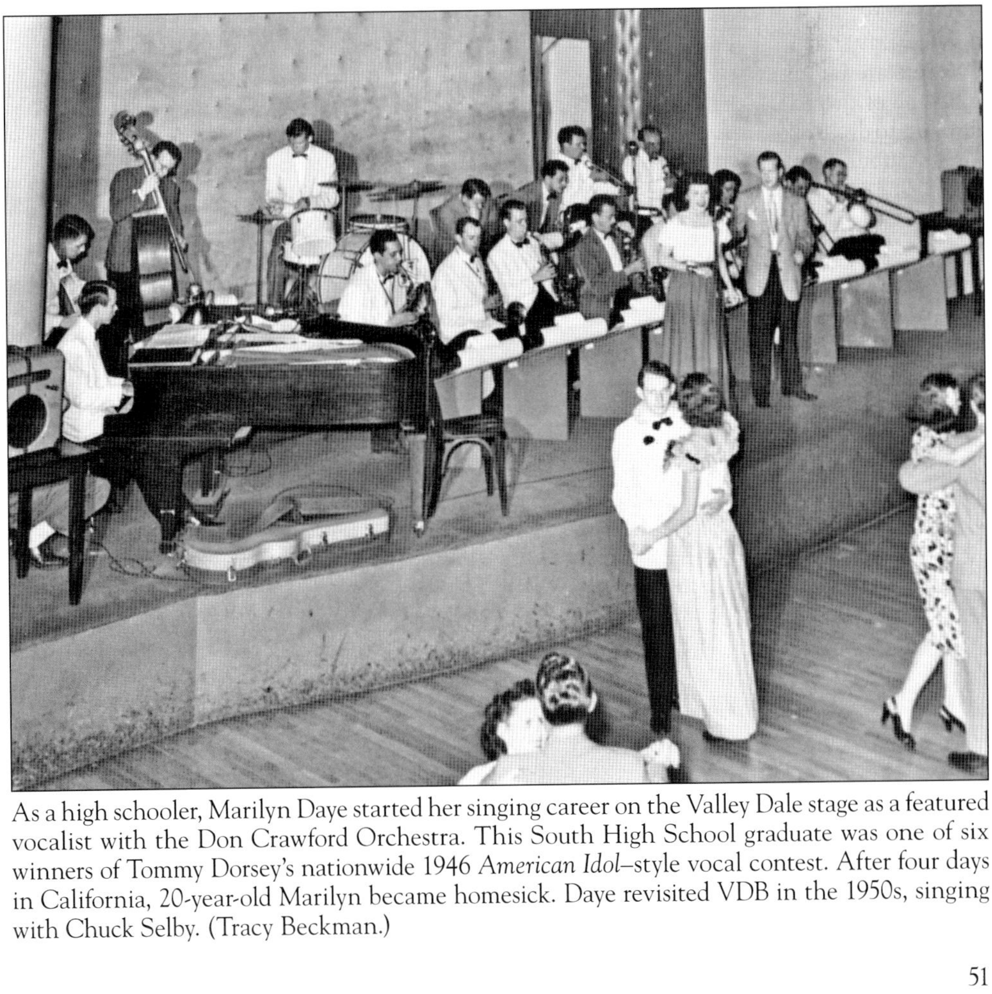

As a high schooler, Marilyn Daye started her singing career on the Valley Dale stage as a featured vocalist with the Don Crawford Orchestra. This South High School graduate was one of six winners of Tommy Dorsey's nationwide 1946 *American Idol*–style vocal contest. After four days in California, 20-year-old Marilyn became homesick. Daye revisited VDB in the 1950s, singing with Chuck Selby. (Tracy Beckman.)

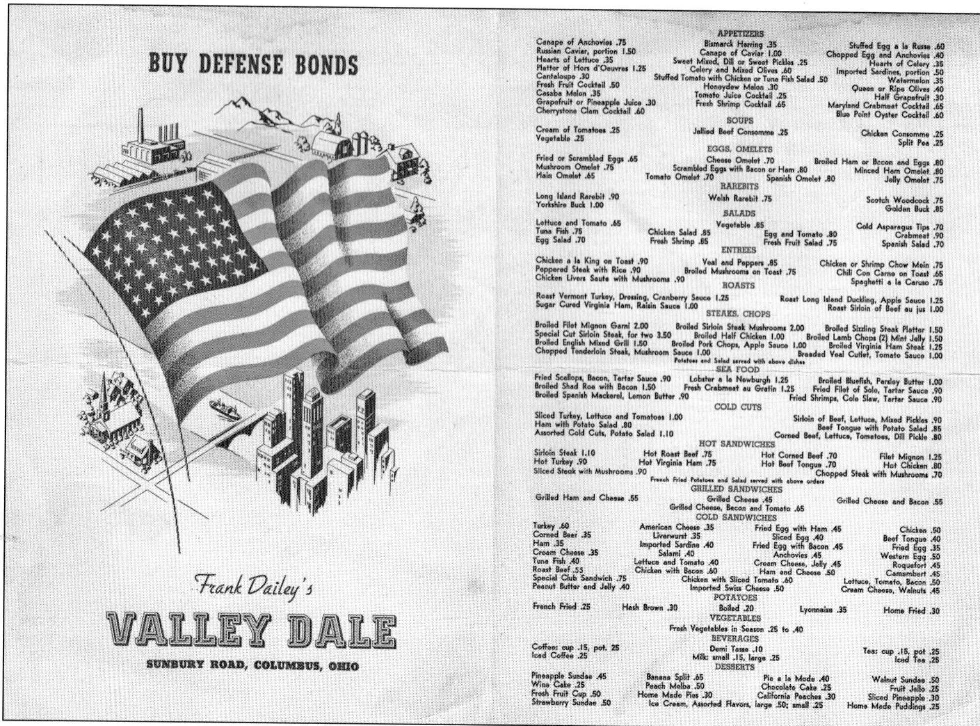

BUY DEFENSE BONDS

Frank Dailey's

VALLEY DALE

SUNBURY ROAD, COLUMBUS, OHIO

APPETIZERS

Canape of Anchovies .75 | Bismarck Herring .35 | Stuffed Egg a la Russe .60
Russian Caviar, portion 1.50 | Canape of Caviar 1.00 | Chopped Egg and Anchovies .40
Hearts of Lettuce .35 | Sweet Mixed, Dill or Sweet Pickles .25 | Hearts of Celery .35
Platter of Hors d'Oeuvres 1.25 | Celery and Mixed Olives .60 | Imported Sardines, portion .50
Cantaloupe .30 | Stuffed Tomato with Chicken or Tuna Fish Salad .50 | Watermelon .35
Fresh Fruit Cocktail .50 | Honeydew Melon .30 | Queen or Ripe Olives .40
Casaba Melon .35 | Tomato Juice Cocktail .25 | Half Grapefruit .30
Grapefruit or Pineapple Juice .30 | Fresh Shrimp Cocktail .65 | Maryland Crabmeat Cocktail .65
Cherrystone Clam Cocktail .60 | Blue Point Oyster Cocktail .60

SOUPS

Cream of Tomatoes .25 | Jellied Beef Consomme .25 | Chicken Consomme .25
Vegetable .25 | Split Pea .25

EGGS, OMELETS

Fried or Scrambled Eggs .65 | Cheese Omelet .70 | Broiled Ham or Bacon and Eggs .80
Mushroom Omelet .75 | Scrambled Eggs with Bacon or Ham .80 | Minced Ham Omelet .80
Plain Omelet .65 | Tomato Omelet .70 | Spanish Omelet .80 | Jelly Omelet .75

RAREBITS

Long Island Rarebit .90 | Welsh Rarebit .75 | Scotch Woodcock .75
Yorkshire Buck 1.00 | Golden Buck .85

SALADS

Lettuce and Tomato .65 | Vegetable .85 | Cold Asparagus Tips .70
Tuna Fish .75 | Chicken Salad .85 | Egg and Tomato .80 | Crabmeat .90
Egg Salad .70 | Fresh Shrimp .85 | Fresh Fruit Salad .75 | Spanish Salad .70

ENTREES

Chicken a la King on Toast .90 | Veal and Peppers .85 | Chicken or Shrimp Chow Mein .75
Peppered Steak with Rice .90 | Broiled Mushrooms on Toast .75 | Chili Con Carne on Toast .65
Chicken Livers Saute with Mushrooms .90 | Spaghetti a la Caruso .75

ROASTS

Roast Vermont Turkey, Dressing, Cranberry Sauce 1.25 | Roast Long Island Duckling, Apple Sauce 1.25
Sugar Cured Virginia Ham, Raisin Sauce 1.00 | Roast Sirloin of Beef au jus 1.00

STEAKS, CHOPS

Broiled Filet Mignon Garni 2.00 | Broiled Sirloin Steak Mushrooms 2.00 | Broiled Sizzling Steak Platter 1.50
Special Cut Sirloin Steak, for two 3.50 | Broiled Half Chicken 1.00 | Broiled Lamb Chops (2) Mint Jelly 1.50
Broiled English Mixed Grill 1.50 | Broiled Pork Chops, Apple Sauce 1.00 | Broiled Virginia Ham Steak 1.25
Chopped Tenderloin Steak, Mushroom Sauce 1.00 | Breaded Veal Cutlet, Tomato Sauce 1.00
Potatoes and Salad served with above dishes

SEA FOOD

Fried Scallops, Bacon, Tartar Sauce .90 | Lobster a la Newburgh 1.25 | Broiled Bluefish, Parsley Butter 1.00
Broiled Shad Roe with Bacon 1.50 | Fresh Crabmeat au Gratin 1.25 | Fried Filet of Sole, Tartar Sauce .90
Broiled Spanish Mackerel, Lemon Butter .90 | Fried Shrimps, Cole Slaw, Tartar Sauce .90

COLD CUTS

Sliced Turkey, Lettuce and Tomatoes 1.00 | Sirloin of Beef, Lettuce, Mixed Pickles .90
Ham with Potato Salad .80 | Beef Tongue with Potato Salad .85
Assorted Cold Cuts, Potato Salad 1.10 | Corned Beef, Lettuce, Tomatoes, Dill Pickle .80

HOT SANDWICHES

Sirloin Steak 1.10 | Hot Roast Beef .75 | Hot Corned Beef .70 | Filet Mignon 1.25
Hot Turkey .90 | Hot Virginia Ham .75 | Hot Beef Tongue .70 | Hot Chicken .80
Sliced Steak with Mushrooms .90 | Chopped Steak with Mushrooms .70
French Fried Potatoes and Salad served with above orders

GRILLED SANDWICHES

Grilled Ham and Cheese .55 | Grilled Cheese .45 | Grilled Cheese and Bacon .55
Grilled Cheese, Bacon and Tomato .65

COLD SANDWICHES

Turkey .60 | American Cheese .35 | Fried Egg with Ham .45 | Chicken .50
Corned Beef .35 | Liverwurst .35 | Sliced Egg .40 | Beef Tongue .40
Ham .35 | Imported Sardine .40 | Fried Egg with Bacon .45 | Fried Egg .35
Cream Cheese .35 | Salami .40 | Anchovies .45 | Western Egg .50
Tuna Fish .40 | Lettuce and Tomato .40 | Cream Cheese, Jelly .45 | Roquefort .45
Roast Beef .55 | Chicken with Bacon .60 | Ham and Cheese .50 | Camembert .45
Special Club Sandwich .75 | Chicken with Sliced Tomato .60 | Lettuce, Tomato, Bacon .50
Peanut Butter and Jelly .40 | Imported Swiss Cheese .50 | Cream Cheese, Walnuts .45

POTATOES

French Fried .25 | Hash Brown .30 | Boiled .20 | Lyonnaise .35 | Home Fried .30

VEGETABLES

Fresh Vegetables in Season .25 to .40

BEVERAGES

Coffee: cup .15, pot. 25 | Demi Tasse .10 | Tea: cup .15, pot .25
Iced Coffee .25 | Milk: small .15, large .25 | Iced Tea .25

DESSERTS

Pineapple Sundae .45 | Banana Split .65 | Pie a la Mode .40 | Walnut Sundae .50
Wine Cake .25 | Peach Melba .50 | Chocolate Cake .25 | Fruit Jello .25
Fresh Fruit Cup .50 | Home Made Pies .30 | California Peaches .30 | Sliced Pineapple .30
Strawberry Sundae .50 | Ice Cream, Assorted Flavors, large .50; small .25 | Home Made Puddings .25

Starting in 1941, fine dining was introduced to the ballroom. Waiters, linen table cloths, crystal, and china complemented the full menu displayed here. The addition of alcohol was also welcomed at VDB. A feast before a band performance or a light supper after a show was very high brow for Columbus at that time.

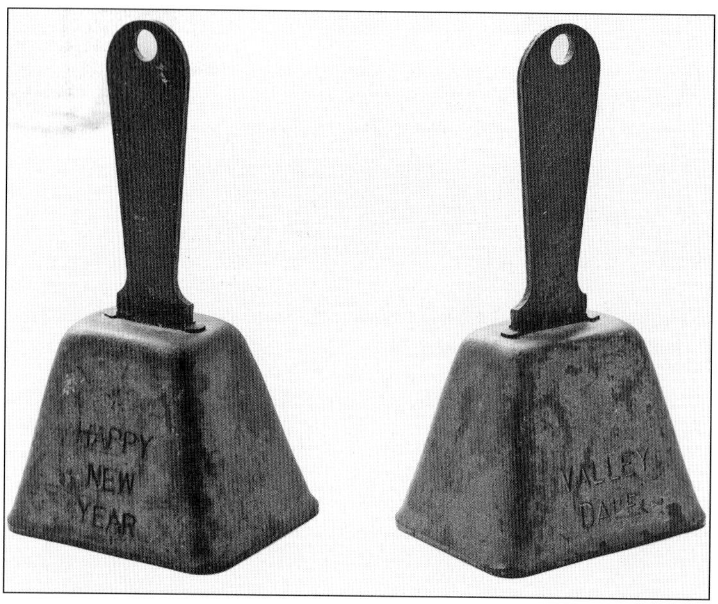

The cofounder of the Fabulous Forties big band, Dale Groves, cherished his personal VDB New Year's Eve memorabilia. Groves scooped up this souvenir in 1947. According to a sentimental tale from Dale, bells were waiting at each guest's place setting in anticipation of "Auld Lang Syne." (Ron and Ken Groves.)

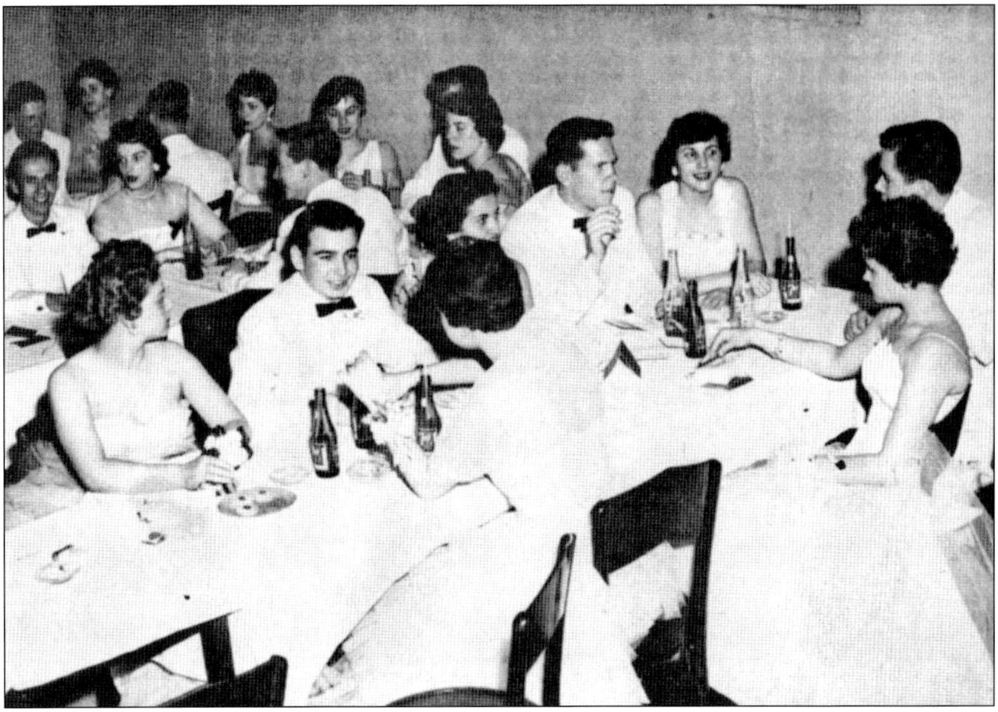

The majority of Columbus high schools held proms and annual themed occasions at VDB. This image from a 1955 Aquinas College High School yearbook stops time, showing what a prom night was like at VDB. This is a rare shot directly off of the dancefloor under the balcony. (Lou Nobile.)

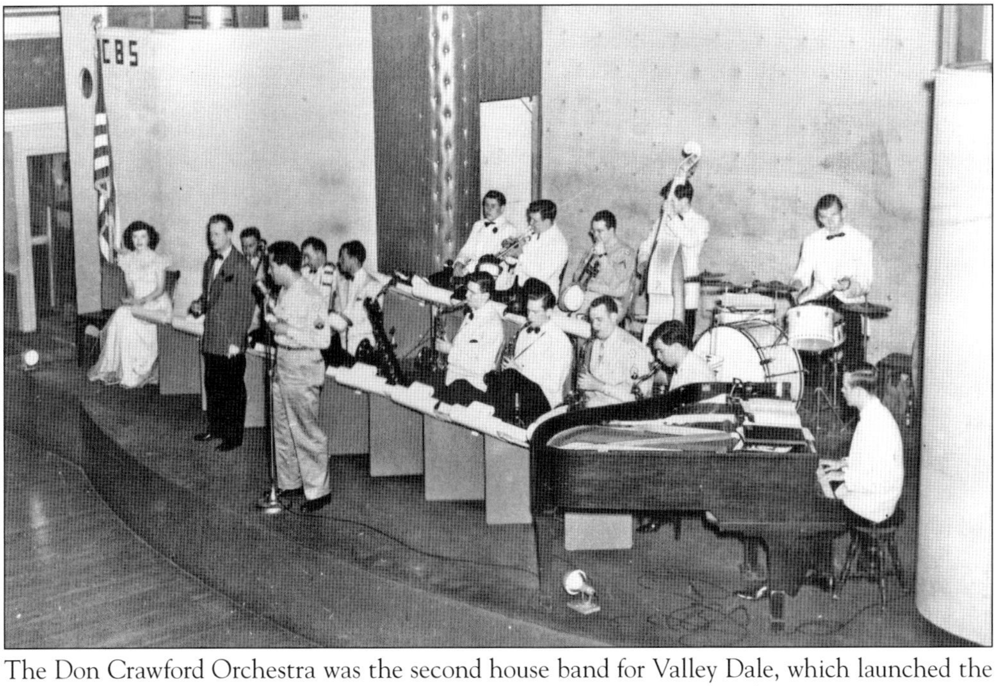

The Don Crawford Orchestra was the second house band for Valley Dale, which launched the careers of many local musicians. The pictured vocalist is a teenage Marilyn Daye.

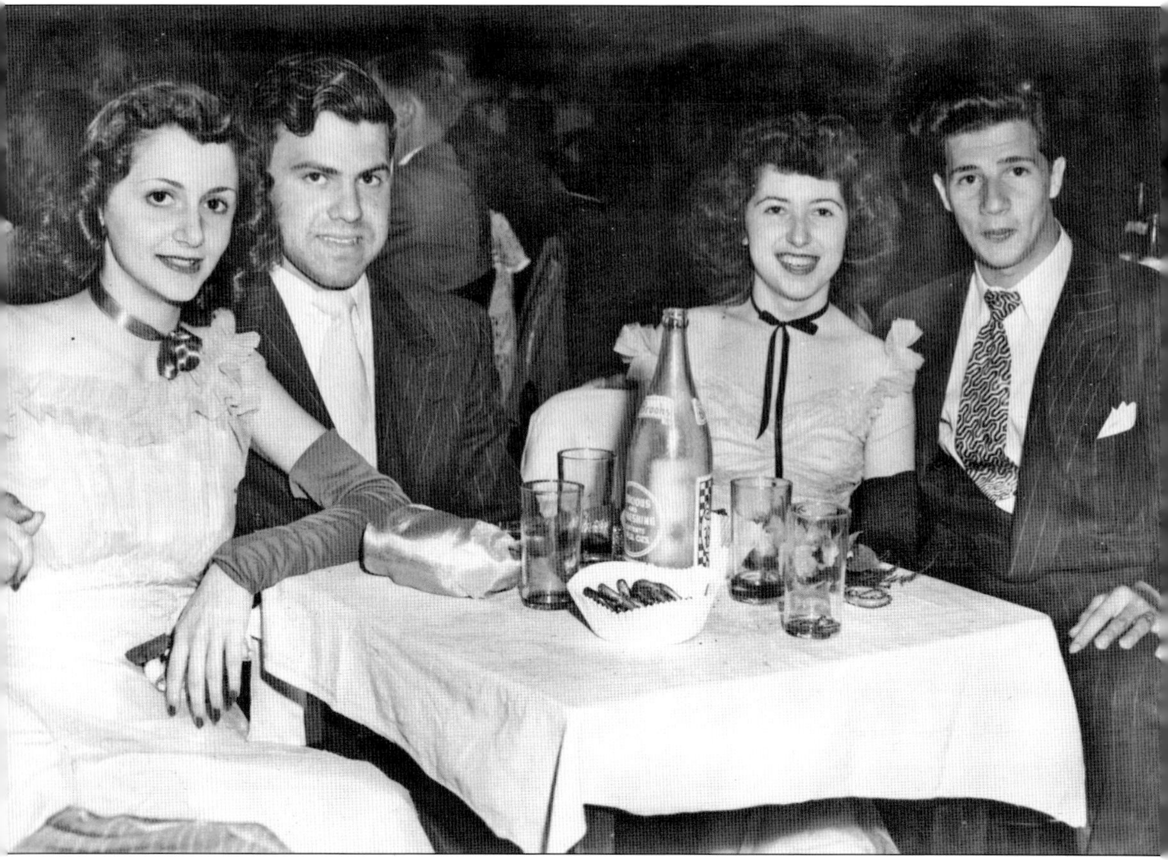

St. Joseph Academy girls often dated the boys of Aquinas College High School. Pictured on June 12, 1947, these girl cousins arc on a double date with boy cousins at the Aquinas Alumni Dance. Between sways and swings on the dancefloor, the couples settled sweetly with pretzels and pop at one of VDB's classic two-foot black square tables. From left to right are Louise Mary Giantonio, John Gallucci, Louise "Wezi" Giantonio, and Bruno Masdea. Valley Dale served as the backdrop for the first and second date of Wezi Giantonio and Bruno Masdea. Masdea married Wezi in 1952. This is where the story unfolds for Bruno, Wezi, and their daughter (the author). (Louise "Wezi" Masdea.)

Five

The Evolution of a Ballroom

The Valley Dale was closed less than four months, remodeled and ready for business October 22 of 1941 . . . the Meadowbrook Ballroom's Frank Dailey of New Jersey, leased VDB from Lou Peppe. Their plan was to make it an even more sensational ballroom. With Dailey's successes at Meadowbrook there was no limit. Frank Dailey's Valley Dale, as it was now named, (smitten newspapers wrote "Dailey's Dale"), offered fine dining and alcohol before the shows and lighter fare after. He remodeled and enhanced with the latest design trends, including plaid wallpaper, teal toned ceilings. Greater attention was placed on the trophy of the ballroom, its national simulcasts of the only twin radio booths in the country. Dailey had hoped to simultaneously run the VDB and his Meadowbrook, through booking orchestras to appear at both locations. This chapter strolls one through the building with a juxtaposition of countless images from past time spans to the present. The Valley Dale was closed less than four months, remodeled and ready for an electrifying business October 22 of 1941 . . . But unknowingly, it was just 46 days before Pearl Harbor brought America into World War II: Frank's calculating intention was to create a phenomenal national presence with his two upscale ballrooms. Reality presented an unwelcomed arrangement, with VDB being poised out of the city limits. War rationing of gasoline, restricted its fans travel to and monies spent at VDB. Dailey had the lease agreement terminated and was back in New Jersey by "The Summer of '42."

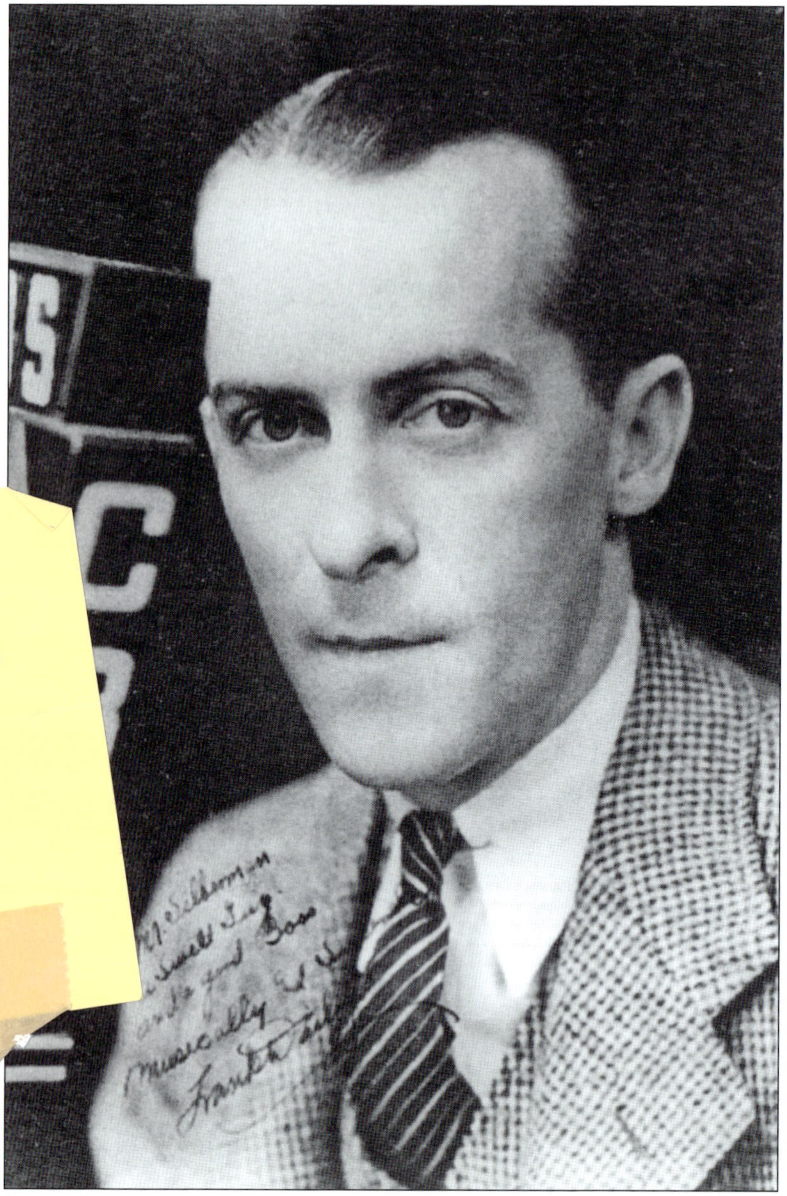

For several months in 1941, VDB closed for remodeling. Frank Dailey, owner, designer and bandleader of New Jersey's renown Meadowbrook Ballroom, arrived in Columbus to manage and freshen the 17-year-old VDB interior. VDB had a bowstring truss wood ceiling, open to the rafters. A paint of teal blue-green was his selected ceiling color. Ivory paint covered walls, balcony and outer staircase. Dailey, added a coral toned leather which he used as an accent textile to warm and enhance the hardwood surfaces. His leather treatment, was tufted and quilted in a diamond pattern applied to multiple surfaces, including the staircase rectangular and radius up-stage detail. Balcony fronts were upholstered with paneled inserts repeated above the dance floor. Carpeting blend consisted of browns and taupe weave. The iconic radio booths were also painted ivory. A balcony-level semi-circular Art Deco bar, a marvel at the time, was also treated with a tufted front, its bar back presented plaid wall covering in tans and browns. Beginning during the 1970s, the VDB began its first refresh since 1941. (Phillip Read Meadowbrook Ballroom.)

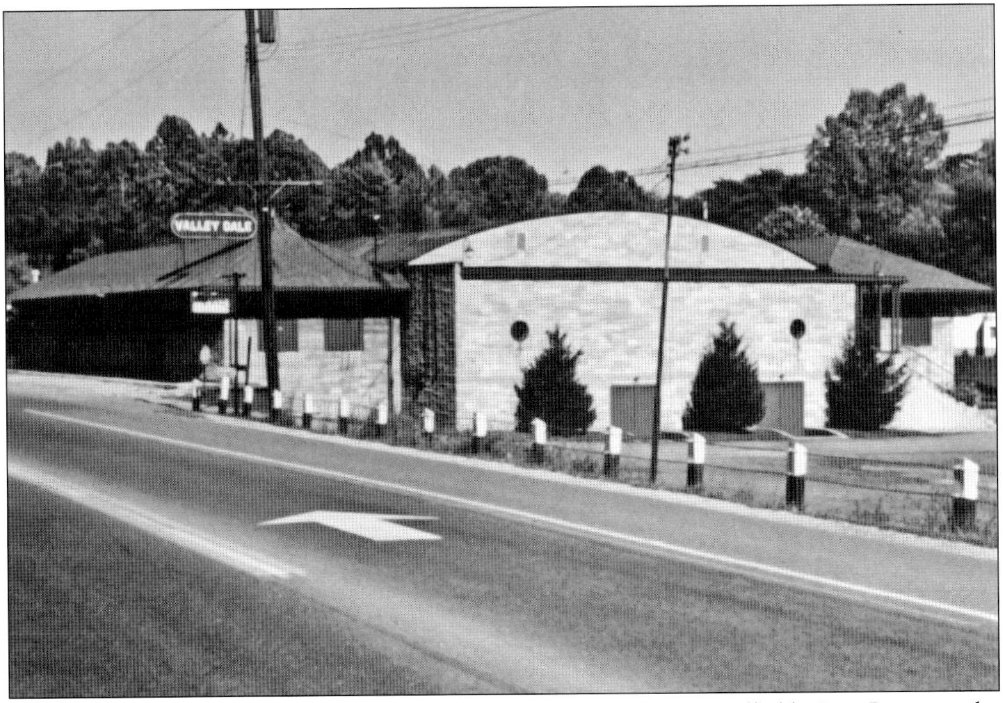

A mid-1950s photograph of the Valley Dale shows the neon sign installed by Lou Peppe in the early 1950s. The facade was enhanced with ledge stone. The front entrance was enclosed, and the area in front of the pine trees was used as a parking lot.

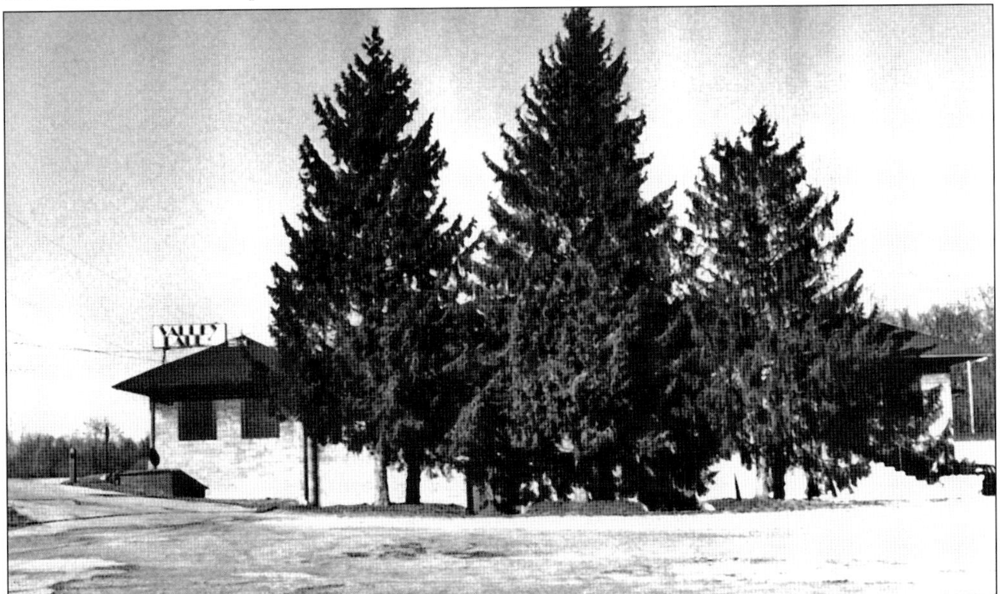

After the city's wrecking-ball plans for the Valley Dale were wrecked in 1980, intense updating and modifications began to take place. An innovative sign was designed for the exterior with a shooting star positioned at the tip of the *Y* in "Valley." The updated logo would be used through the next 18 years. This 1987 *Columbus Dispatch* image is the last documentation of the pine trees, which were removed shortly after Finta family took over operations in 1989.

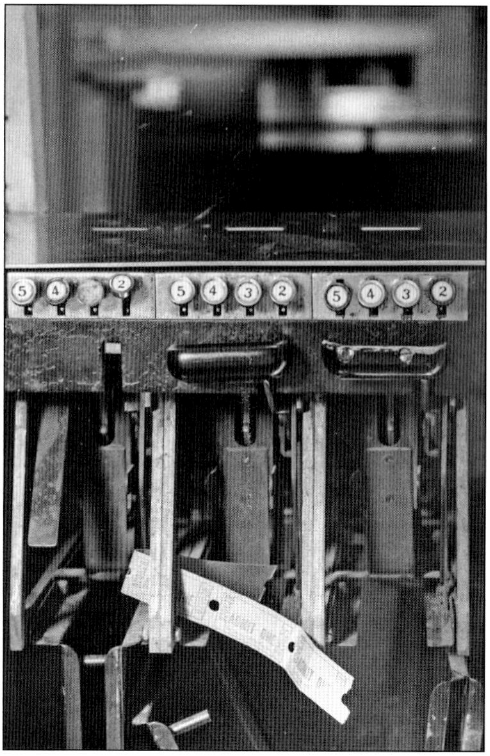

A now-antiquated ticket machine was once used by patrons to purchase tickets to the hall. As people passed through double doors, they were directed left towards the ticket booth. Two knee walls led guests to the ticket booth, separating those who had purchased tokens. Frank Daily redesigned the space in 1941; the booth was completely dismantled and removed in 2016. (*Columbus Dispatch.*)

VDB owner Mike Peppe thoughtfully remembers: "my dad continually used these passes up until he sold the Dale to me." These slips were sent to entertainment reporters, businesspeople, radio announcers, and anyone Lou Peppe was trying to promote the Dale to for business or social reasons. Mike Peppe softly sighed as his hand glided over the pieces. "Yep, way back in the early days, basically as long I can remember, they were in use."

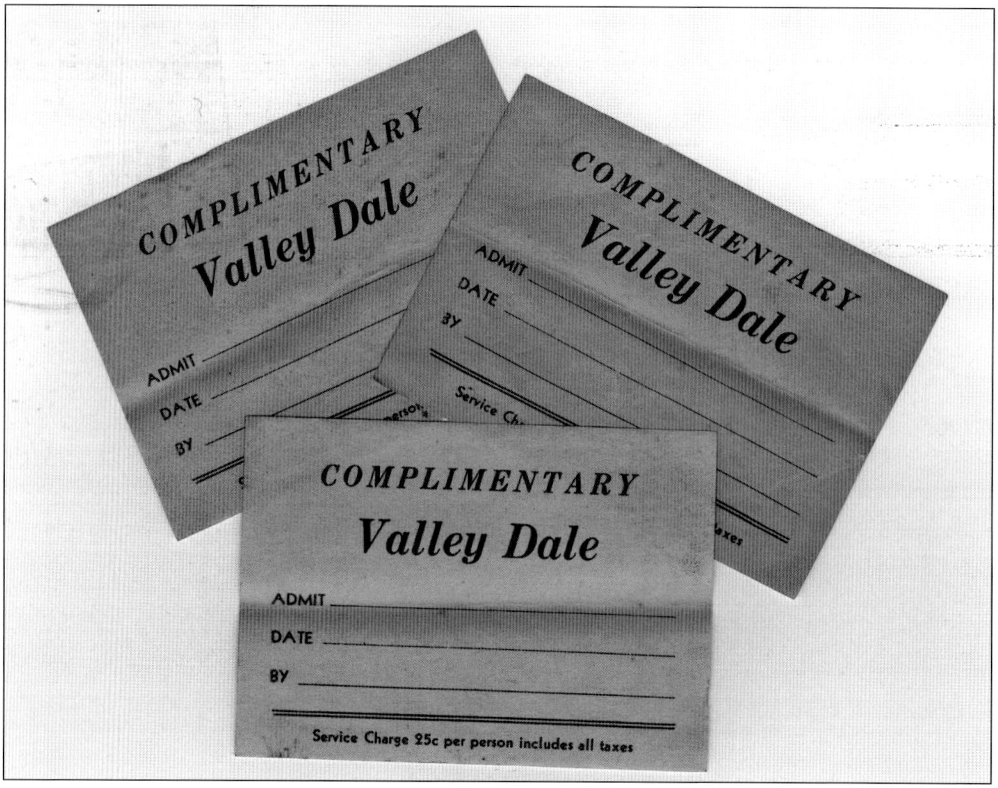

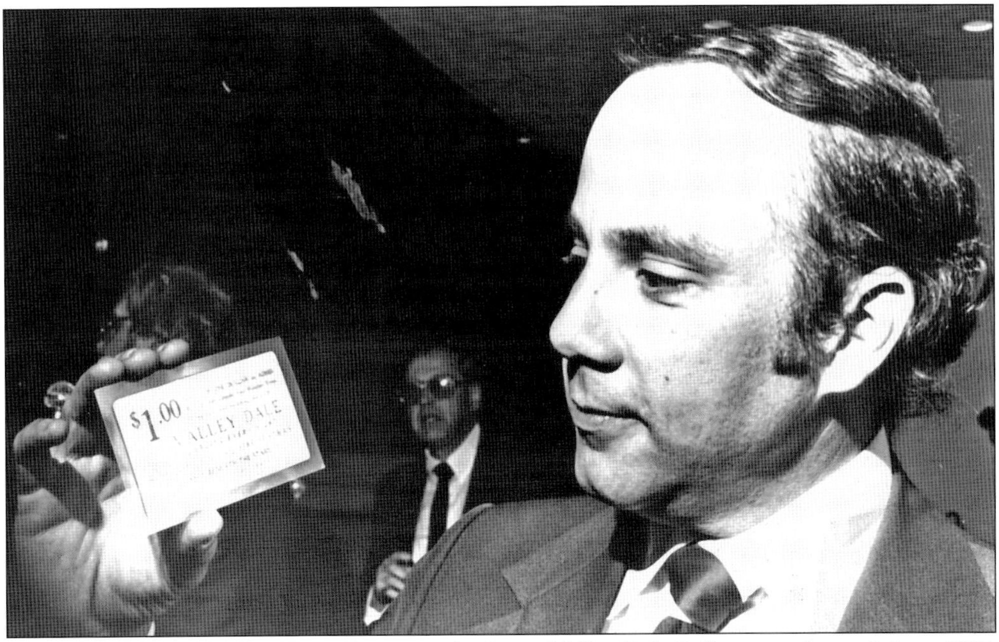

In this photograph from 1981, Mike Peppe displays a Valley Dale Ballroom ticket stub from 1927. The ticket states: "GOOD FOR ONE DOLLAR on ADMISSION of one couple any Monday evening up to and including Oct. 3, 1927—VALLEY DALE—DANCING EVERY NIGHT—WORLD'S LEADING ORCHESTRAS—'DANCE BENEATH THE STARS'—NOT GOOD ON HOLIDAYS." (*Columbus Dispatch*; photograph by Ken Chamberlain.)

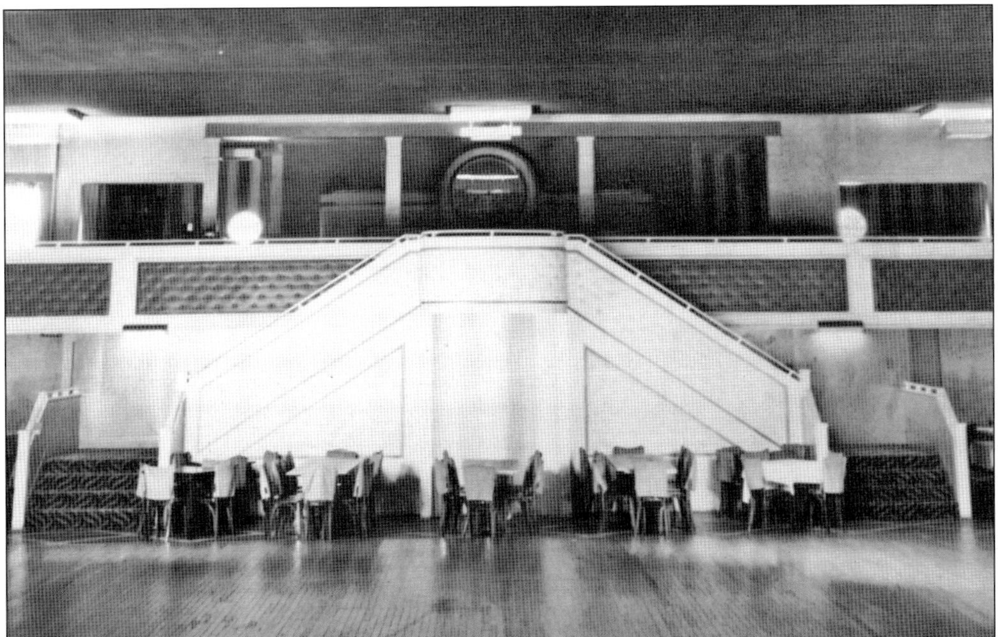

Before 1950, this vantage from the dancefloor shows the original glass entry doors at left and the ticket booth, art deco bar, and coat check, all on the balcony level. This image shows an uncommon view of a closed-in ceiling painted teal.

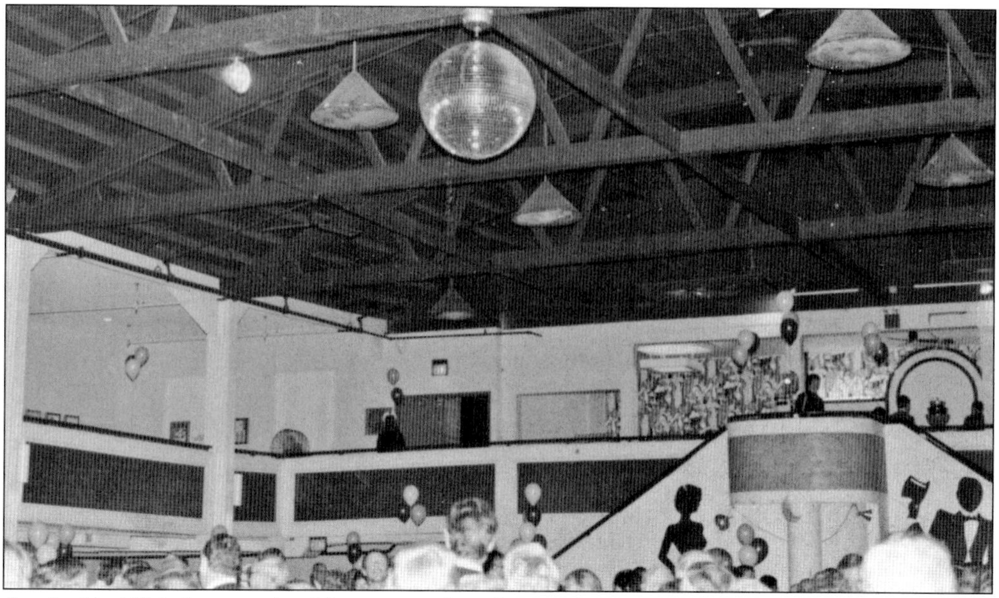

A valuable 1984 photograph of the open ceiling depicts the raw, unpainted wood truss and rafters. Notice the exit sign denoting the main entrance, the ticket booth, and the art deco bar space with black and white wall covering replacing the former brown and tan plaid wallpaper of 1941. (Graham Brannon Photography.)

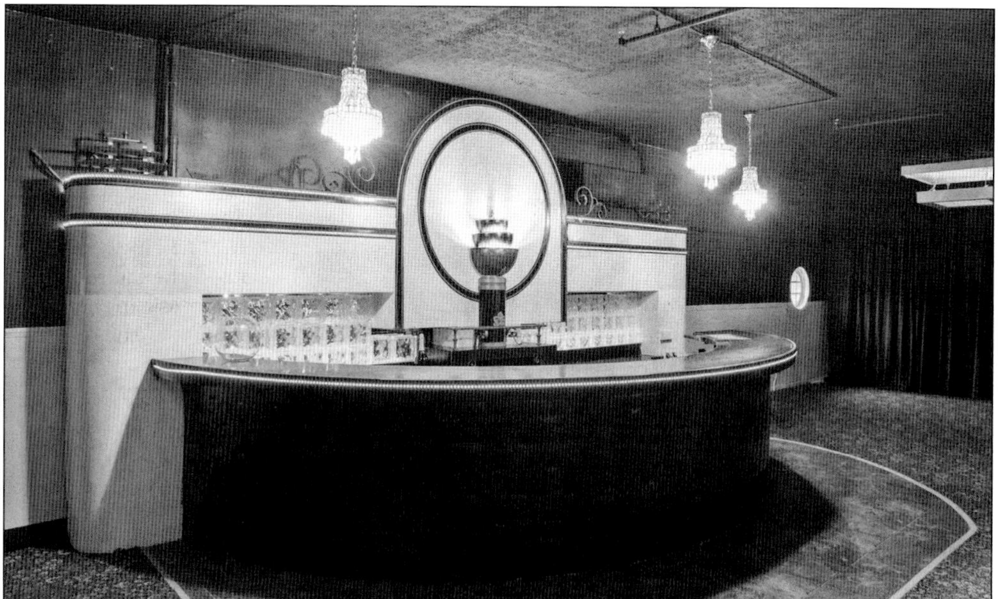

This image gives a crisp view of the art deco bar in 2018. The round mirror disappeared in 1980; only its shape remains. The bar walls are painted forest green instead of papered. It is a thrill to see the original tiered light sconce celebrating VDB's 78th year. Lighting is a favorite way to enhance a space, and the rope lighting outlining the bar and the chandelier pendants (mini versions of the eight chandeliers suspended over the ballroom floor) were added in 2016. The circular bar dates from 1941. Black enamel was painted over the leather during the 1970s. For an image of Dailey's original bar design, refer to page 49. (Graham Brannon Photography.)

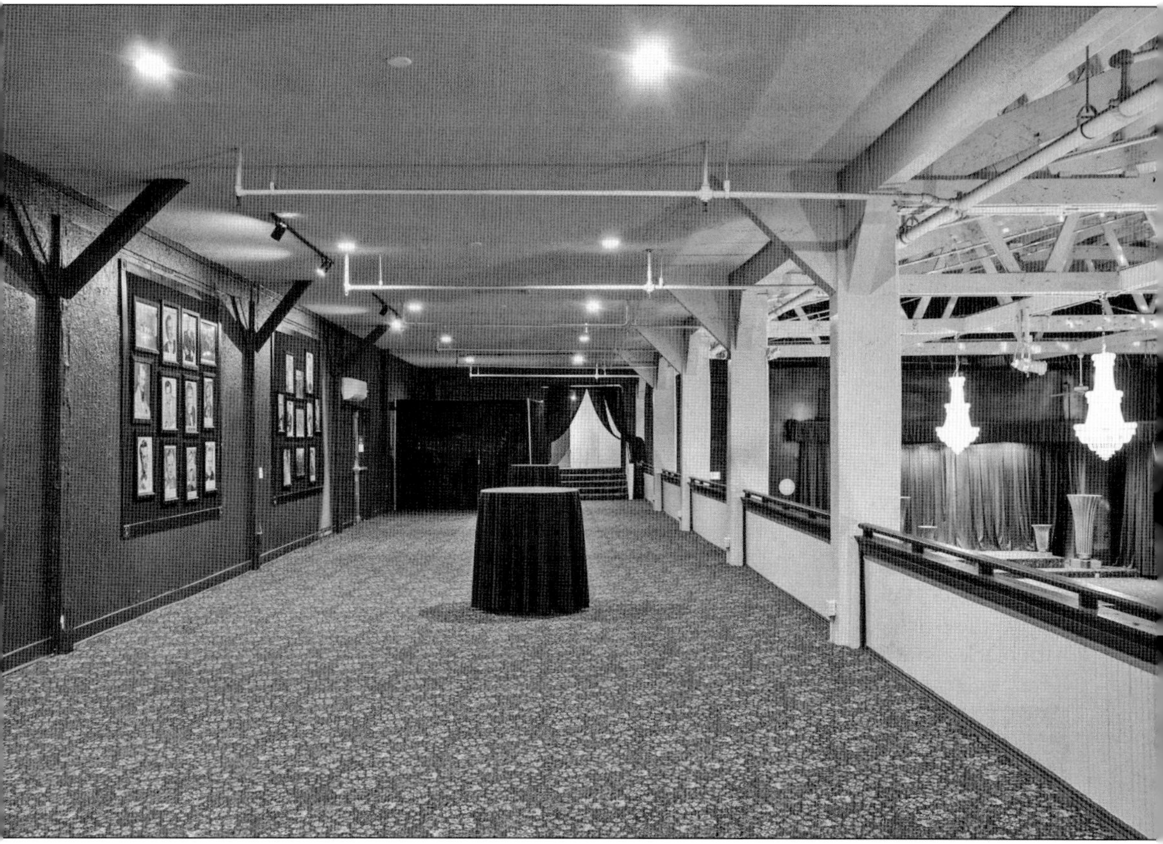

Linen eight-tops were scattered with nibbled wedding cakes. Where fragrant centerpieces earlier welcomed guests, loose petals were strewn on tabletops littered with wine-splashed goblets. At evening's end, VDB proprietors Dana and Marty Finta assisted the dwindling crew through the knotty pine bar, bolting the steel back door as the last server headed home. The Fintas flicked the switches turning off the lights and the sound system. The couple scanned the ballroom as they picked at a late-night snack. They paused at hearing almost indecipherable music in the hall. Dana moved back to the sound system and found that it was still off; she unplugged the system, but the nostalgic melody played on. The duo briskly covered the ballroom, looking for a radio or a CD player that may have been left on by the wedding party. As they searched the balcony and ballroom level, the music increased to an almost deafening volume. "It was an orchestra, I believe it was Tommy Dorsey's Orchestra's playing," remarked Marty. "Even when we turned off everything to almost entire darkness," added Dana, "the orchestra played uninterrupted . . . they froze, absorbed in the grand unexplainable moment." With passing time, the music faded. In May 2018, a new VDB employee heard a crowd of people dancing and cheering to a big band in the ballroom. The ballroom had been emptied for hours. (Graham Brannon Photography.)

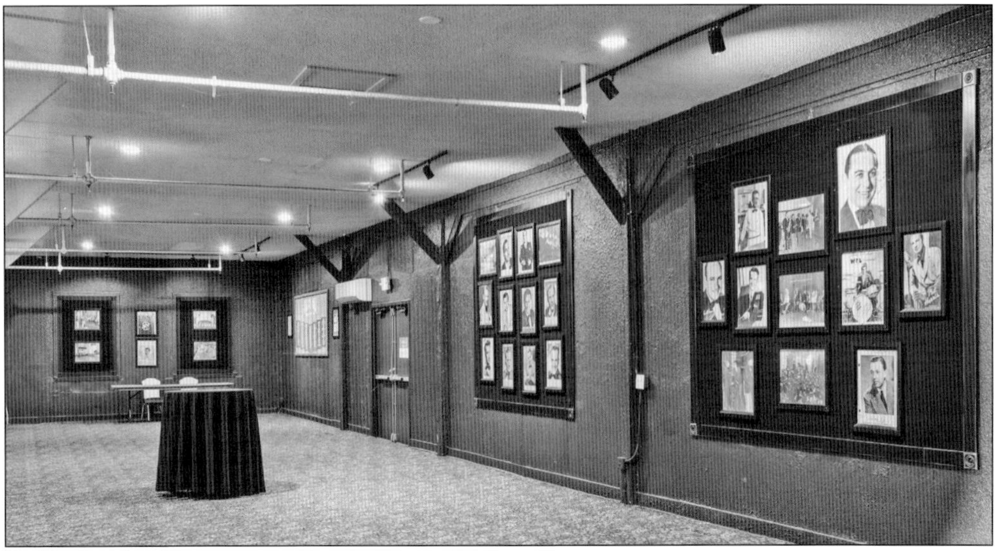

When visiting the Valley Dale, tour the portrait gallery on all the balcony walls overlooking the dancefloor. The Cavalcade of Stars is a framed plaque inscribed with a substantial number of artists who have played VDB. Frank Sinatra's photograph hangs in this section. Walls of fame consist of photographs or illustrations of performers, many autographed with dedications to the Valley Dale and members of the Peppe family. Several date back to the late 1930s. Deana Martin was the most recent addition in 2013. (Graham Brannon Photography.)

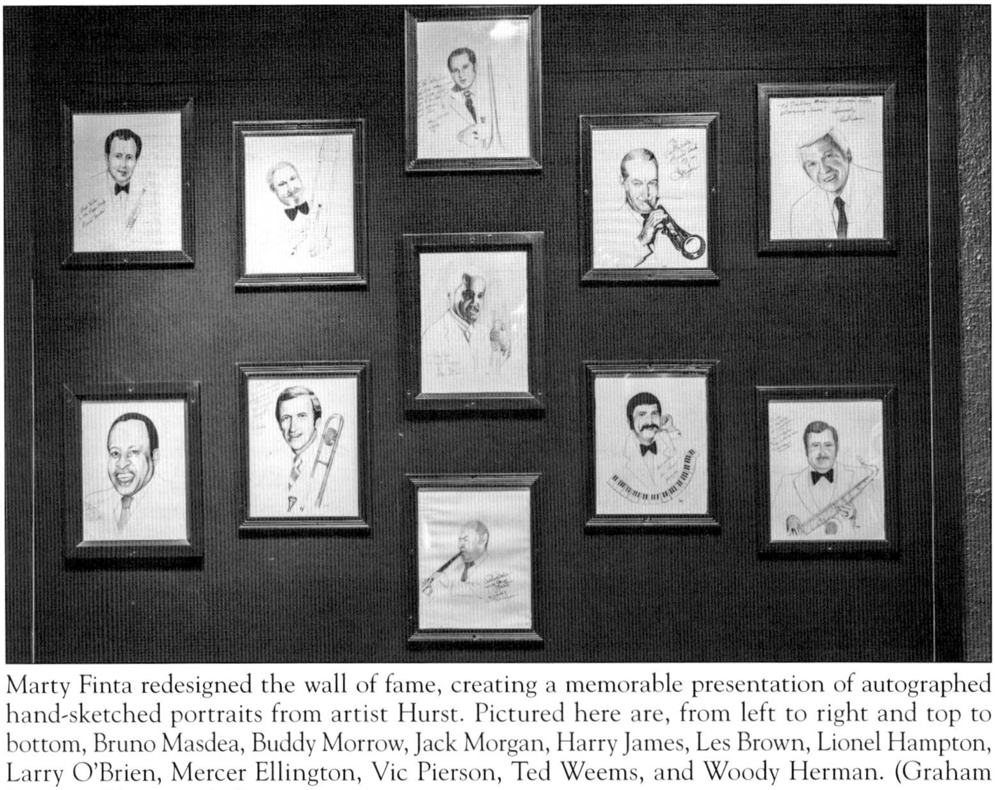

Marty Finta redesigned the wall of fame, creating a memorable presentation of autographed hand-sketched portraits from artist Hurst. Pictured here are, from left to right and top to bottom, Bruno Masdea, Buddy Morrow, Jack Morgan, Harry James, Les Brown, Lionel Hampton, Larry O'Brien, Mercer Ellington, Vic Pierson, Ted Weems, and Woody Herman. (Graham Brannon Photography.)

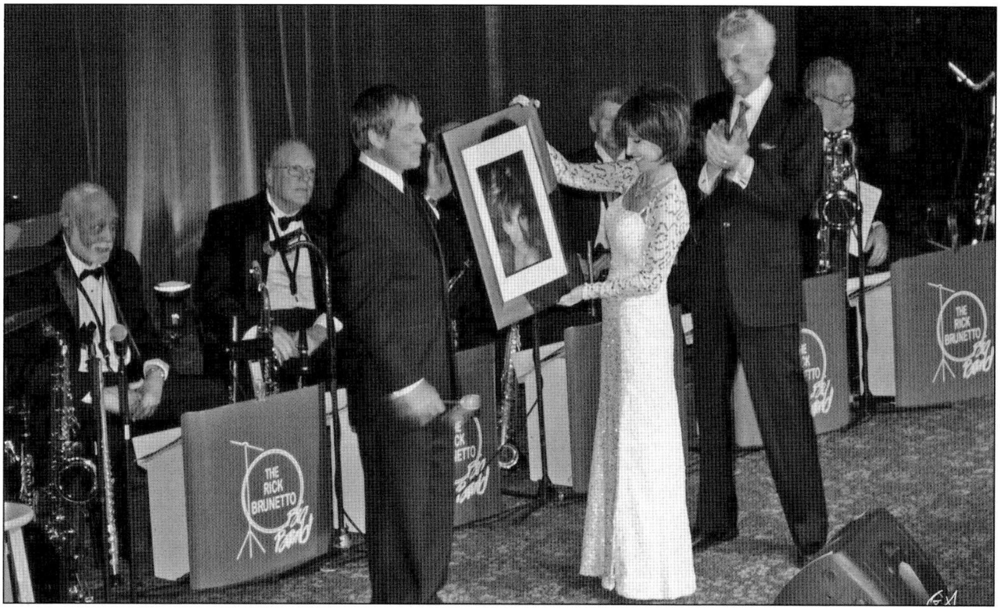

This official autographed portrait of Deana Martin is installed on the VDB wall of fame. Martin's surprise induction took place moments before her Christmas show in 2012. Deana's appropriate salutation was fitting: "Memories Are Made of This" also served as the title of her autobiography. Deana is an artist quite familiar with the VDB; it was only fitting to invite her to write a foreword from her intimate perspective as daughter and performer. Pictured here are, from left to right, (first row, in front of band) Marty Finta, Deana Martin, and John Griffith; (second row) Rick Brunetto Big Band musicians Sonny McBroom, Tom Schwieterman, Gordon Shaffer, and Bob Carpenter. (Graham Brannon Photography.)

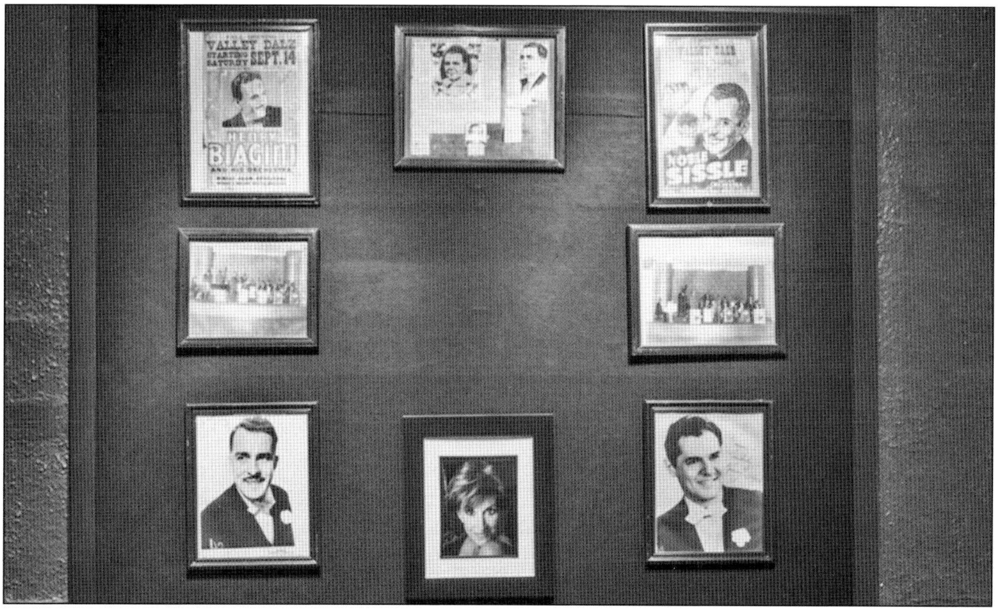

Pictured is the wall of fame with a list of artists' names. Clockwise from top left are Henry Biagini, Jim Peppe, Nobile Sissel, Earl Hood, Glen Gray (see page 24), Deana Martin, and Kenny August (see page 24). (Graham Brannon Photography.)

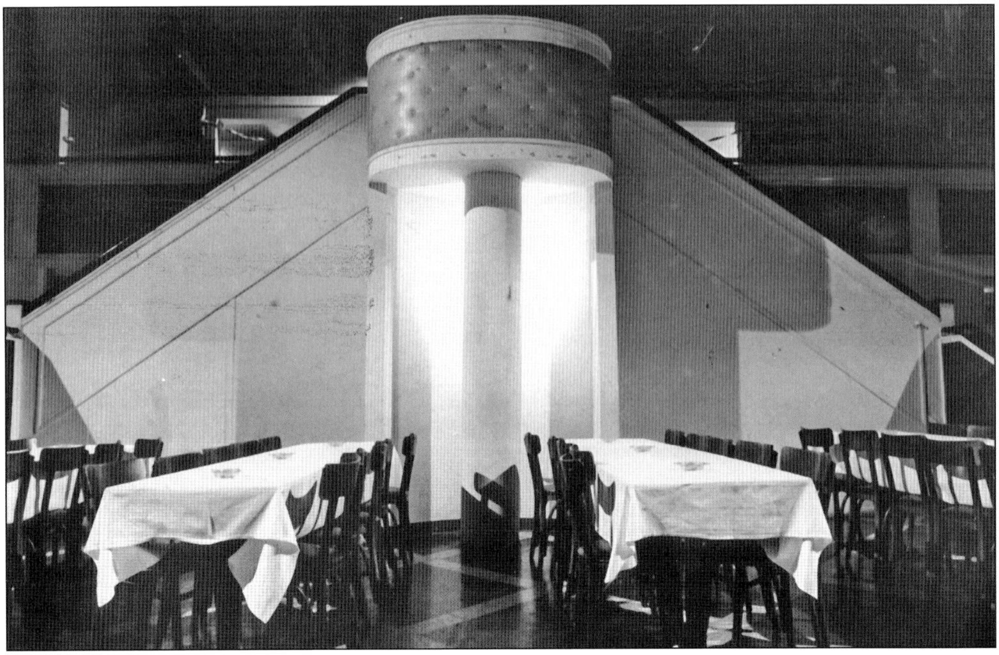

A 1987 photograph taken from the *Columbus Dispatch* portrays an older view of the ballroom with the double staircase and the illuminated radius wall enhancing VDB merriments.

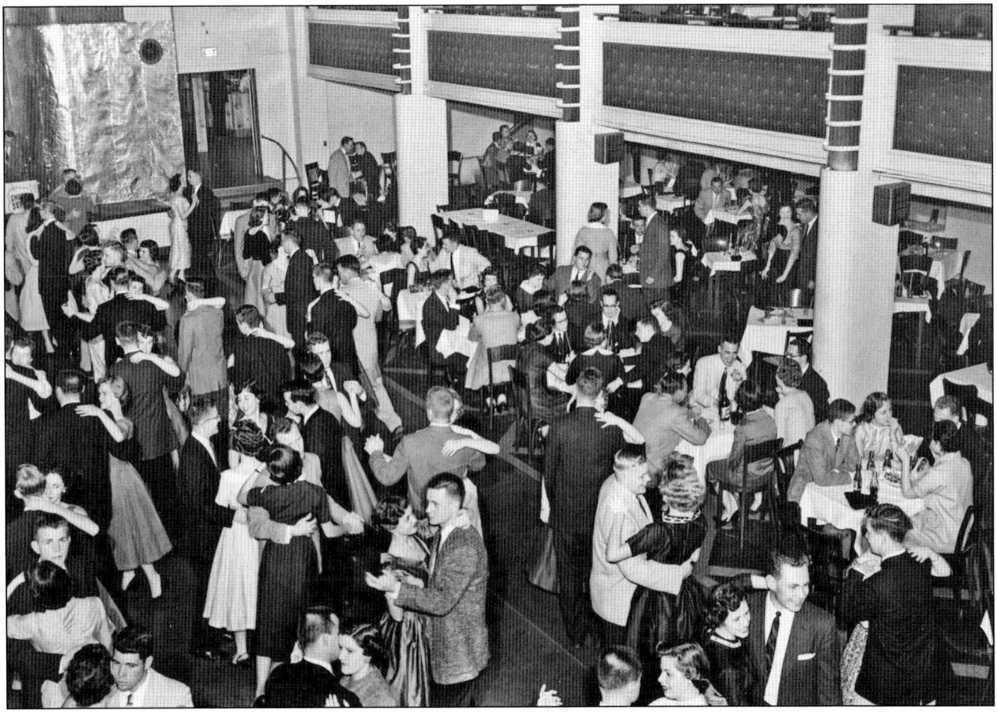

This balcony view was snapped during the 1950s. The artistic touches of Frank Dailey include lighting fixtures placed vertically on the balcony. Their ambient lighting was an enhancement that had not been present at VDB. Gaze toward the radio booths; they are covered in aluminum foil, maybe updating the ballroom for the space age.

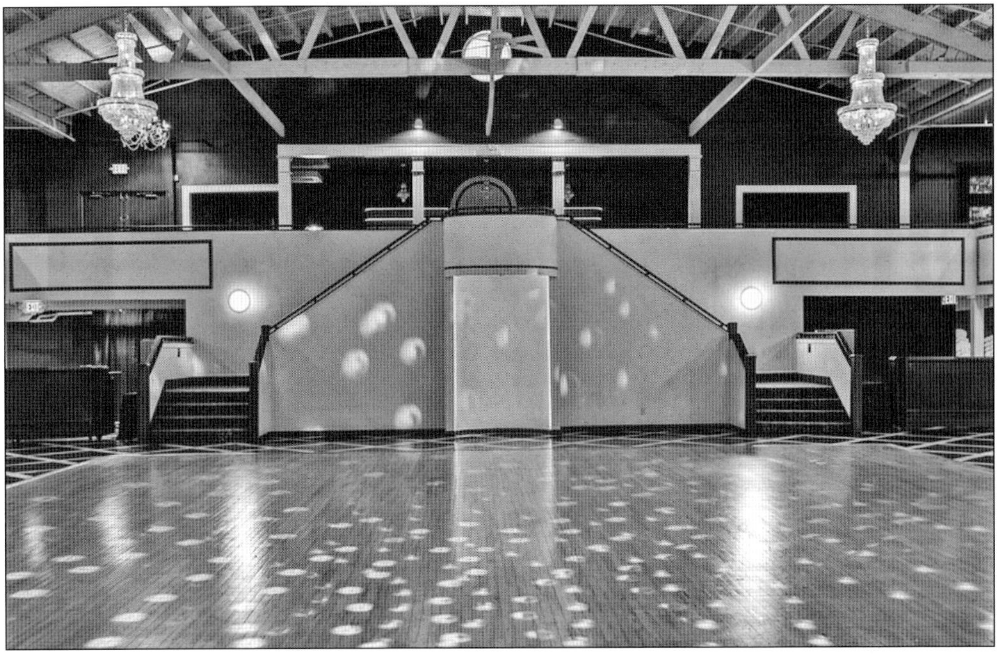

A 2018 view shows the ballroom's double staircase, the hardwood floor, and a spinning mirrored ceiling globe. (Graham Brannon Photography.)

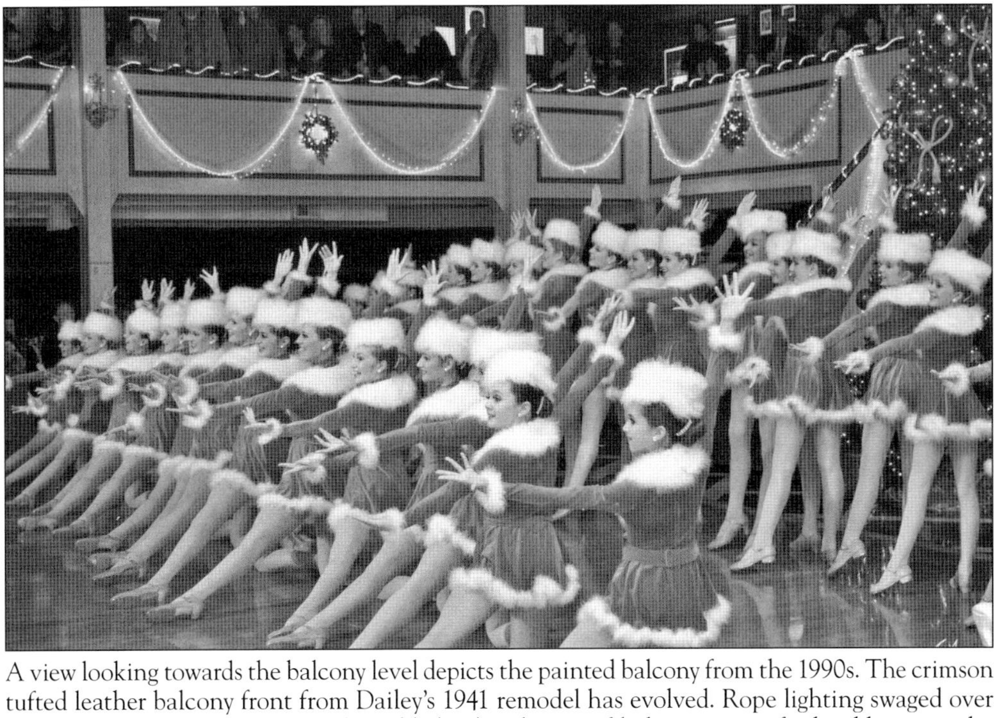

A view looking towards the balcony level depicts the painted balcony from the 1990s. The crimson tufted leather balcony front from Dailey's 1941 remodel has evolved. Rope lighting swaged over the balcony and sconces were also added. This degree of lighting was a fresh addition to the ballroom. The photograph was taken during Deana Martin's 2013 Christmas show, presenting a kickline of over 100 Straub Center dancers from Westerville, Ohio. Notice the crowded balcony. This evening had a gate of over 800 guests. (Graham Brannon Photography.)

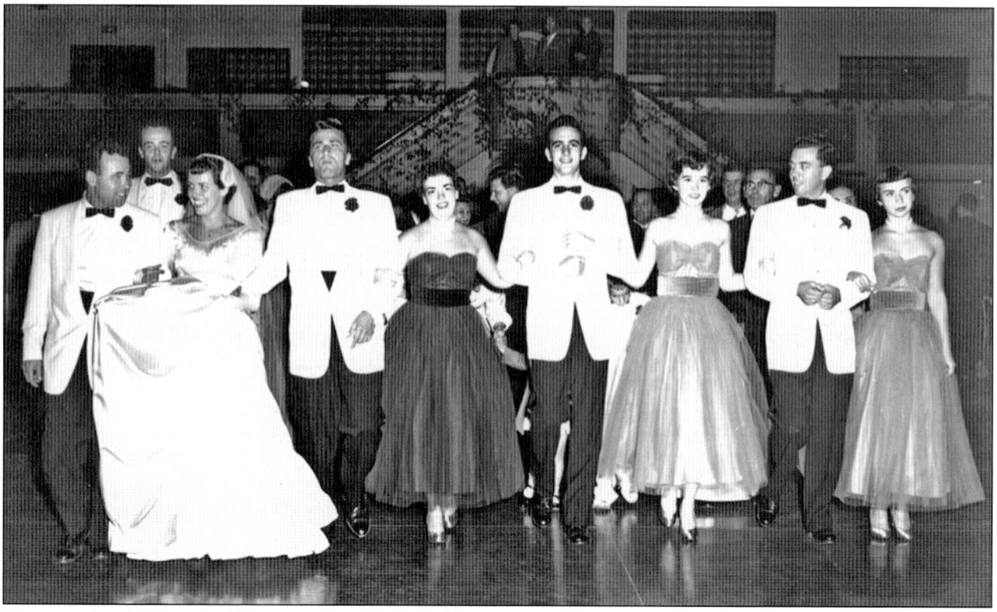

During the 1950s, the VDB evolved into a favorite venue for weddings, replacing the nightly live band dances of the 1930s and 1940s. The wedding of Joe Cua and Elois Lefebure on September 16, 1953, presents a rare glimpse of the upper balcony; from left to right are the entry doors, ticket booth, and walk-up bar (three openings) and the coat check. Flooding destroyed the hardwood maple dancefloor beyond repair, revealing the cement foundation slabs depicted in this photograph as the dance surface of the future. The VDB would not be refurbished again until the 1970s. The hardwood plank dancefloor would not return until 1992. Joseph Cua Jr., L to R Gary Sigrist, Elois Lefebure Cua, Carmen Davirro, Delores Lefebure, (?) Marita Mulherin, Henry Lefebure, Maureen Mulherin. (Michael Cua.)

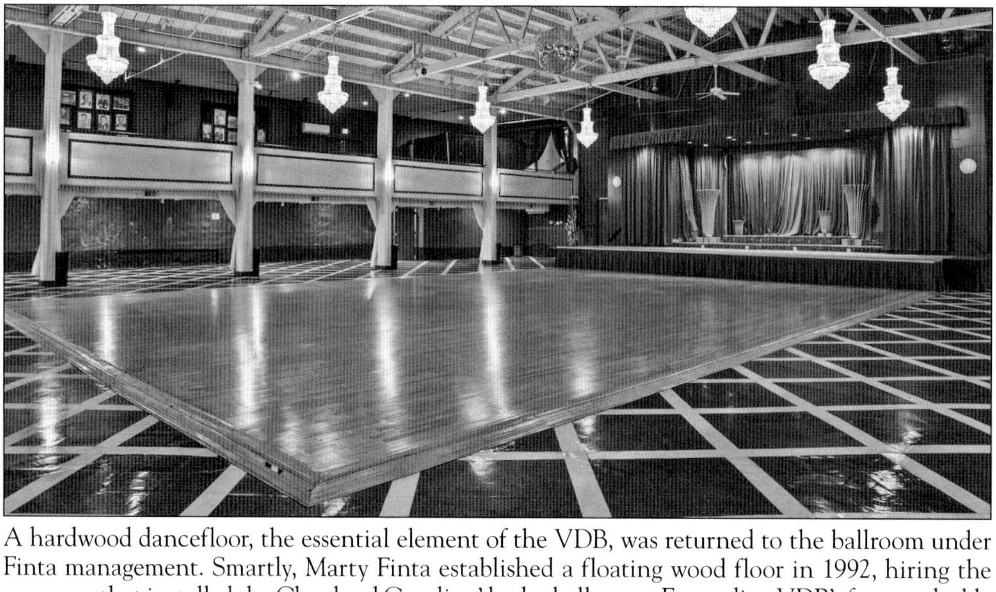

A hardwood dancefloor, the essential element of the VDB, was returned to the ballroom under Finta management. Smartly, Marty Finta established a floating wood floor in 1992, hiring the company that installed the Cleveland Cavaliers' basketball court. Expanding VDB's future saleable uses, the dancefloor could occasionally double as a basketball court. Black and white tile frames the 60-foot-by-90-foot dancefloor, creating a stronger impact. (Graham Brannon Photography.)

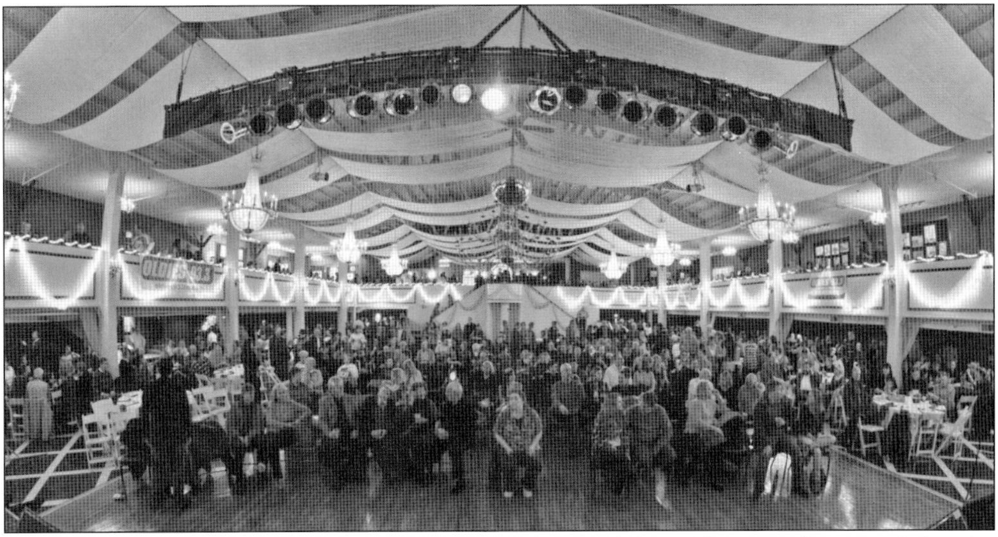

From the 1990s through 2014, Dana Finta displayed swaged sheer fabric panels suspended under the barrel-vaulted ceiling. This presented a finished and dramatic enhancement to the great hall. With increasing code restrictions, the fire marshal ordered all non-fireproof fabric removed. In 2018, the ceiling is void of textiles. The fabric appointment is one of the most missed items of the ballroom, especially by brides. The festooned light strands in the balcony were removed in 2015. This perfect view of VDB was taken during the February 9, 2014, tribute to the Beatles on *The Ed Sullivan Show* and shows over 900 audience members suffering from Beatlemania. (Graham Brannon Photography.)

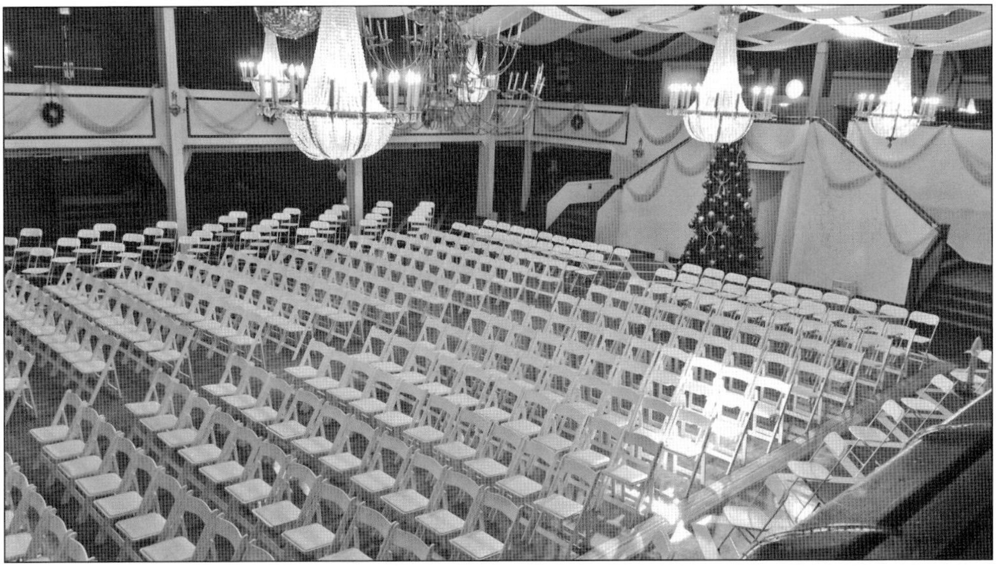

The Fintas pay homage to Frank Dailey. Almost 50 years after Dailey redesigned VDB, the Finta organization enhanced the ballroom by installing chandeliers almost identical to those that once lighted Dailey's Meadowbrook Ballroom. Such irony! Finta did not initially purchase these fixtures for the VDB, but purchased the lighted pendants for another venue. Marty Finta studied ballrooms across the country, deciding Dailey's Meadowbrook had the elegant look he was seeking for the Hartman Ballroom some 15 years before they were even managers at VDB. (Graham Brannon Photography.)

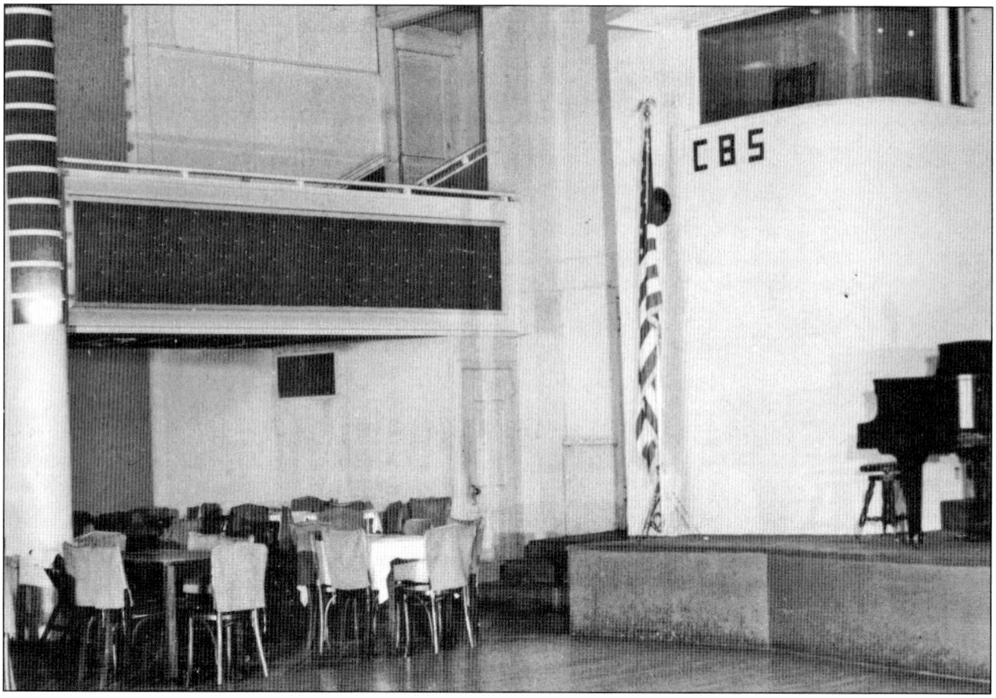

The iconic maple dance floor installed under the stage in 1925 allowed for controlled contraction and expansion. Tables were in place since the 1930s with chair slipcovers. The steps at side of stage head to the knotty pine bar backstage. The former radius-front stage was enlarged and squared in 1992. A CBS booth behind radius glass gives any radio host a bird's-eye view while broadcasting the evening's events.

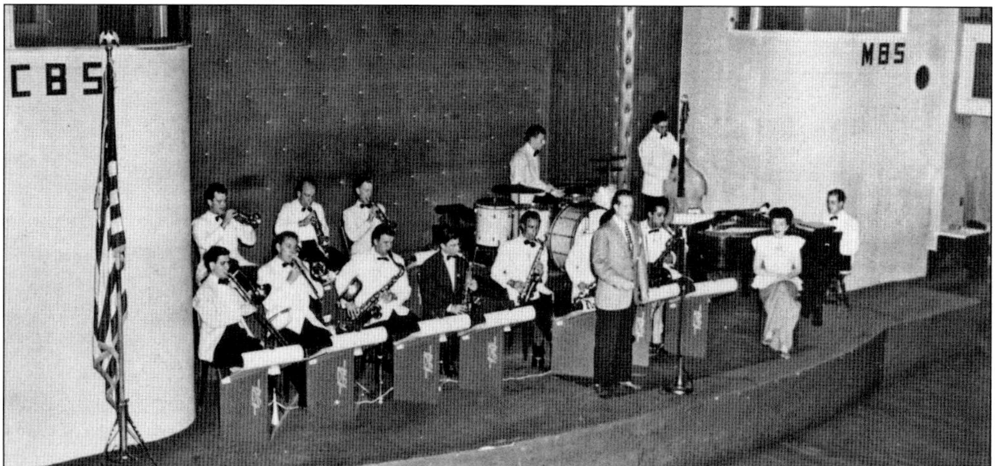

VDB was the only location in America to have live simultaneous broadcasts over CBS (1927–present) and MBS (1934–1999); the twin radio booths flanked the VDB stage. When viewing other photographs in this book, always look for the booths' evolution. NBC also aired from the VDB, but its live shows were only permitted to broadcast from the stage, not the booths. View Dailey's upholstered tufted leather backdrop wall and radius sidewalls. When visiting VDB today, notice the respective call letters painted on the booth walls, still admired today as an homage to the 1930s. Here, the Don Crawford Orchestra plays with vocalist Margie Alden (Coyle).

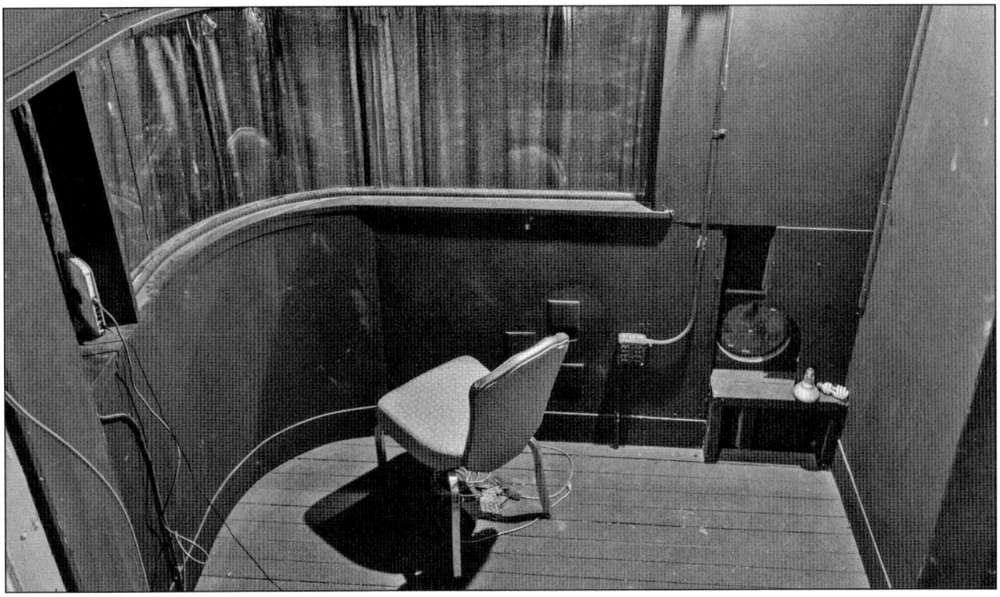

This is a rare glimpse inside the booths flanking the VDB stage. Teens squealing in the ballroom and parents listening from home would hear "From the beautiful Valley Dale Ballroom in Columbus, Ohio, we bring you Harry James and his Orchestra." The radio announcer opening the musical show with these words is still remembered distinctly 77 years later. Drifting over the airwaves next would be the sweetest trumpet solo of James's theme song, "Ciribiribin." Microphones on stage connected to audio mixers in the booths that sent the signal via telephone line back to WBNS, then on to New York for nationwide broadcasts. Mike Peppe recalled that during 1980 renovations, "Transmission hook-ups from six radio networks were uncovered in the radio booth." A more detailed explanation of the transmissions is presented in Arcadia's title *Columbus Radio*, by Mike Adams. (Graham Brannon Photography.)

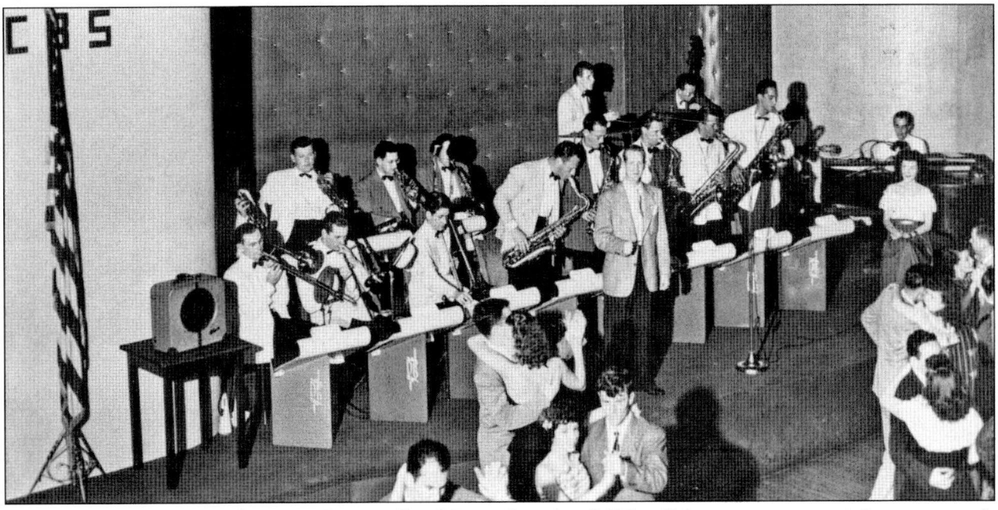

The talkback cue speaker, on the small table under the CBS call letters, was used for a network announcer, maybe from New York, to introduce the band and cue it to start playing. Sometimes, the network used a director and hand signals. Mike Adams pointed out since there was no announcer in the booth, this could have been a small-budget show with just an engineer. The Don Crawford Orchestra performs here with vocalist Marilyn Daye.

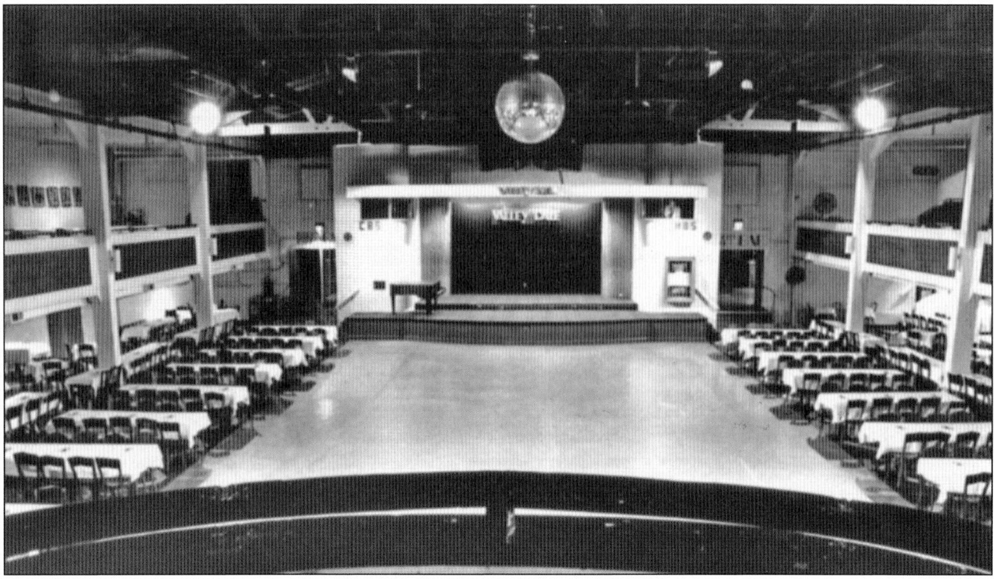

Here is a ballroom view from 1987. VDB's fresh logo is placed on the stage. The famed radio booths crowned with radius glass have been present since the 1930s. Notice the tufted balconies still in place, along with portraits of beloved bandleaders from a generation before installed horizontally on the upper balcony; 15 years later, this would change. Tables and chairs are from the 1940s. The piano was used by most of the classic big band artists, including Count Basie; it was removed in 1990 but still exists in a private collection. (*Columbus Dispatch*.)

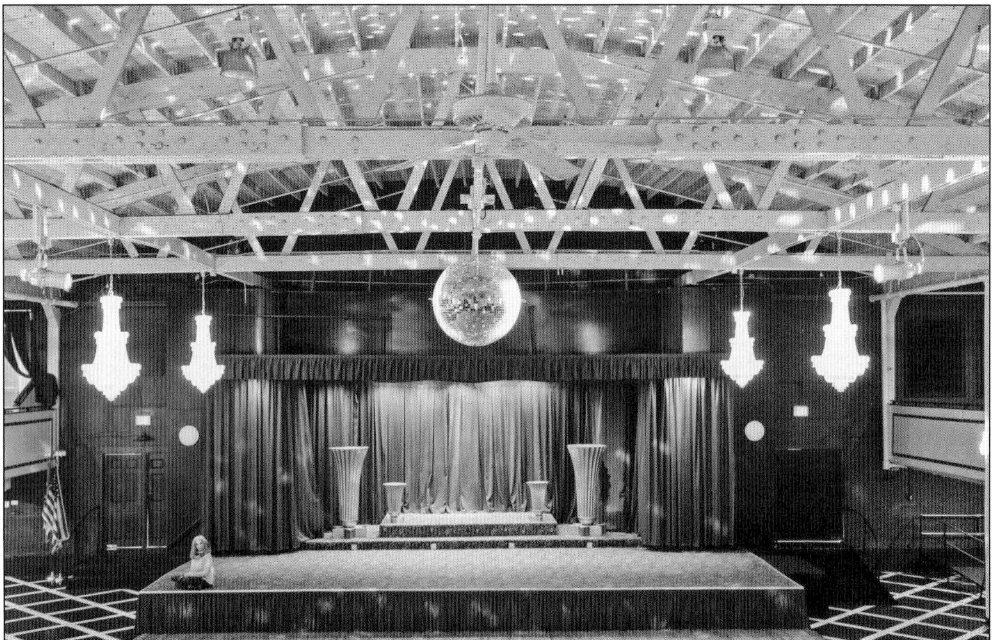

The theatrical staging in 2018 displays radius draperies. When preferred, these may be removed to expose the radio booths. Sadly, today, these iconic radio booths are not as appreciated as they were at the ballroom's zenith. The Finta organization extended the former stage radius of eight decades and made it rectangular in 1992. (Graham Brannon Photography.)

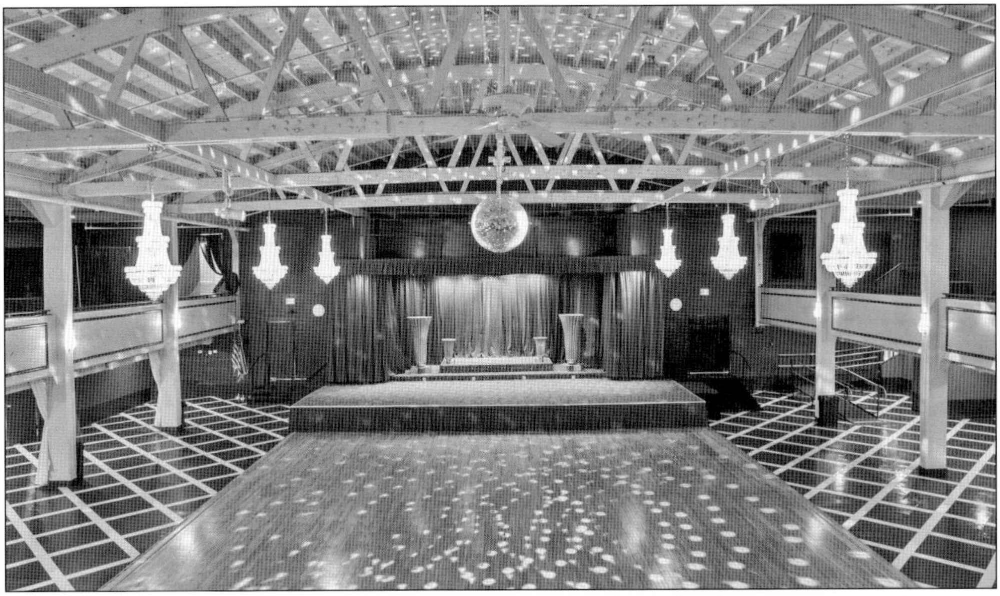

A 2018 ballroom view includes the chandeliers. Multicolor light shows in time to the music enhance the crowd's mood. The lighting evolves in color and intensity throughout the evening. It was installed at Valley Dale and presented for New Year's Eve, 2015. On December 25, 1932, the *Columbus Citizen Journal* announced that the ballroom portion of VDB was given a separate name, the New Star Salon, and welcomed Duke Ellington on December 28, 1932. Touting chandeliers with 1,000 color changes, a newsprint ad described the pendant lighting as "Gorgeous, Glittering & Modernistic." (Graham Brannon Photography.)

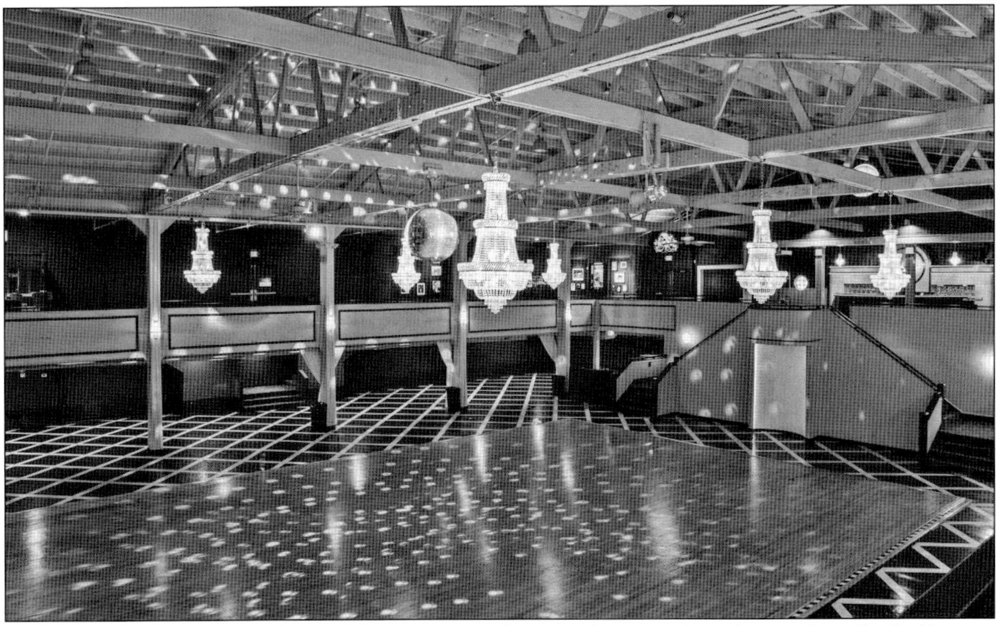

Wood in the ceiling and on the dancefloor enhances the sound quality within the ballroom. The bow truss wooden ceiling includes six wood trusses, complimented by the ballroom's plank dancefloor. The wood lends acoustical warmth to the music in a space that is never overly reverberant. Musicians frequently comment on the marvelous sound quality of the venue.

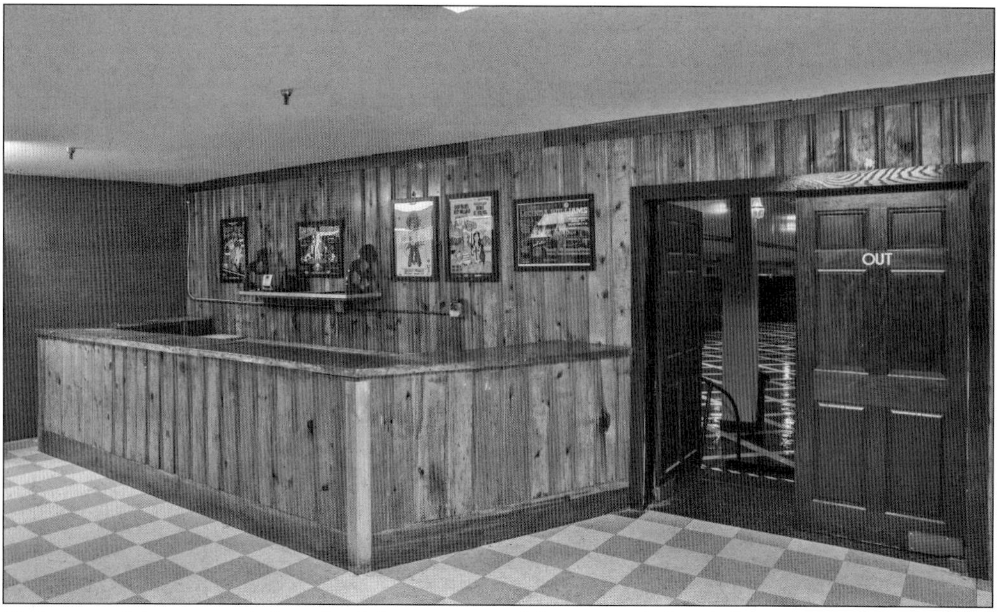

Only one of the original three back bars remains. This space behind the stage, the knotty pine bar, is accessible from the ballroom through double doors on either side of the stage. This 2018 photograph depicts the final remaining bar with its glistening worn copper countertop from the 1980 refresh. (Graham Brannon Photography.)

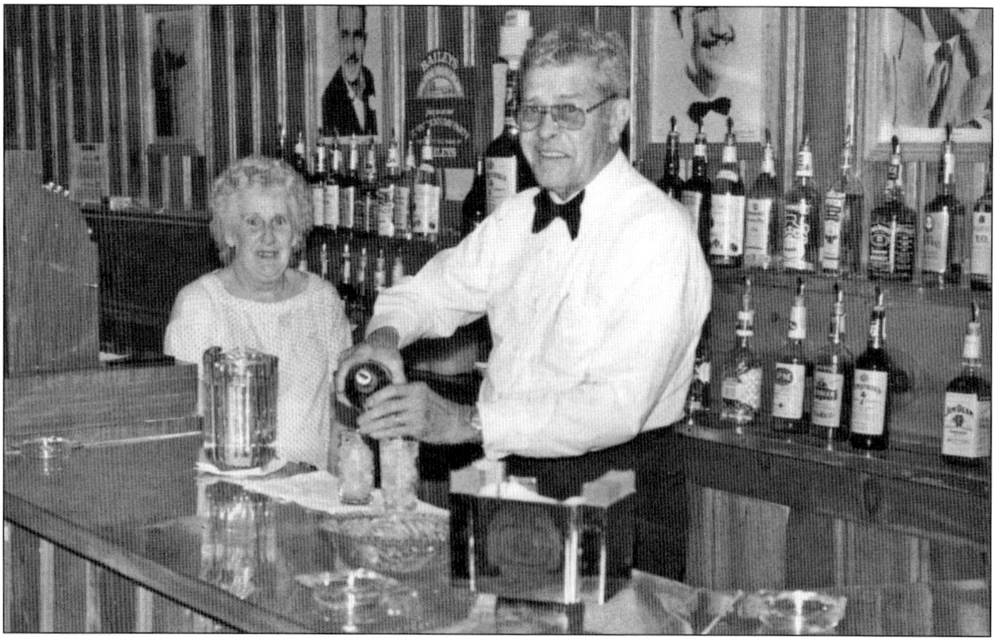

In the late 1950s, clarinetist and bandleader Benny Goodman posed as spokesperson for Smirnoff Vodka. Mike Peppe relates that VDB owner Lou Peppe once purchased a drink for Goodman from the bar with a large-denomination bill. When the change was presented, Goodman swooped in, pocketing the significant handful of bills. In this 1984 image, notice the placement of band portraits. The bartenders' names were Mike Sullivan and LaRue Wilson. (Graham Brannon Photography.)

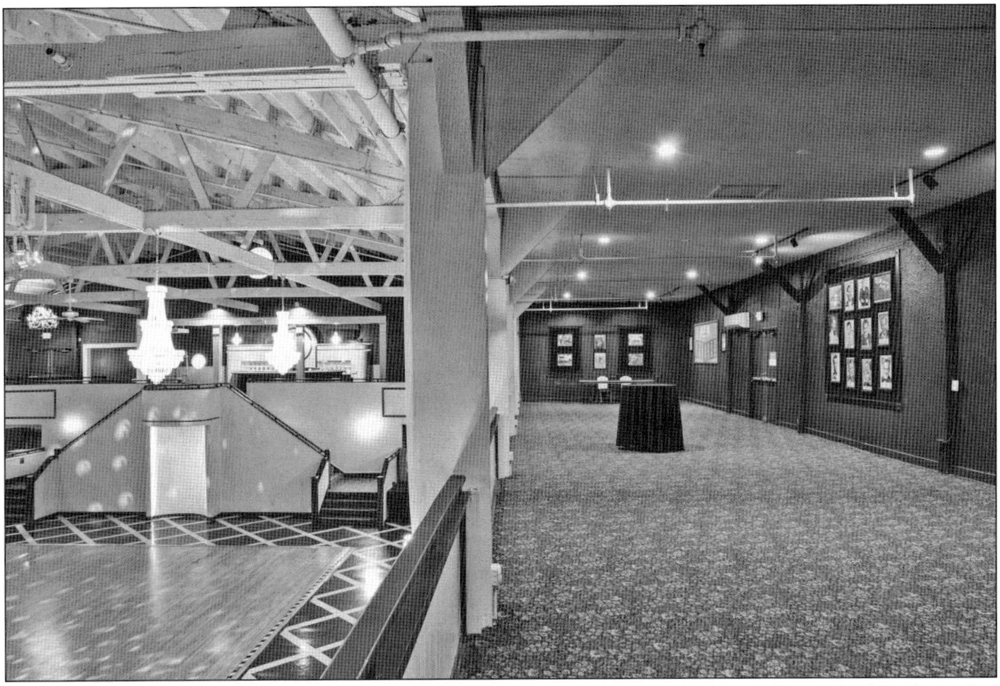

In this 2018 photograph of the second-level balcony, and first-level dancefloor, the bandstand is at lower left. The wall of fame gallery includes autographed photographs shown throughout this publication. (Graham Brannon Photography.)

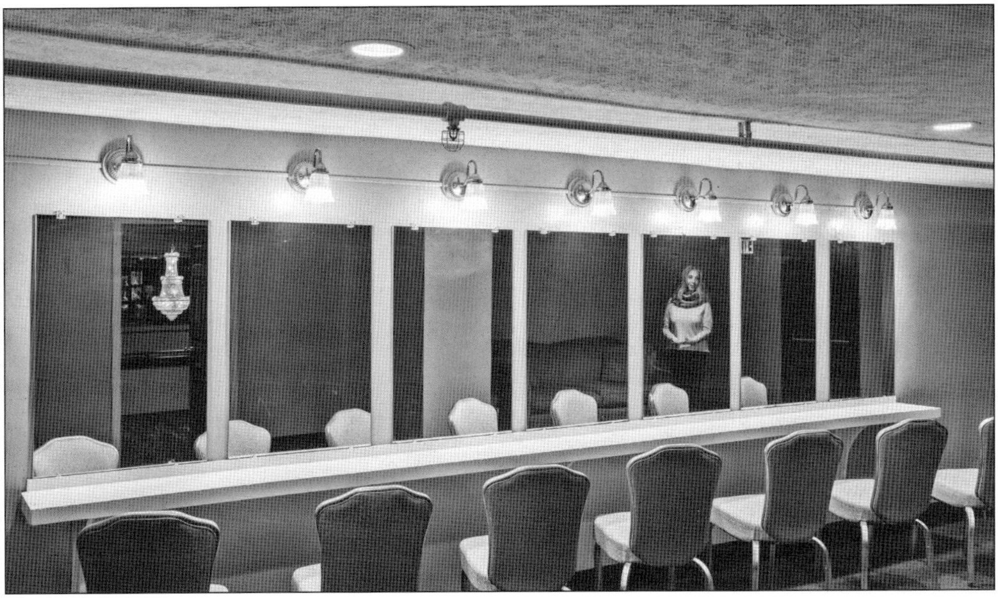

The main dressing room is off the balcony ladies' room. The musicians of the early years, like Helen O'Connell, Ray Eberle, Frank Sinatra, and Dino Martini; dancers like Hot Chocolate from the 1930s; modern icons such as Natalie Cole and Alice Cooper; local musicians; and most every celebrity mentioned in this book used this area to prepare for their performances. Wedding parties and their brides use this space, and even Santa Claus has combed his snowy beard in front of these mirrors. (Graham Brannon Photography.)

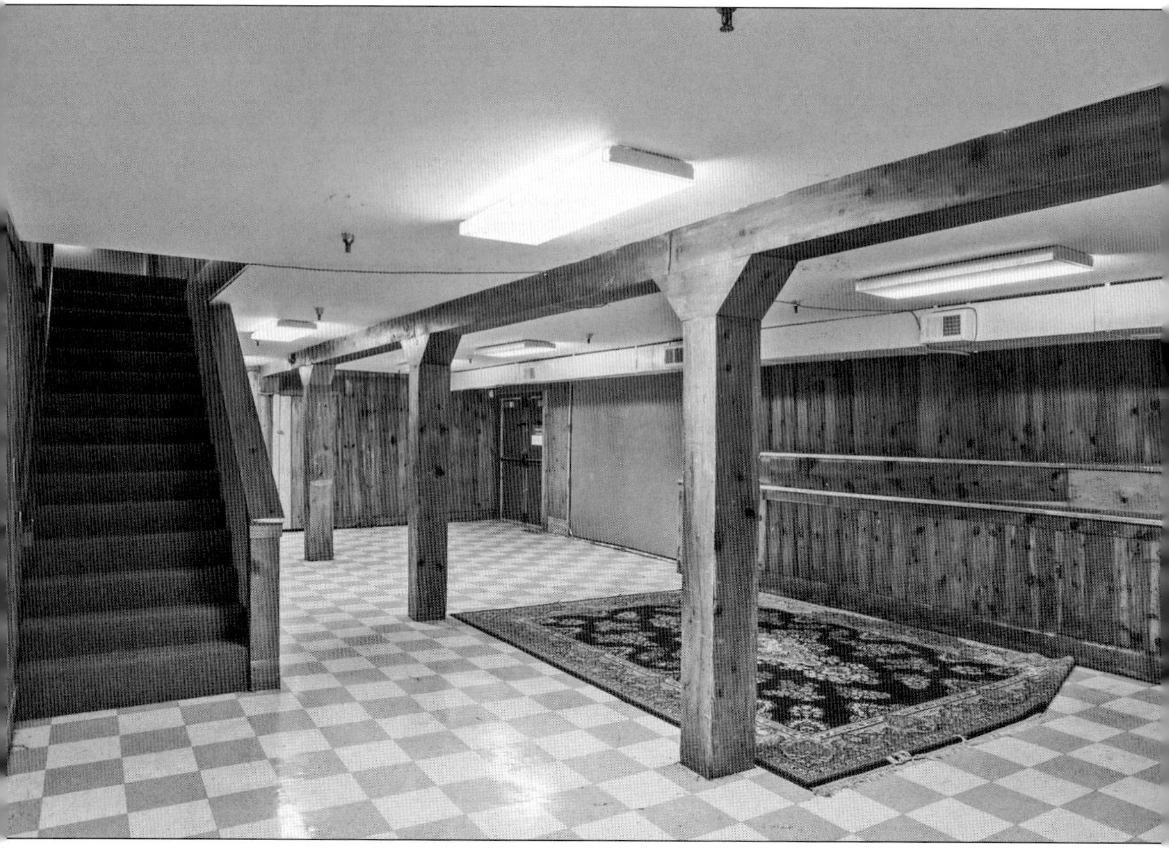

After ushering a future bride and groom through the expectations of their wedding day at Valley Dale, the engaged couple and VDB manager Dana Finta headed through a narrow hall to the fashionable office space to ink the final contract. While seated comfortably on upholstered sofas, Dana stopped the conversation to see who was running through the famous knotty pine bar. The couple followed her. The three believed they had escorted everyone out before locking the door. As the trio approached the bar, they again heard the brisk step of someone running in stiletto heels. When they called out, the steps stopped. Dana turned to her clients, and they exchanged startled glances. They all heard it twice, but no one was ever seen. In May 2018, working late one evening alone in the ballroom, a new employee heard dancing music and a celebratory crowd, when she ran to the ballroom, she faced complete darkness with deafening silence. (Graham Brannon Photography.)

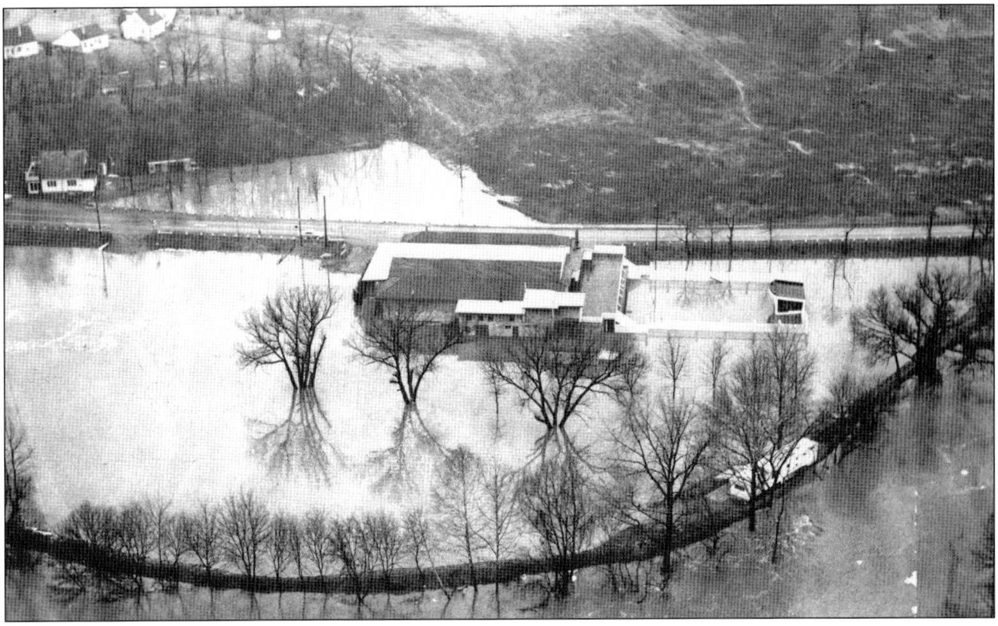

This flood struck in 1963 and presents an unbelievable account of damage at VDB. The first devastating flood was in 1927.

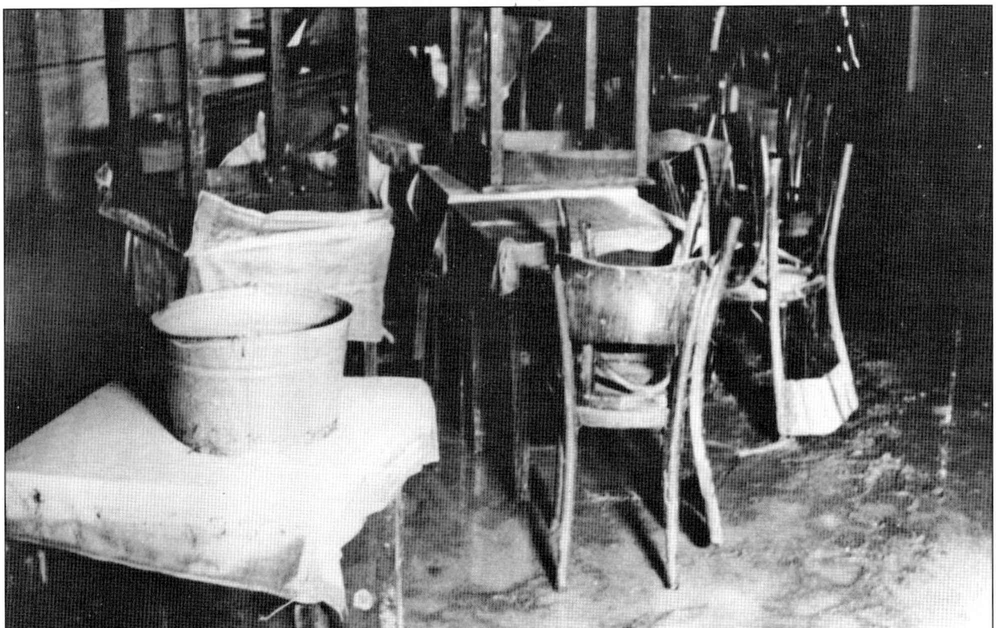

VDB house bandleader Chuck Selby also became house manager in 1960. Selby's longest running VDB gig was not a prom or charity dance but a continual three-day, three-night vigil during the ravaging Columbus flood of 1963. As maritime tradition dictates that the captain is the last to leave his ship, Selby passed 78 hours at VDB attempting to keep the thick, damaging floodwaters at bay. He was aided by his fans, not wearing sassy dance shoes but showing up in rubber boots carrying sacks of boiled ham sandwiches, bottles of water, and fresh-baked chocolate chip cookies to provide sustenance to their leader.

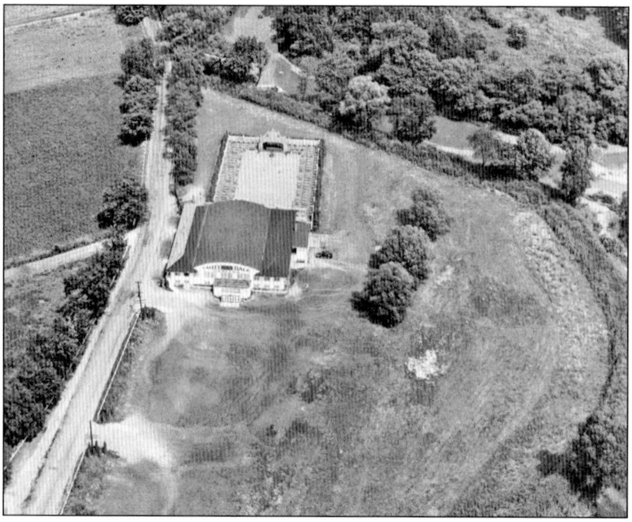

This bandstand photograph is from the original outdoor dance pavilion that opened in 1924. This structure fell into ruins and was closed in 1961. This incline has been a source of parking issues during inclement weather. In the 1930s, attendants would stop the north-and-south traffic on Sunbury Road giving the Model Ts a running start up the steep incline. Some eight decades later, the incline is still present.

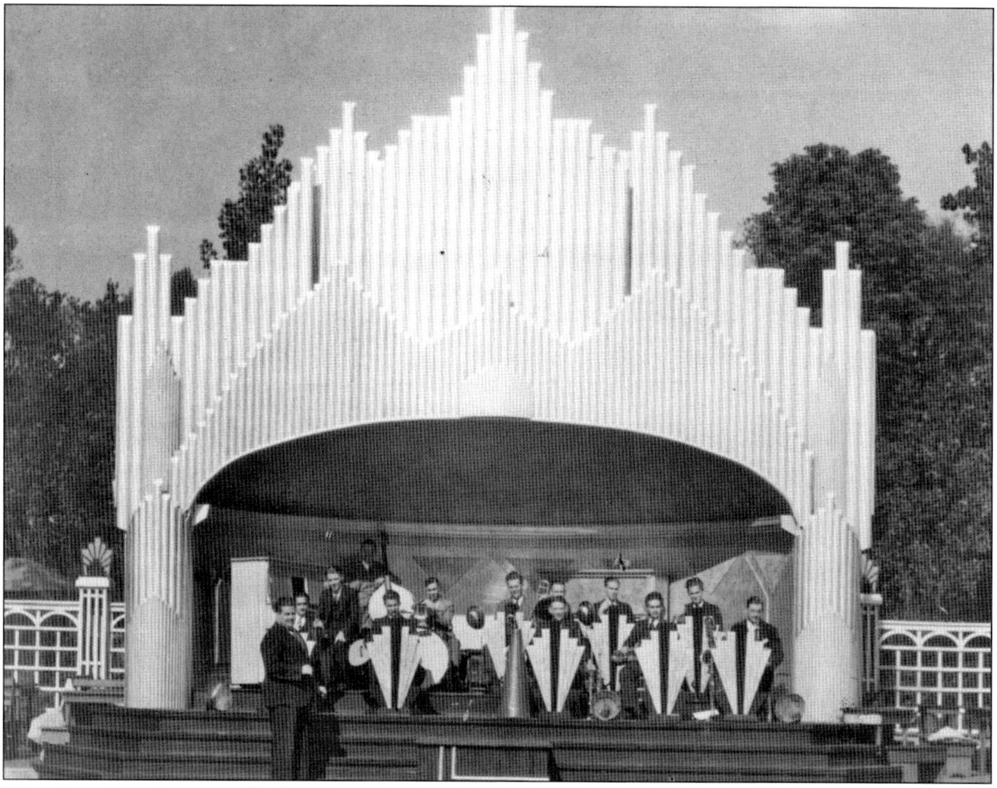

Months after the so-called New Year's Eve Fire of 1924, an innovative outdoor pavilion was constructed on the grounds of the original Valley Dale Hall; this is a bandstand snapshot from the original outdoor performance space. The area around the original indoor dancefloor became a poured cement outdoor dance surface. Rosebushes were placed around the floor, creating an additional open-air dance space with a newly constructed stage that opened on June 7, 1924. The bandstand fronts echo the architectural fashion of the bandshell, following the linear design of the 1920s art deco period. With an indoor and outdoor dancefloor, more than 5,000 people could enjoy VDB.

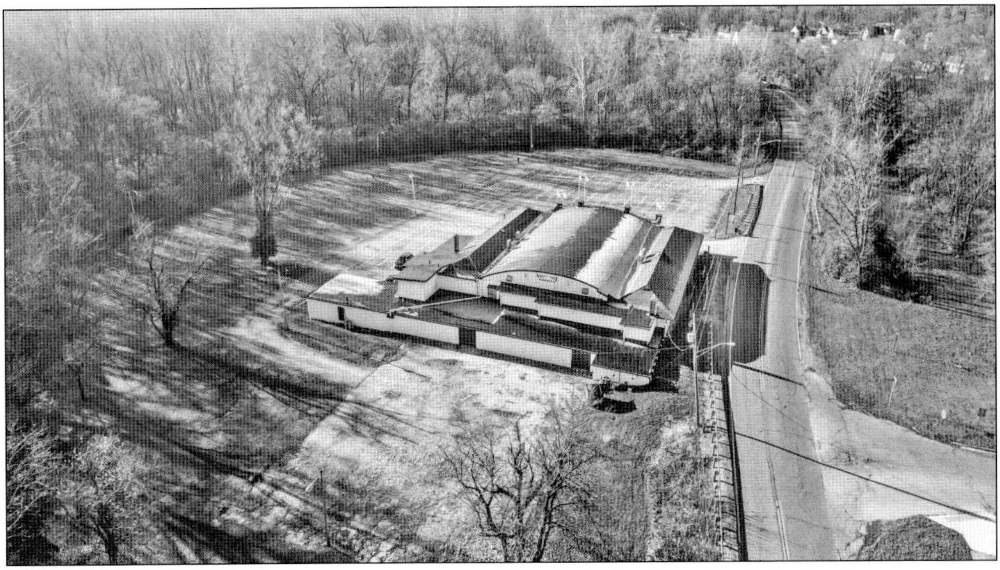

The outdoor dance pavilion had several names—Moonlight Gardens, Starlight Gardens, or Sunken Gardens. Rudy Vallee appeared here on his 36th birthday, July 28, 1937, the second biggest night for the Moonlight Gardens; the largest was Guy Lombardo. For a time, bands would play three or four sets in the evening air. If it became too cool or rainy, the band would be moved inside while on break. Before the 1950s, it was very common to have a band inside and another band outside, one playing while the other was on break. In 2018, the outline of this pavilion and its disjointed cement slab are still visible behind the Valley Dale site. (Larry Pishitelli.)

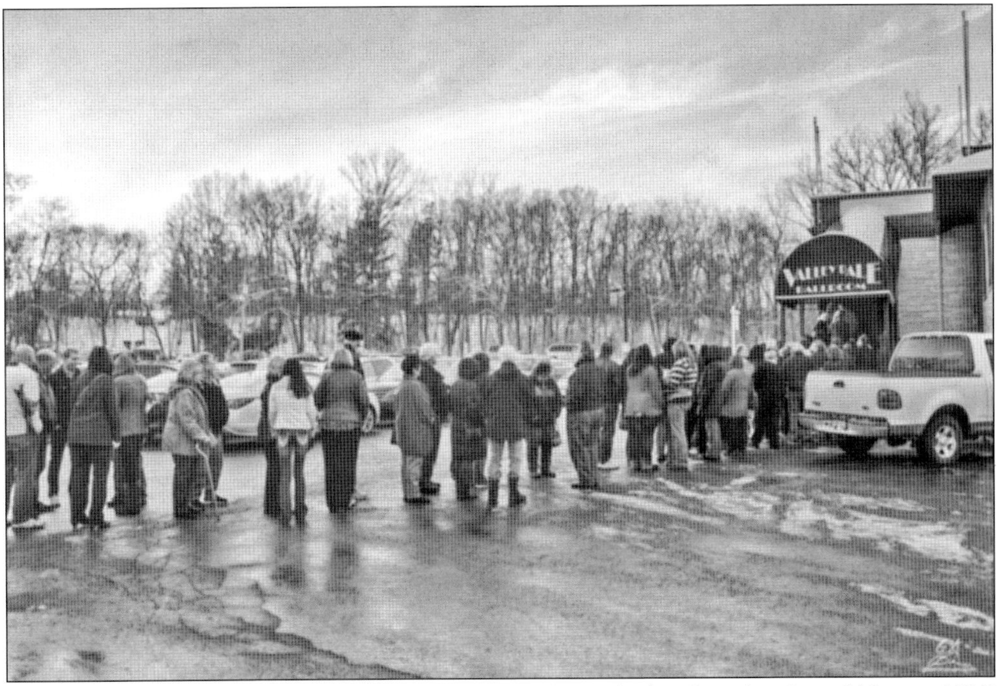

Cars are backed up on Sunbury Road creeping into the packed parking lot. It could be any VDB decade or event, but this night is February 9, 2014, the 50th anniversary of the Beatles on *The Ed Sullivan Show*. (Graham Brannon Photography.)

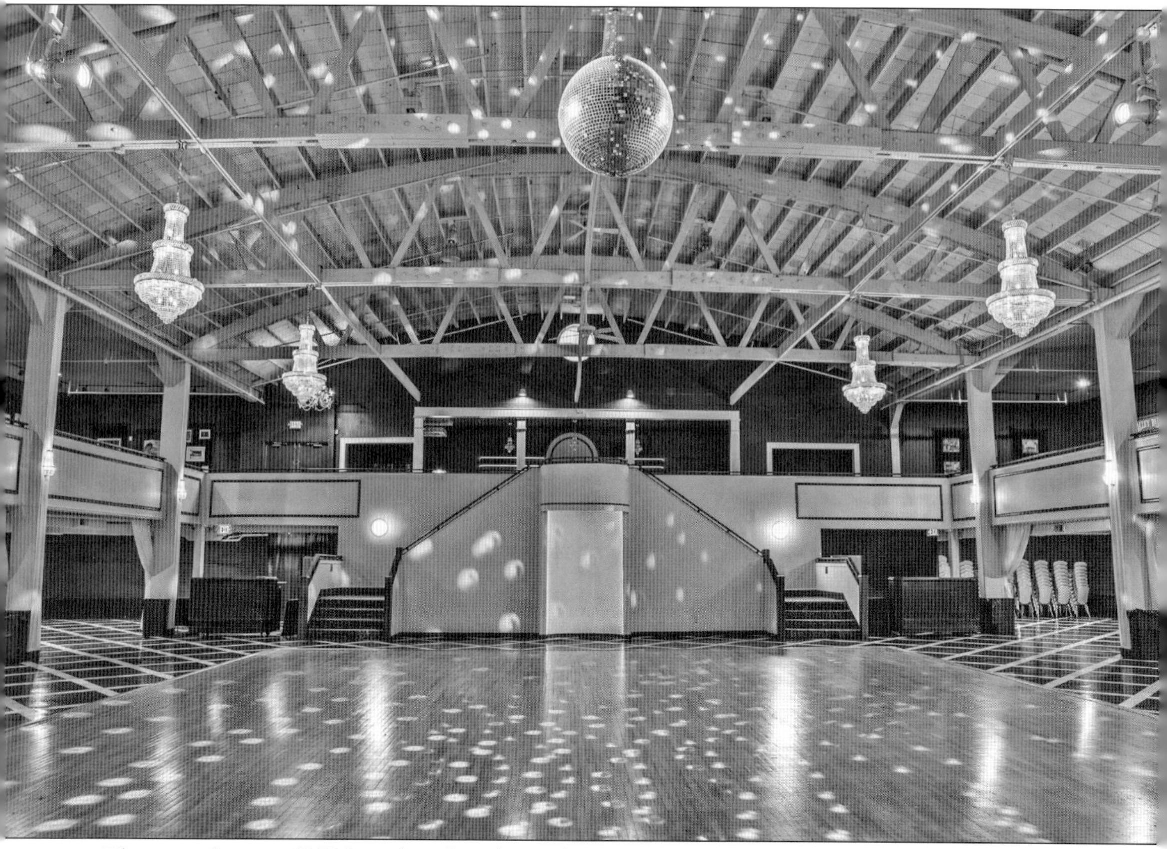

The crystal tiara of VDB is placed at the midpoint of the bowstring truss ceiling. The crowning placement of the rotating mirror ball reflects the elegance and nostalgia of past ballroom days, much like the honor and reverence felt when wearing one's great-grandmother's diamond locket. The debut of the faceted sphere dates back to an 1897 ballroom in Boston. The next appearance of a reflective globe was in a nightclub scene in a German silent film released in 1927. The Valley Dale has possessed four mirrored spheres over the last 90 years. The one in the picture replaced the third, changed during the renovation and updates of 1980. Kathy Peppe expressed: "We liked the larger size and how it sparkled across the ballroom floor." Mike and Kathy Peppe gifted VDB its largest-ever mirror ball. The ballroom's turning mirror ball echoes lightning bugs on summer nights gliding just out of fingertip reach. (Graham Brannon Photography.)

Six

Singers, Combos, and Bands, Oh My!

By the early 1960s, the decades of the true big band era had faded from VDB. World War II was over; its impact on big band music and songs was finished. The Korean War was not discussed. Vietnam's impact was not yet felt; its protests had not yet started. It was a complacent time. The main debate of the day was from exactly which two James Bond movies "shaken and not stirred" or "stirred not shaken" was uttered and how the spoken line was phrased. America was living the calm before the storm. A counterculture of beatniks and coffee houses was mushrooming underground. The few groups playing locally contained three to ten musicians, most arrangements were stock charts. Jazz trios and combos were cropping up across the country and this city. Valley Dale had gone from every night dancing to a maybe one or two a month Saturday night ballroom. The teenagers who could not get enough of VDB had matured, starting families, gaining employment, building life. The mesmerized VDB high school musicians that made up, filled in, or observed many of the 1930s and 1940s stage bands at VDB had returned to VDB, constructing their own bands. Also, most of the high school girl singers were now seasoned some 20 years later and had a following of their own. Becoming a musician and singer was less frowned on at this time and more celebrated, making it easier for the artist and entertainer to embrace one's dreams. This chapter shows how the influence of VDB introduces the local musician to their community.

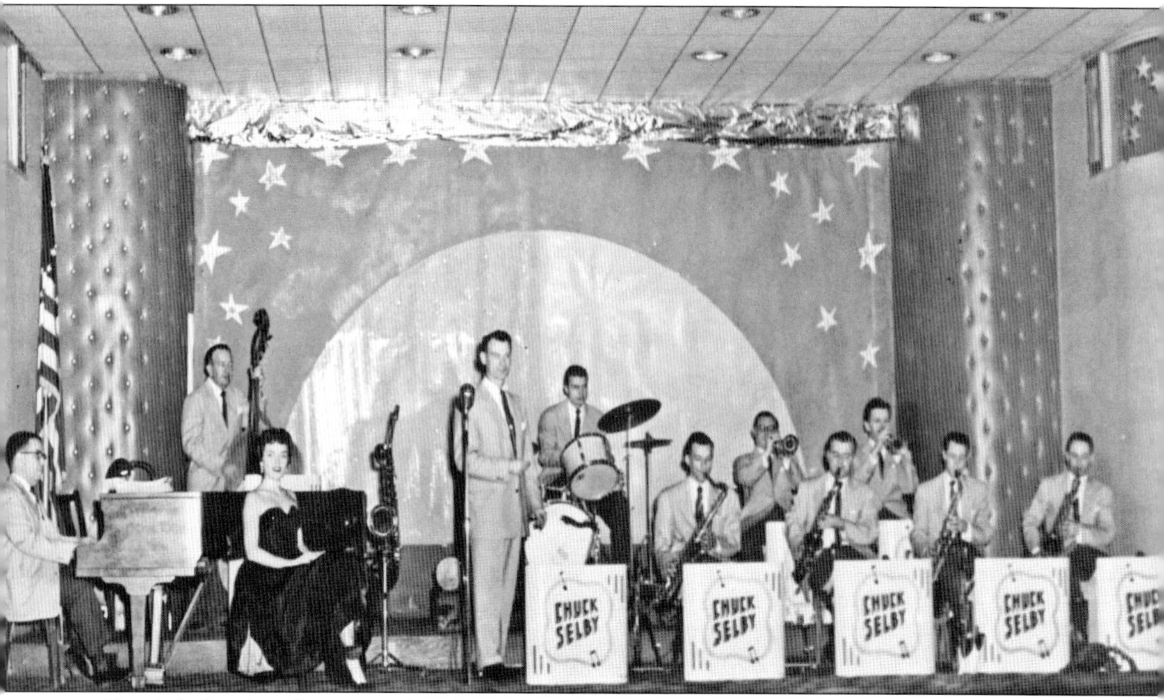

Chuck Selby's band is pictured with vocalist Marilyn Daye. Lovely stories have been told about the kindnesses of Chuck and his wife, Anne Young. In the 1960s, when dance bands' popularity was declining, Chuck Selby became employed for the county clerk of courts. Bill Selby recalled: "I was 10 years old when mom married Chuck, and he was a fantastic stepfather. Chuck, as deputy clerk, was in charge of name changes. When I showed up he was puzzled, asked me why was I there. When I told him it was my birthday, I wanted to change my name to Selby, he began to cry. It was the most emotional I ever saw him. He was so happy, so proud, that he took me around the courthouse, introduced me to his friends, and explained to them why I was there. It was a wonderful day. I recall showing up at the Franklin County Courthouse to change my name to Selby bright and early on my 21st birthday."

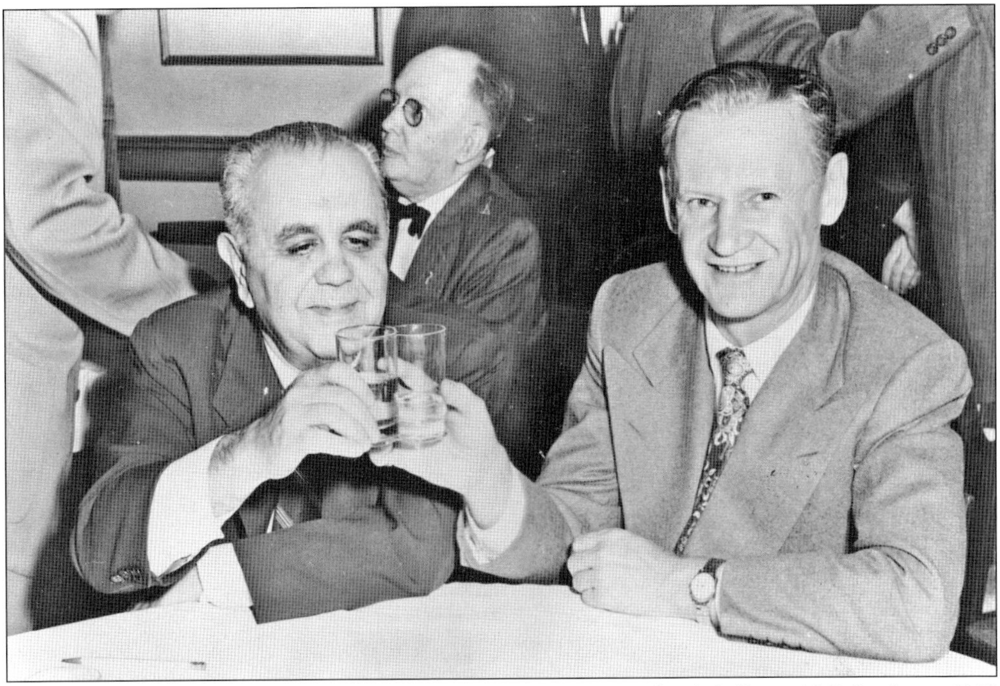

Owner Lou Peppe turned over daily ballroom management to Chuck Selby in 1961. In this c. 1949 photograph, Jim Peppe (left), the Peppe brother who owned the VDB in the early 1930s, spends an entertaining evening with Selby, VDB house bandleader from 1951 to 1977.

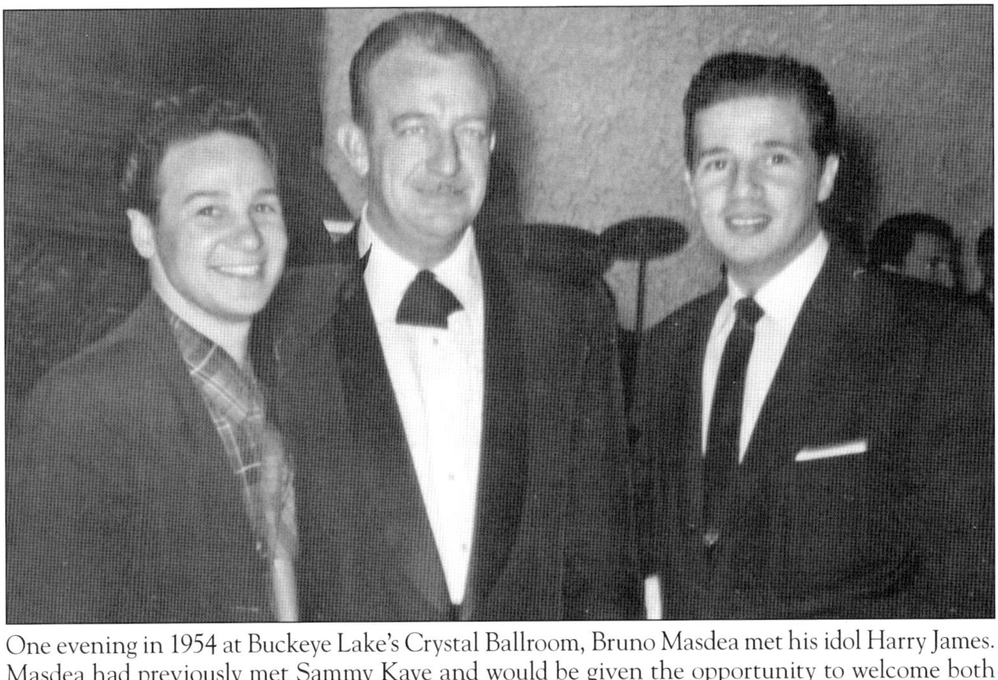

One evening in 1954 at Buckeye Lake's Crystal Ballroom, Bruno Masdea met his idol Harry James. Masdea had previously met Sammy Kaye and would be given the opportunity to welcome both Kaye and James in remarkable, yet to come VDB connections. Masdea (right), a trumpeter, is pictured with his dear friend and future big band vocalist Rocky Latorre (left) and James. (Bruno Masdea archives.)

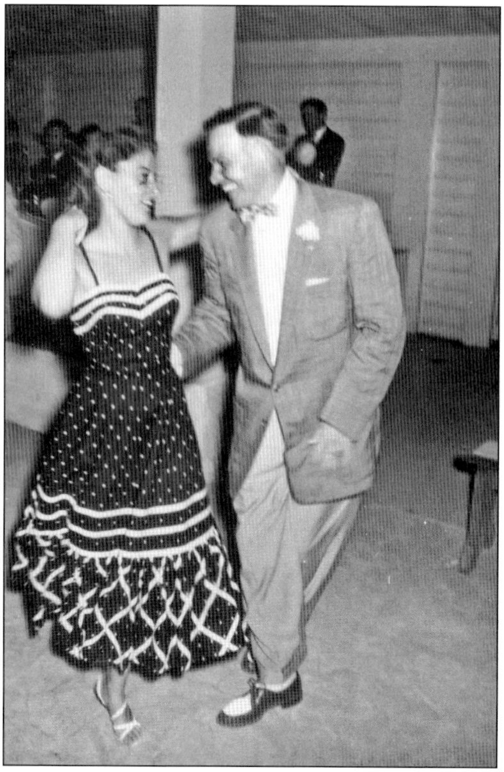

After meeting in 1952, these lovebirds married and spent 55 years dancing at VDB. Frank and Lola Mattox were avid dancers, driving 37 miles from Lancaster, Ohio, most weekends to dance with the Selby band and later the Masdea and Brunetto bands. When the author appealed for an interview and a snapshot, Lola recalled: "I loved them all, it was always a thrill to dress up and dance on that huge dancefloor. The music and our friends were all so special, those were the best days of my life. . . . When they closed the exterior dancefloor I was so brokenhearted, it was my favorite place to dance, but the other ladies just didn't like to get eaten up by the mosquitoes. I told them the way around that is to just dance faster." She provided this photograph, taken on the grounds of the outdoor gardens around 1953. Frank passed in 2008. The author remembered how striking she looked when she would appear at Masdea's VDB dances. It was a thrill for the author to locate Lola after 18 years. (Lola Mattox.)

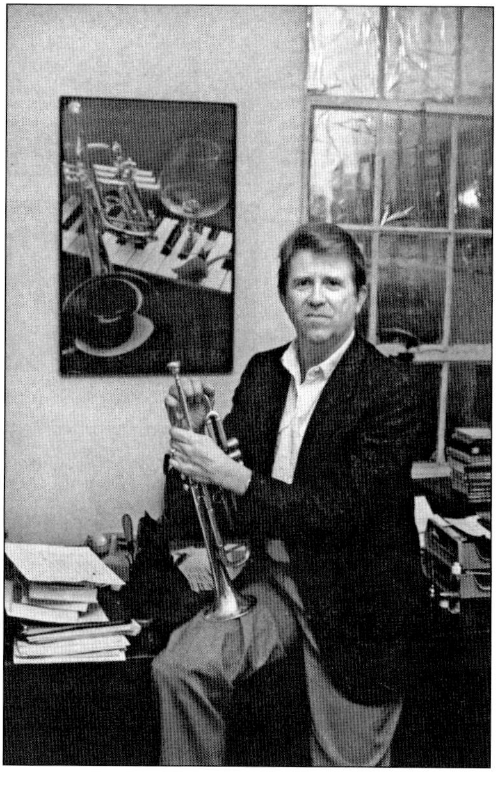

"Roses, that sweet fragrance seemed to envelope the dance floor. That's what I remember, I had taken a date to dance at the outdoor pavilion in the late 1950s." This once Ohio State Marching Band graduate assistant later had his own group, The Embers, playing at VDB. Capital University Professor Ray Eubanks, trumpeter, Jazz Arts Group founder, was asked about his rememberings of VDB, this was his first reflection. "The years of music gigs, playing with the best musicians were always a thrill, especially The Jazz Arts Group's performances at VDB, you got to love playing in that hall, but the roses—I can never forget the scent of the roses." (James Loeffler.)

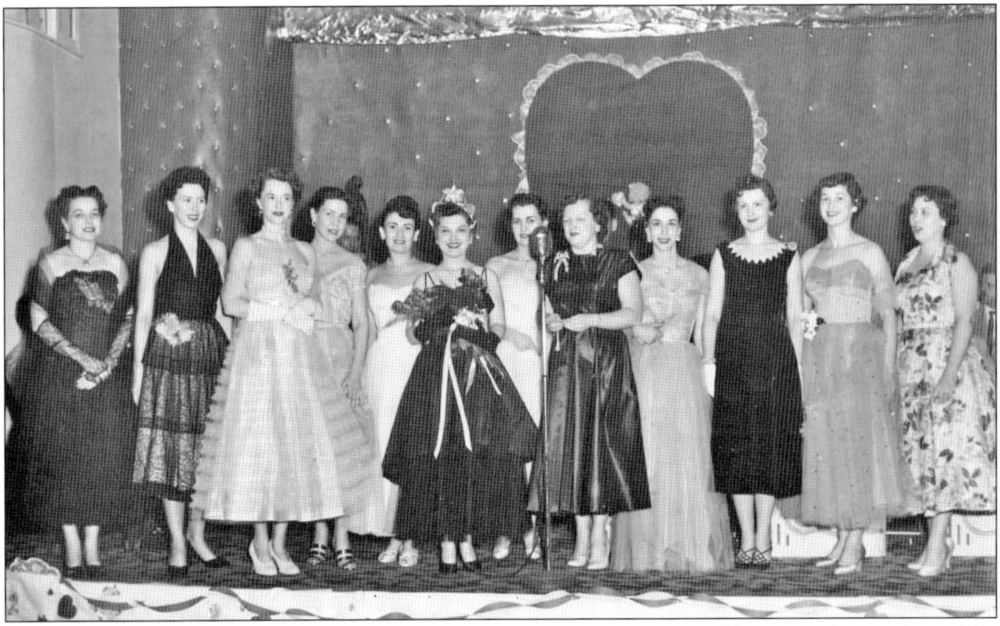

Events and private parties began taking over VDB's dances for weekend business during the 1950s, among them club and sorority dances. This c. 1955 image shows a sweetheart dance, with sorority sisters, court, and queen standing on the Valley Dale stage decorated with hearts. (Bob Stoll.)

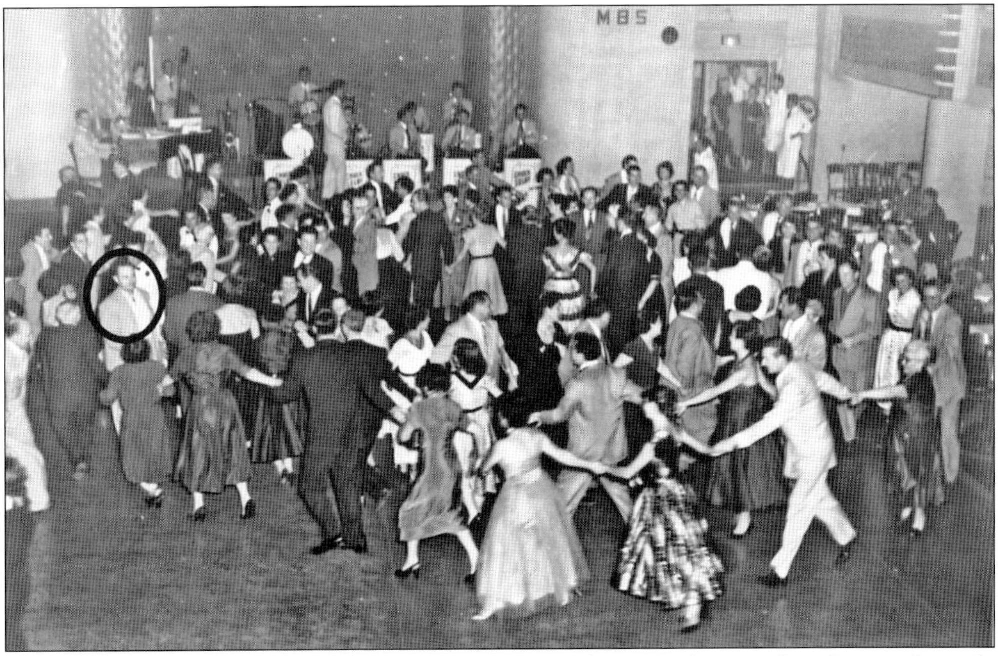

VDB is engaged for weddings over dances. The dance in this 1953 photograph is the grand march, a recognizable event at any Italian wedding. The wedding couple weave through their parading guests, culminating at the wedding cake, led by Columbus's grand march king and noted Seymour Bakery owner Joseph Giantonio (circled). Giantonio is the father-in-law of future 1970s VDB house bandleader Bruno Masdea. Masdea was also co-owner of Seymour Bakery and decorated party and wedding cakes. (Michael Cua.)

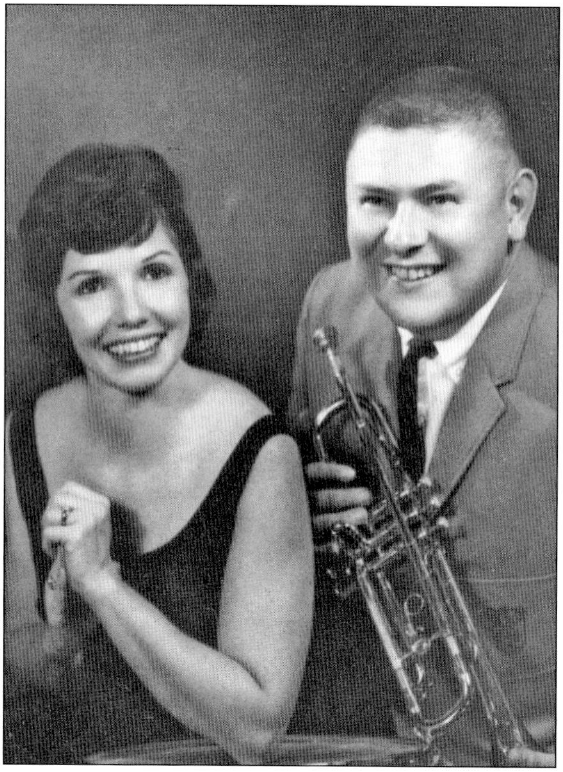

John Philip Sousa's "Stars and Stripes Forever" was recognized as the official march of America under the tutelage of Ziggy Coyle, owner of Columbus's Coyle Music and a legend in supporting music education in Ohio. Before his music store success, the former OSU marching band trumpeter served as East High band director in the early 1950s. Coyle played for the VDB house band under Don Crawford in the late 1950s, when he first met the band vocalist, Margie Alden. He later played a smattering of VDB dances with his Ziggy Coyle Orchestra in the 1960s. Then he married Margie, later featuring her as his vocalist. This picture is from around 1960. Ziggy died in December 1997. (James Loeffler.)

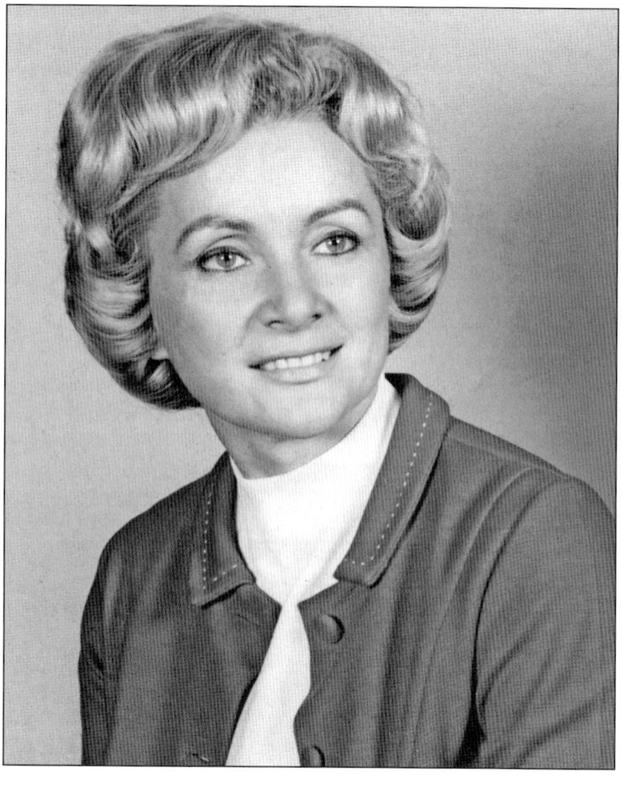

Jeanne Cummins was a favored vocalist with Chuck Selby and a cousin to Margie Alden Coyle. Cummins also sang with Al Waslon and was the featured vocalist for Bernie Cummins. Jeanne met Bernie's brother, Walter, playing in the band. She married Walter in 1946. In a recent chat, Jeanne Cummins marveled at the passing of years and how she still remembers the lyrics to countless tunes. At the printing of this book, she is a spry 93 years old. (Dale Groves archives.)

During the 1950s, Marilyn Daye sang with Chuck Selby. Once married to sportscaster Marty De Victor of WBNS, Daye was selected as the vocalist with the WBNS studio band. According to her son, Tracy Beckman, in 1972, Daye started the Capital City Jazz Band, where she was the vocalist. She is pictured singing at VDB with Selby. (Tracy Beckman.)

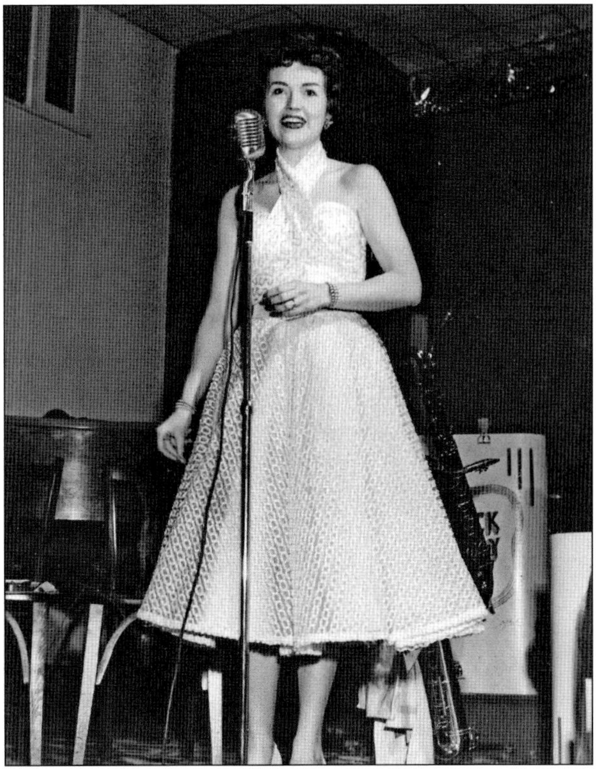

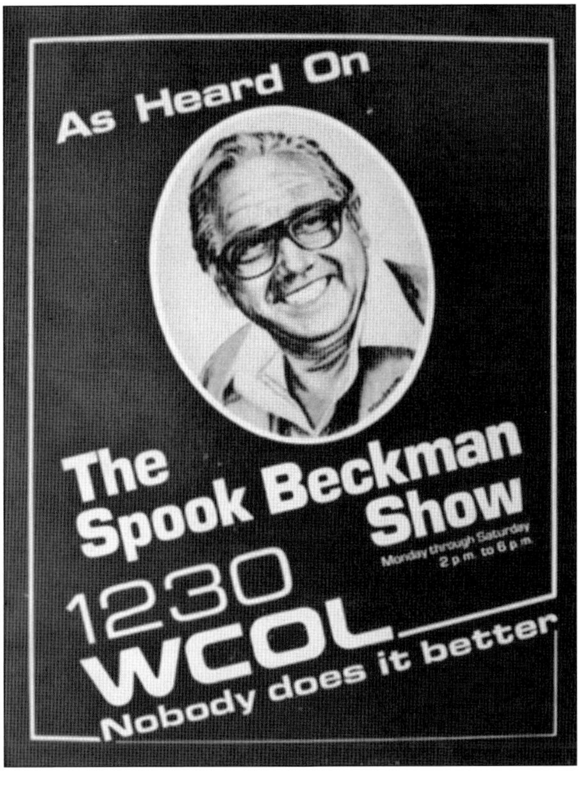

Chuck Selby's vocalist, Marilyn Daye, was not spooked away from radio personality Spook Beckman of WCOL's *Bumper to Bumper* drive time fame. They married, and she enjoyed her life with the man who emceed many Selby VDB frolics. Several dances with Spook are still available on the internet. The admired broadcaster passed away 32 years before his wife; Marilyn passed in 2011. (Mike Adams.)

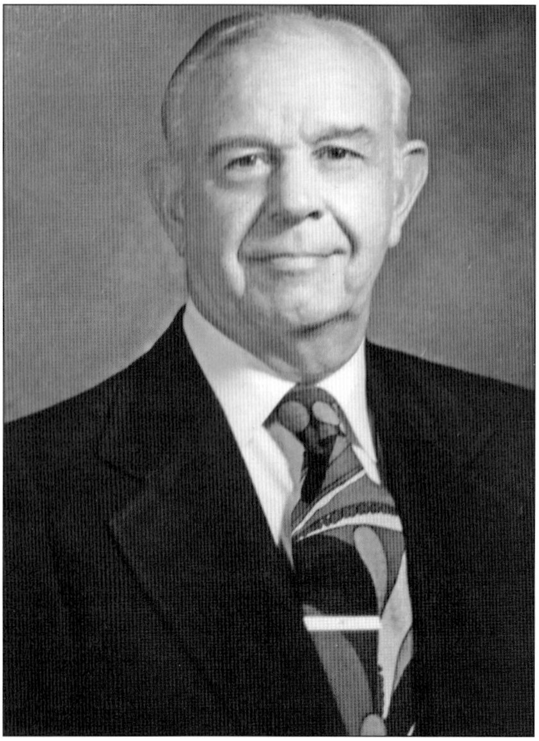

Dr. Robert Everhart, a general practitioner, began performing at VDB in 1951, holding biannual dances until the early 1980s. According to his instrumentalist son Bobby, countless musicians became patients of the well-respected physician. His avocation of music established an unmatched Columbus big band tradition. (Bobby Everhart.)

Doc Everhart's band of 10 in the early 1950s grew to 33-plus onstage musicians by the 1980s, essentially doubling the size of a standard big band. Doc would host free dances for his larger-than-life band and audience, personally paying the VDB rental fee himself. Dr. Everhart's quarterly dances drew 800–1,000 very healthy patients. (Bobby Everhart.)

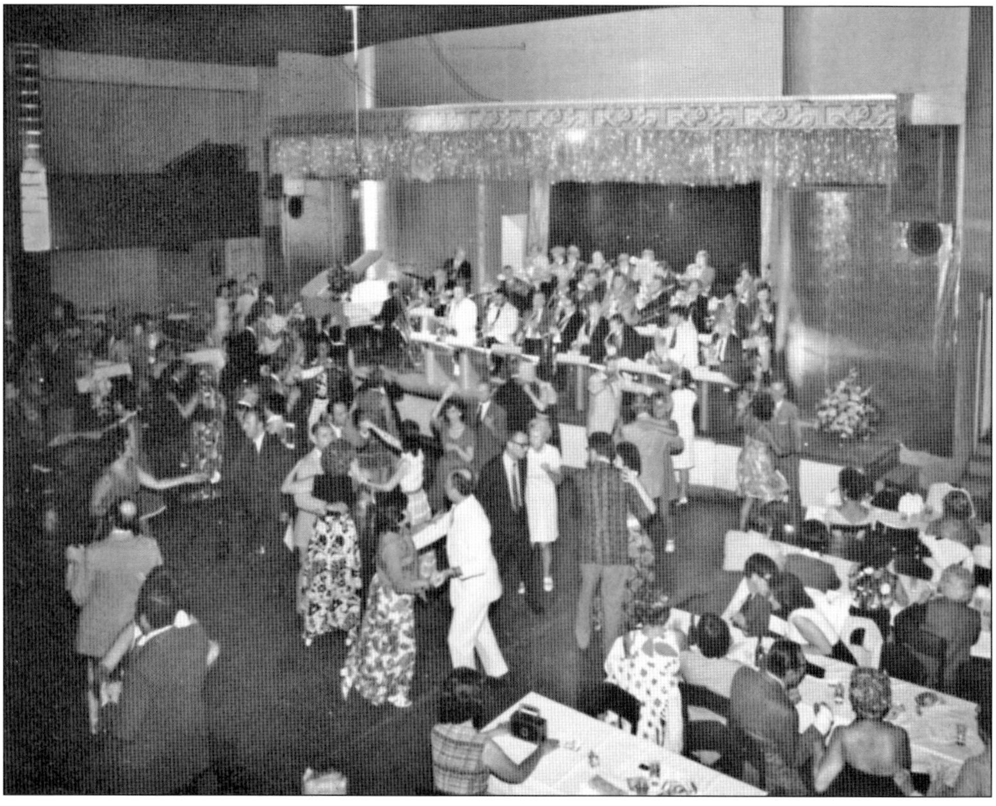

Seven

It's a Sign of the Tymes

The 1960s counterculture may have put a hatchet in the back of once mainstream orchestras and big bands. However the sands of time were tumbling, there was one lone teen band emerging to combat the rock revolution: The Sounds of Tyme. With a hip name and musical message, their compositions turned a restructured corner.

The 1960s did corner Sunday afternoons at VDB as a rock-room in place of the ballroom. For the first time VDB had two masters, classic big band and rock. The flavors were different there was even a rebellion happening, the division was established. The 1930s and 1940s swing music was drastically different from 1960s and 1970s rock tones. The dress once polite and modest was now neither, the idea was to shock. However the kids may have appeared, the teens' passion for their music was identical to those teens of generations gone by.

Unlike the first generation of teenagers where the music was at VDB long before its teenagers discovered their cathedral, the 1960s teenagers flooded VDB, bringing their music with them.

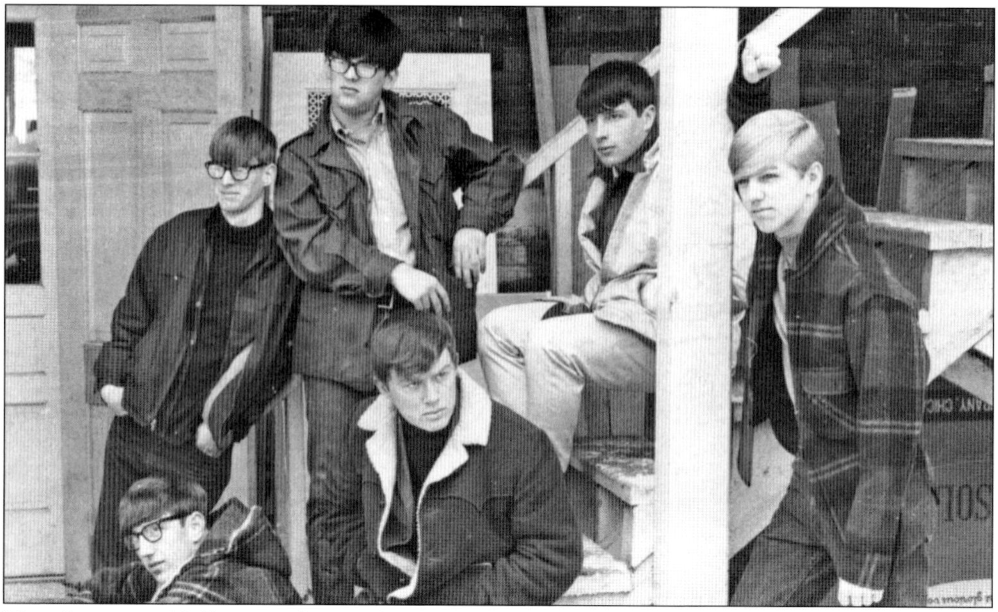

The Grayps, a 1965 group from Whetstone High School, bloomed with a win at the 1966 Northland Battle of the Bands and were the first rock band to play VDB. They backed up Sonny and Cher, the Beach Boys, and the Byrds, making these musicians a unique bunch. In later years, each member had a thriving entertainment career. Don Kettler was a sound engineer for Meatloaf and Kiss, later working on Broadway. Dan Lawson worked with Kris Kristofferson; Jon Townley created visual effects in the Denzel Washington movie *Virtuosity*. Sterling Smith toured with J.D. Blackfoot and the Beach Boys starting in the 1960s, periodically continuing through 2018. From left to right are Don Kettler (seated on first step), Charlie Censer (seated on second step), Bud Dillahunt (seated on third step), and standing are Mike Bauman, Tom Ramseyer, and Ed Mikusa. Dan Lawson, Jon Townley, and pianist Sterling Smith are not pictured. (Sterling Smith.)

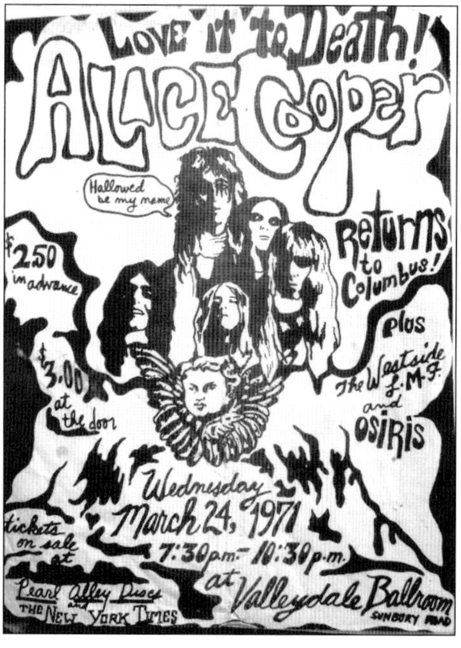

While the Grayps were the first Columbus rock group introducing the second group of teenagers to VDB, Chuck Selby believed that bringing in top 1960s acts could bring fresh teenage energy back to the ballroom. Selby engaged a list of stars: Ike and Tina Turner, Little Anthony, Al Green, B.B. King, Booker T & the MG's, Chubby Checker, Otis Day and the Knights, the Dave Clark Five, Herman's Hermits, The Buckinghams, Linda Ronstadt and the Stone Ponies, Leon Russel, Three Dog Night, Gary Puckett and the Union Gap, Tommy James, the Four Seasons, and the Velvet Underground. Herman's Hermits lead singer Peter Noone was contacted during the writing of this book, kindly answering he did not remember playing VDB. Peter's performance was in 1990. This poster introduces the Grayps opening for Alice Cooper in 1971. (Sterling Smith.)

For a decade from the 1960s through the early 1970s, WLWC NBC television showed *Dance Party* on Saturdays, showcasing bands and their high school fans and hosted by Columbus disc jockey Jerry Rasor. Rasor promoted WLWC's weekly live televised shows from VDB featuring the Rebounds, Four O'Clock Balloon, the Edicates, and others. The Dantes caused an April 1966 disturbance for the Righteous Brothers' Billboard number-one ballad "Soul and Inspiration" by thwacking it off the top of the local chart with "Can't Get Enough of Your Love." (Lynn Wehr.)

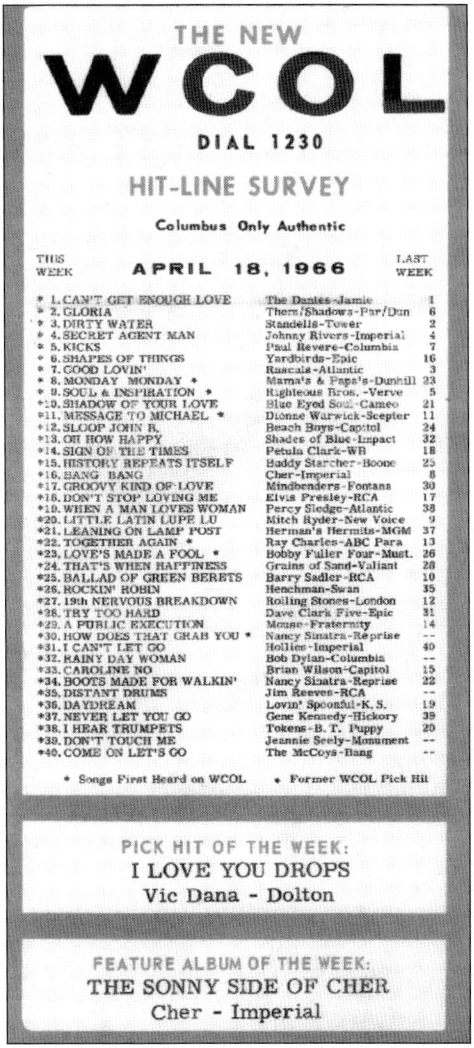

THE NEW

WCOL

DIAL 1230

HIT-LINE SURVEY

Columbus Only Authentic

THIS WEEK	APRIL 18, 1966		LAST WEEK
* 1.	CAN'T GET ENOUGH LOVE	The Dantes-Jamie	1
* 2.	GLORIA	Them/Shadows-Par/Dun	6
* 3.	DIRTY WATER	Standells-Tower	2
* 4.	SECRET AGENT MAN	Johnny Rivers-Imperial	4
* 5.	KICKS	Paul Revere-Columbia	7
* 6.	SHAPES OF THINGS	Yardbirds-Epic	16
* 7.	GOOD LOVIN'	Rascals-Atlantic	3
* 8.	MONDAY MONDAY *	Mama's & Papa's-Dunhill	23
* 9.	SOUL & INSPIRATION *	Righteous Bros. -Verve	5
*10.	SHADOW OF YOUR LOVE	Blue Eyed Soul-Cameo	21
*11.	MESSAGE TO MICHAEL *	Dionne Warwick-Scepter	11
*12.	SLOOP JOHN B.	Beach Boys-Capitol	24
*13.	OH HOW HAPPY	Shades of Blue-Impact	32
*14.	SIGN OF THE TIMES	Petula Clark-WB	18
*15.	HISTORY REPEATS ITSELF	Buddy Starcher-Boone	25
*16.	BANG BANG	Cher-Imperial	8
*17.	GROOVY KIND OF LOVE	Mindbenders-Fontana	30
*18.	DON'T STOP LOVING ME	Elvis Presley-RCA	17
*19.	WHEN A MAN LOVES WOMAN	Percy Sledge-Atlantic	38
*20.	LITTLE LATIN LUPE LU	Mitch Ryder-New Voice	9
*21.	LEANING ON LAMP POST	Herman's Hermits-MGM	37
*22.	TOGETHER AGAIN *	Ray Charles-ABC Para	13
*23.	LOVE'S MADE A FOOL *	Bobby Fuller Four-Must.	26
*24.	THAT'S WHEN HAPPINESS	Grains of Sand-Valiant	28
*25.	BALLAD OF GREEN BERETS	Barry Sadler-RCA	10
*26.	ROCKIN' ROBIN	Henchman-Swan	35
*27.	19th NERVOUS BREAKDOWN	Rolling Stones-London	12
*28.	TRY TOO HARD	Dave Clark Five-Epic	31
*29.	A PUBLIC EXECUTION	Mouse-Fraternity	14
*30.	HOW DOES THAT GRAB YOU *	Nancy Sinatra-Reprise	--
*31.	I CAN'T LET GO	Hollies-Imperial	40
*32.	RAINY DAY WOMAN	Bob Dylan-Columbia	--
*33.	CAROLINE NO	Brian Wilson-Capitol	15
*34.	BOOTS MADE FOR WALKIN'	Nancy Sinatra-Reprise	22
*35.	DISTANT DRUMS	Jim Reeves-RCA	--
*36.	DAYDREAM	Lovin' Spoonful-K. S.	19
*37.	NEVER LET YOU GO	Gene Kennedy-Hickory	39
*38.	I HEAR TRUMPETS	Tokens-B. T. Puppy	20
*39.	DON'T TOUCH ME	Jeannie Seely-Monument	--
*40.	COME ON LET'S GO	The McCoys-Bang	--

* Songs First Heard on WCOL • Former WCOL Pick Hit

PICK HIT OF THE WEEK:
I LOVE YOU DROPS
Vic Dana - Dolton

FEATURE ALBUM OF THE WEEK:
THE SONNY SIDE OF CHER
Cher - Imperial

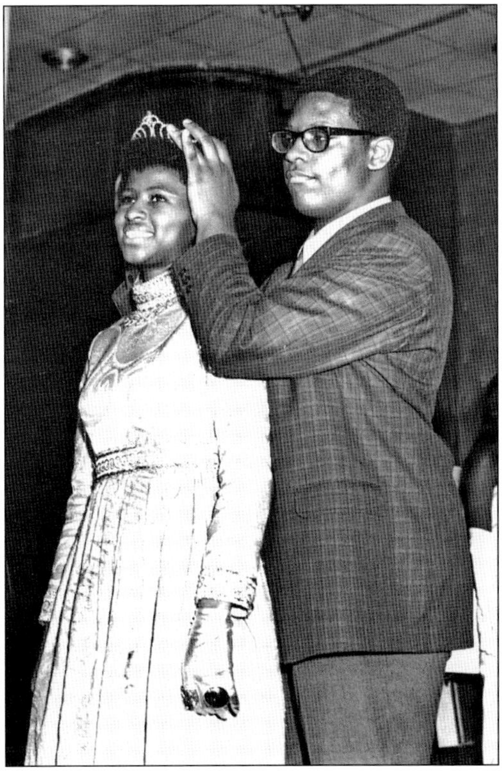

The musicians and vocalists of the big band era were replaced by an array of events such as cotillions and pageants. Mildred Billups, 19 at the time, represented Columbus in the state finals of the 1970 Miss Americolor Contest, once held in Dayton, Ohio. The winner competed for the national title in New York City. Roger Stowe, vice president of the Youth Council of the Columbus NAACP, which sponsored the Columbus contest, crowned Billups after she won at VDB. (*Columbus Dispatch*.)

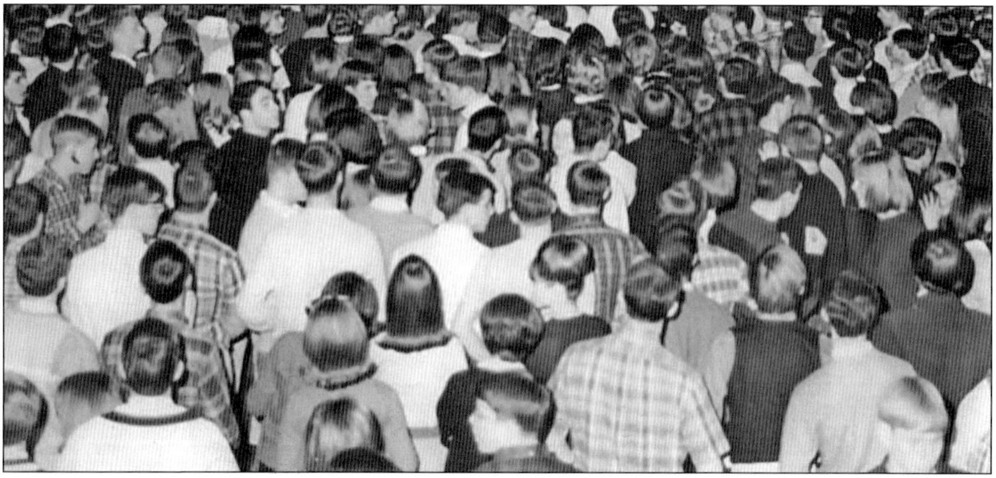

It started with high school garage bands entering battles of the bands. The wise and tasteful Jerry Rasor and VDB's savvy manager, Chuck Selby, thought Sunday afternoon teen dances of the 1960s might replace the tea-dances of the 1950s to save the failing "Dale." Rasor would publicize VDB as the Sunday place to be during his Saturday *Dance Party*. The Sunday "Dance a Rama" was a success due to the impact the new generation of teenagers had on the music scene. VDB hosted over 1,000 teenagers each Sunday afternoon. Note the 1960s "flip" hairstyle many of the teen girls are sporting.

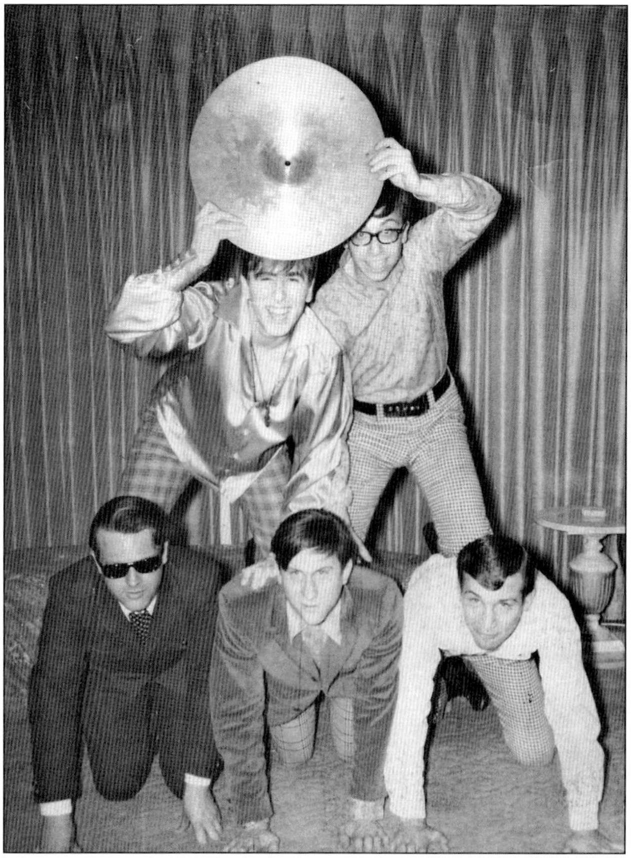

Noted for sing-a-long songs dipped in cotton-candy flavors, the 1910 Fruitgum Company performed Valley Dale Ballroom between 1969 and 1971. Svengali producers preferred the group's road to fame to be a sweet concoction of chords with repetitive harmonies. Decades later, critics are still unkind, categorizing the band as expendable as a gum wrapper. Original vocalist and guitarist Frank Jeckell is not so quick to agree. Some 50 years later, he is humble and gracious about the band's three gold records and its Billboard charting at four and one. Members were disillusioned by the reality of not recording the music they wrote, influenced by Cream, Vanilla Fudge, and Hendrix (who played VDB in 1966). The closest they came to recording their own music was "Reflection of a Looking Glass," the B side of their hit "Simon Says." (Frank Jeckell.)

Lead guitarist Lynn Wehr recalls how the Dantes got their name. It involved a happenstance gaze, a slight head tilt to the left, and a label on a cologne bottle perched by a stack of books on a dresser. The 14th-century poet might have enjoyed his comedic divinity of intervention as the cologne of the day became linked to one of Columbus's most memorable bands of the 1960s. (Lynn Wehr.)

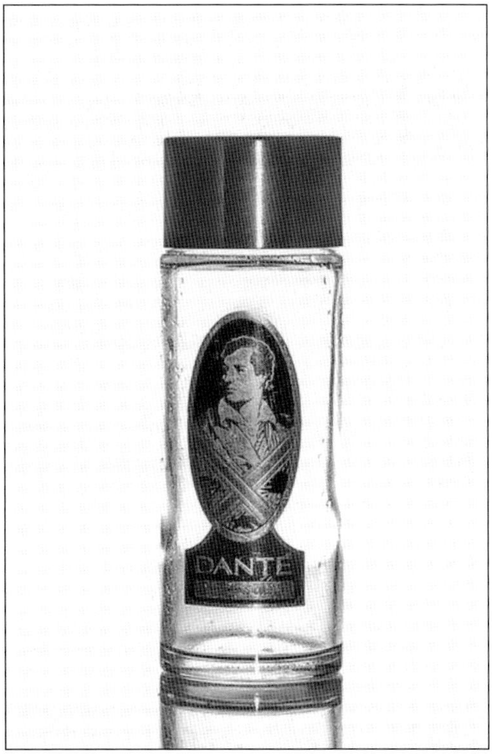

In the 1960s, a handful of local bands really changed the complexion of VDB. One was Sir Timothy and the Royals, later becoming the Ohio Express. Another success between 1964 and 1969 was Worthington High School's Dantes. First being defeated at the Northland Battle of Bands then winning the rock-off at VDB cemented this garage band in the hearts of local 1960s teens. The Dantes' energized performances with "Loads" of other bands each Sunday afternoon, magnetized the 1960s minors at VDB dances. From left to right are Dave Workman, Lynn Wehr, Carter Holliday, Joe Hinton, and Barry Hayden. (Lynn Wehr.)

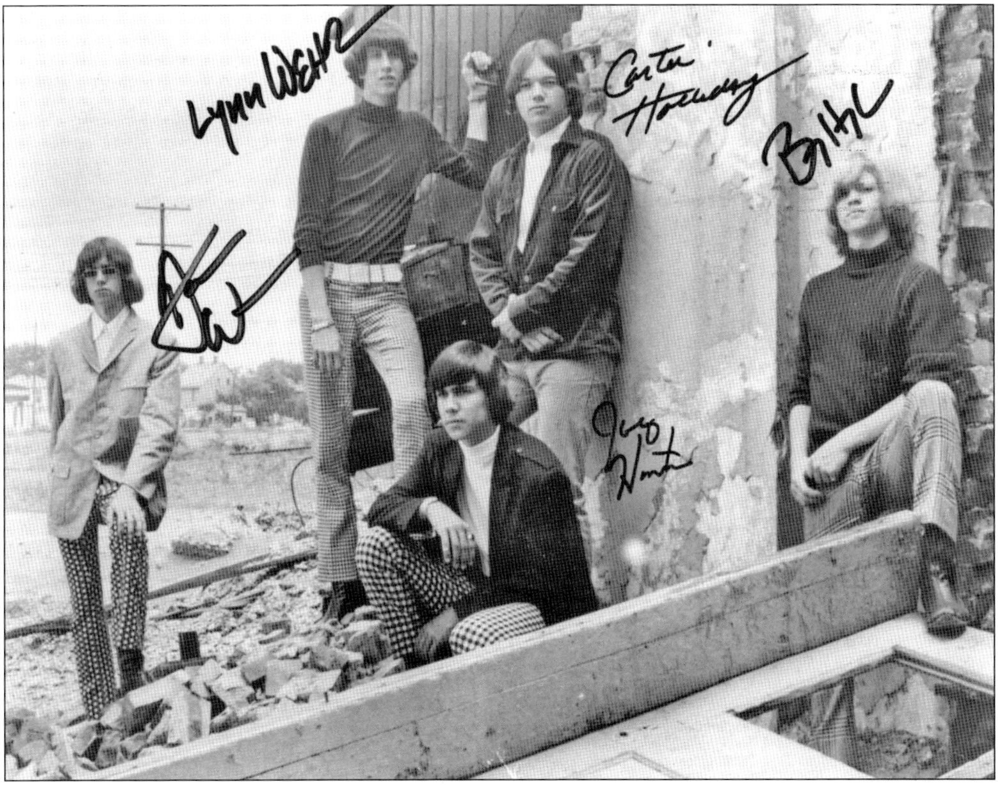

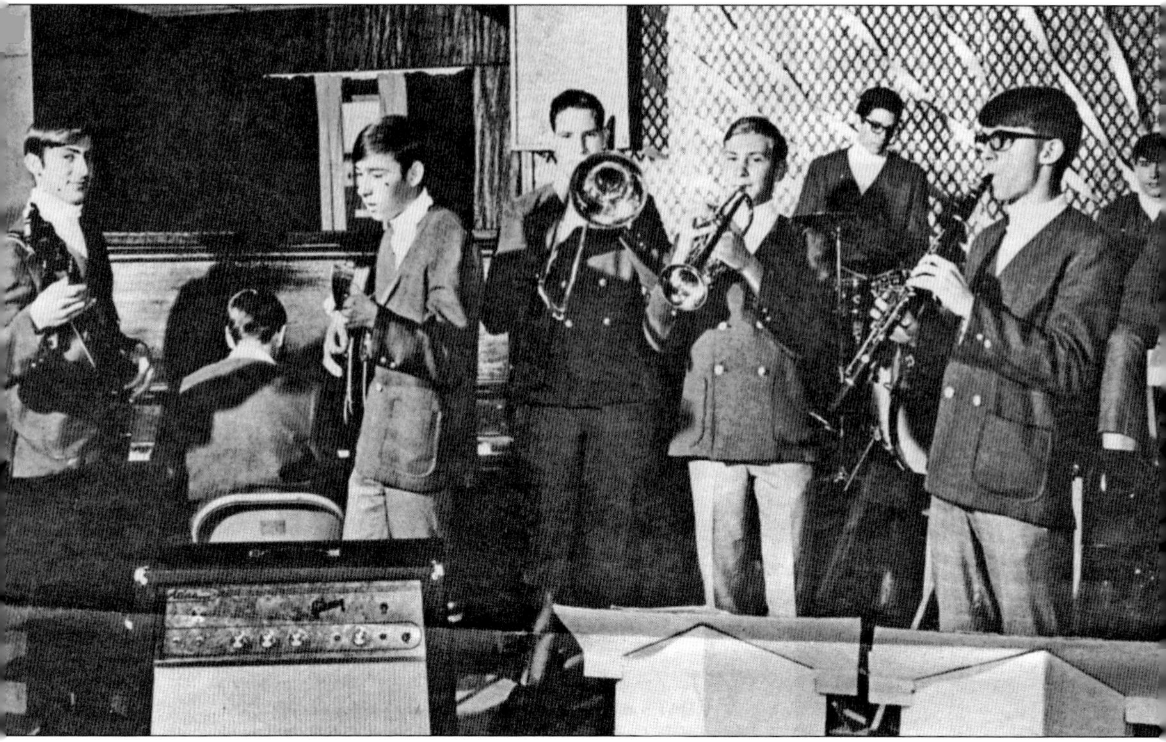

Musical tastes evolved away from big bands in the 1960s. The British Invasion presented the final blow to the once-beloved traveling dance bands. No-nonsense Dale Groves actively fought that battle. Casually holding court in his garage, Dale encouraged musical history chats with the neighborhood kids. He wrote his friend Les Brown, director of the Band of Renown, for advice; Brown responded with a package of music charts to start his group. Using the sheet music to present instrumental history to the Baby Boomer generation, Dale created a big band made up entirely of central Ohio teenagers. The first engagement for the youth jazz band Sounds of Tyme was at Valley Dale in 1967. Decades later, while Groves strolled on a Columbus street, a former teen band member approached with an outstretched hand and said, "Mr. Groves, you saved my life, without the focus of music in my teens, I fear to think where I could have ended up." Groves, a stoic, tall, slender fellow, was tremendously moved by the encounter, to the point that his wife, Glenna, believed flecks of dust blurred his vision. (Ken Groves.)

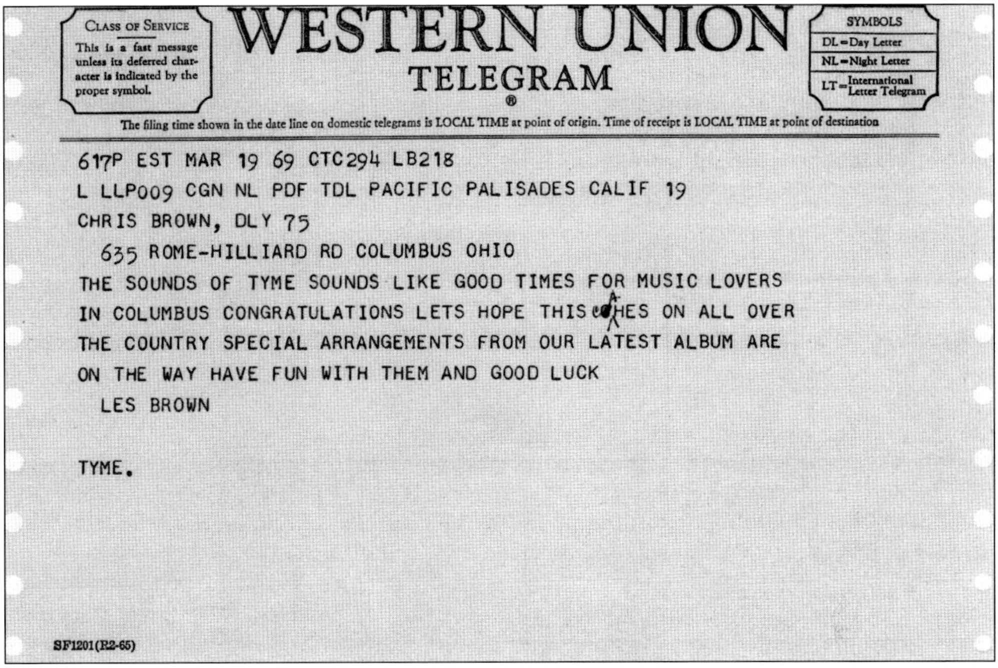

CLASS OF SERVICE
This is a fast message unless its deferred character is indicated by the proper symbol.

WESTERN UNION
TELEGRAM

SYMBOLS
DL=Day Letter
NL=Night Letter
LT=International Letter Telegram

The filing time shown in the date line on domestic telegrams is LOCAL TIME at point of origin. Time of receipt is LOCAL TIME at point of destination

617P EST MAR 19 69 CTC294 LB218
L LLP009 CGN NL PDF TDL PACIFIC PALISADES CALIF 19
CHRIS BROWN, DLY 75
635 ROME-HILLIARD RD COLUMBUS OHIO
THE SOUNDS OF TYME SOUNDS LIKE GOOD TIMES FOR MUSIC LOVERS
IN COLUMBUS CONGRATULATIONS LETS HOPE THIS CATCHES ON ALL OVER
THE COUNTRY SPECIAL ARRANGEMENTS FROM OUR LATEST ALBUM ARE
ON THE WAY HAVE FUN WITH THEM AND GOOD LUCK
LES BROWN

TYME.

SF1201(R2-65)

Dale Groves found success with the first-of-its-kind teenage big band Sounds of Tyme between 1966 and 1970. Groves received a congratulatory telegram from Les Brown and the Band of Renown, the house band for Dean Martin's TV show. (Dale Groves archives.)

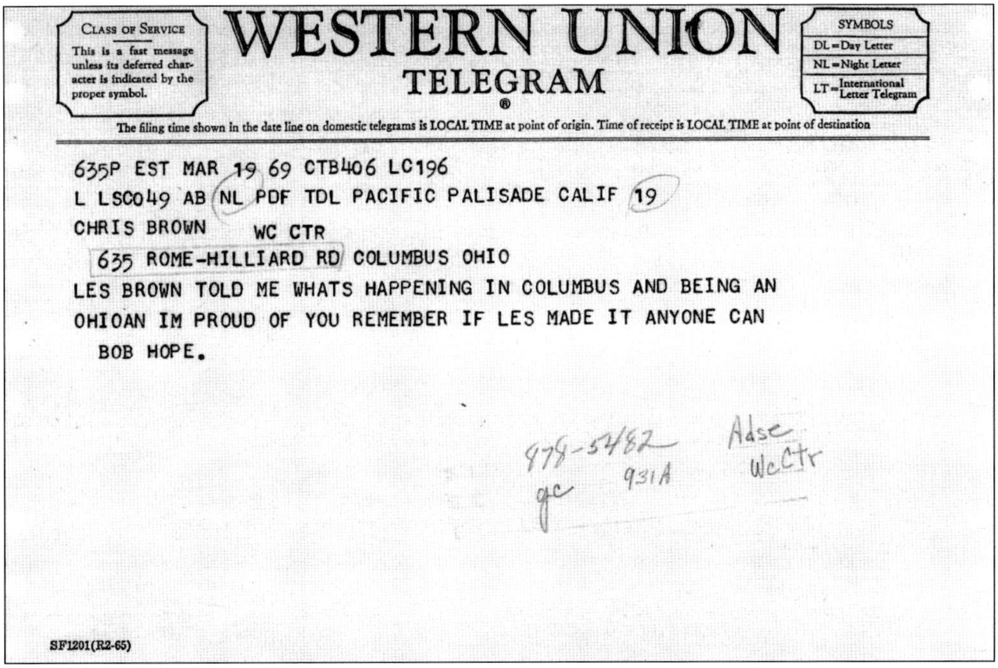

CLASS OF SERVICE
This is a fast message unless its deferred character is indicated by the proper symbol.

WESTERN UNION
TELEGRAM

SYMBOLS
DL=Day Letter
NL=Night Letter
LT=International Letter Telegram

The filing time shown in the date line on domestic telegrams is LOCAL TIME at point of origin. Time of receipt is LOCAL TIME at point of destination

635P EST MAR 19 69 CTB406 LC196
L LSC049 AB NL PDF TDL PACIFIC PALISADE CALIF 19
CHRIS BROWN WC CTR
635 ROME-HILLIARD RD COLUMBUS OHIO
LES BROWN TOLD ME WHATS HAPPENING IN COLUMBUS AND BEING AN
OHIOAN IM PROUD OF YOU REMEMBER IF LES MADE IT ANYONE CAN
BOB HOPE.

SF1201(R2-65)

A humorous quip from Bob Hope shows his Ohio pride. Groves received a congratulatory telegram for Sounds of Tyme from the legendary comedian. A third congratulatory telegram hailed from Corky Corchran of the Harry James Orchestra. (Dale Groves archives.)

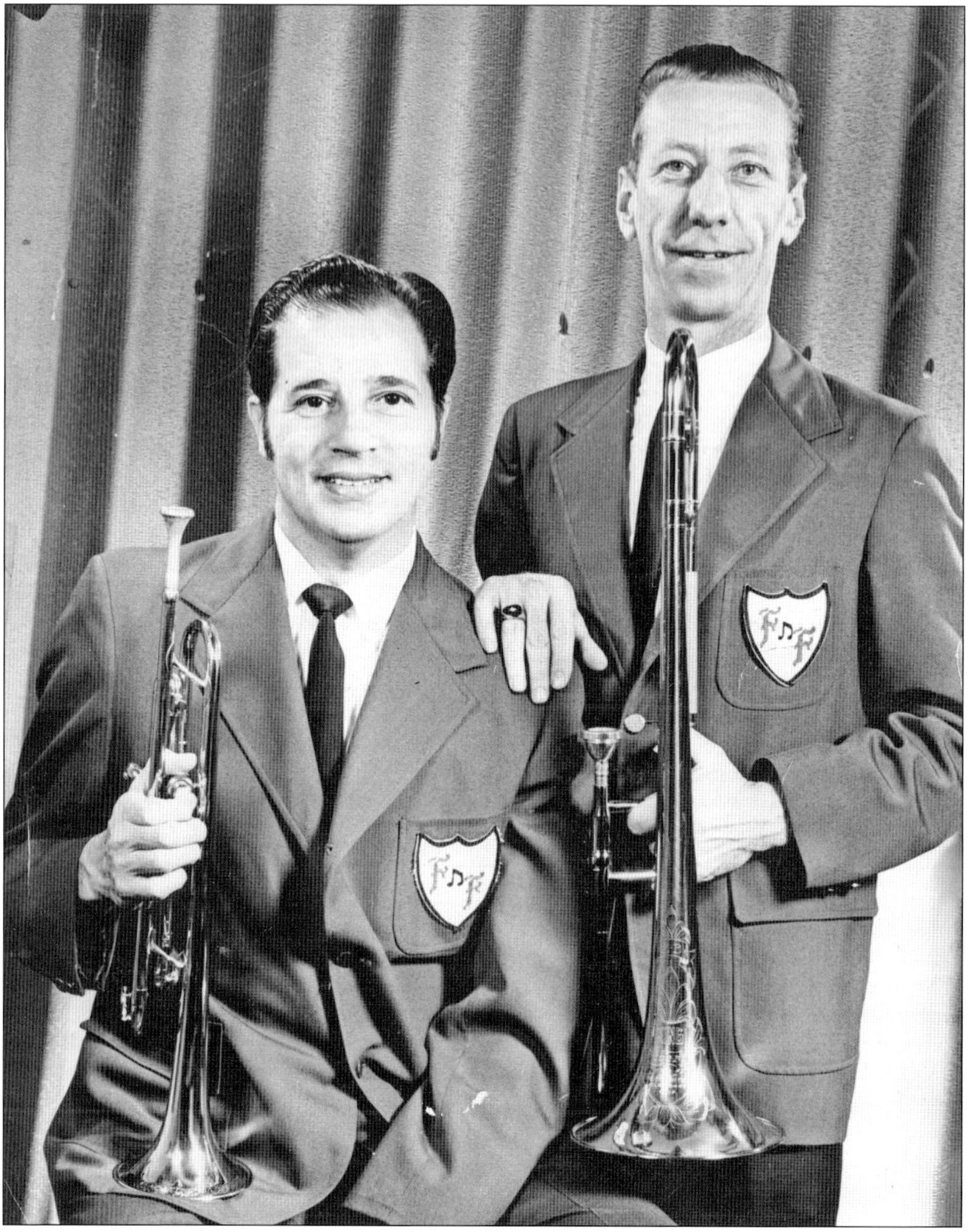

Once the successful students of Sounds of Tyme graduated high school in 1970, Dale Groves headed to see a friend, bringing another stellar dream with him. It was almost 25 years since the end of the big band era. Groves, brimming with ideas, headed to Bruno Masdea's Seymour Bakery, the two baked up a terrific recipe to start a big band. Dale Groves, a trombonist, taught by Fritz Hummel, (see p.24) and Bruno Masdea, a trumpeter trained since he was six years old by his Columbus Concert Band Director father, Joseph Masdea, brought the 18-piece sound back to VDB with their fresh "Fabulous Forties" dance band. Their VDB date with history was June 5, 1971, theirs was the first of the new wave of big bands returning to VDB. (Dale Groves archives.)

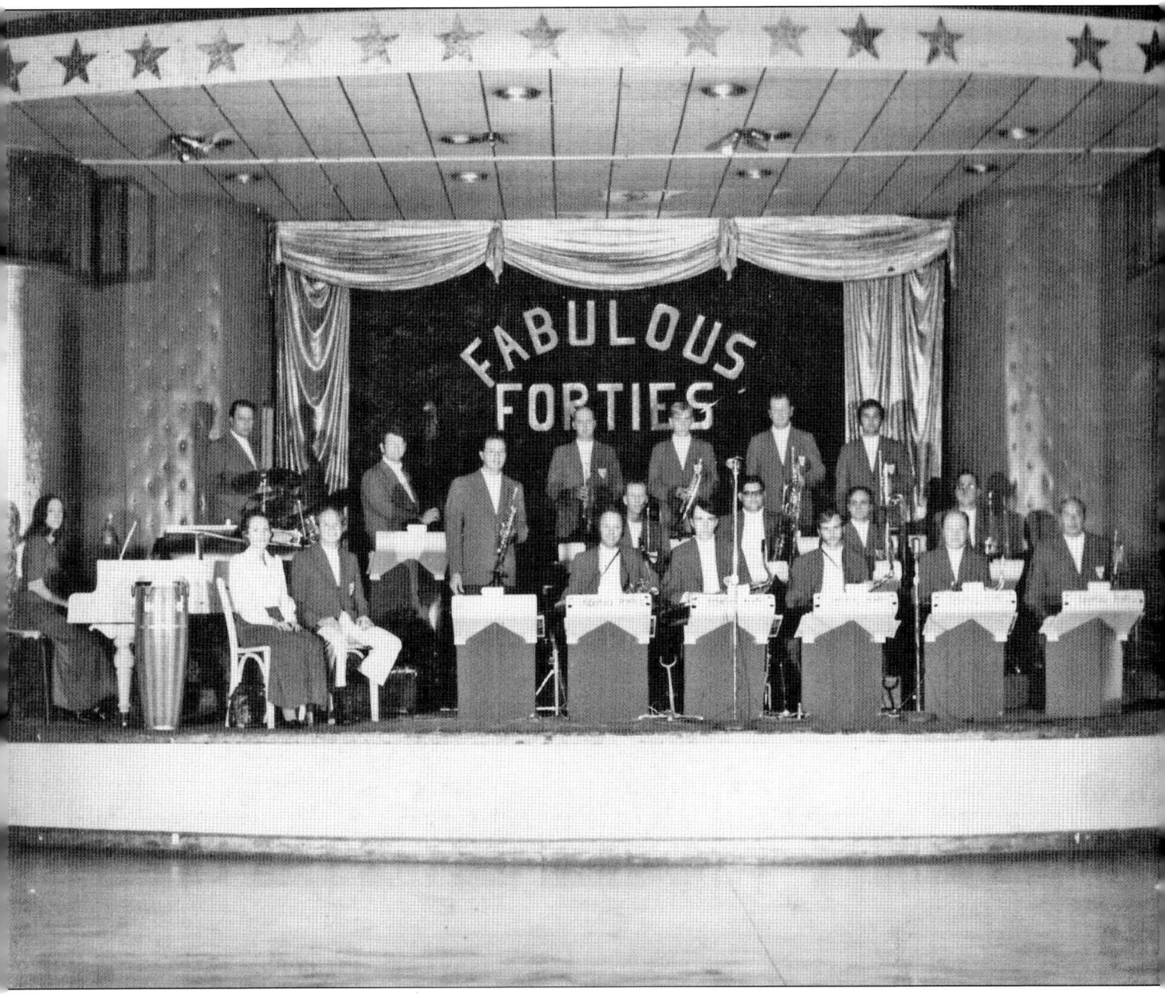

"The Fabulous Forties were mostly over 40 and mostly fabulous," opened a report by journalist Jim Bradshaw describing a Saturday evening VDB show by the group led by Dale Groves and Bruno Masdea in the September 25, 1972, *Columbus Dispatch*. "A packed house deep into the balconies at Valley Dale last Saturday night, the band does not have to be concerned about the national revival of the Big-Band Sound: its members have successfully resurrected it locally. . . . To Masdea the VDB, where the new group got its start 1 ½ years ago, will always be his favorite. . . . This report, while intended to be flattering—deservedly so—has not included any musical critique. It wasn't music they were playing, it was memories—some already treasured, some in the making." The final quoted line is the anthem of this book on the Valley Dale Ballroom. The Fabulous Forties are pictured on the Valley Dale stage in 1971. Dale Groves' sons were F.F. musicians, Ken, a vocalist and trumpeter, Ron, a trombonist, young Kevin the roadie. The daughters of; Groves, Cherrie and Candy and Masdea's Margi, all under nine years old, would play in the radio booths gleefully looking out its window at the twirling dancers during their fathers' VDB engagements. (Dale Groves archives.)

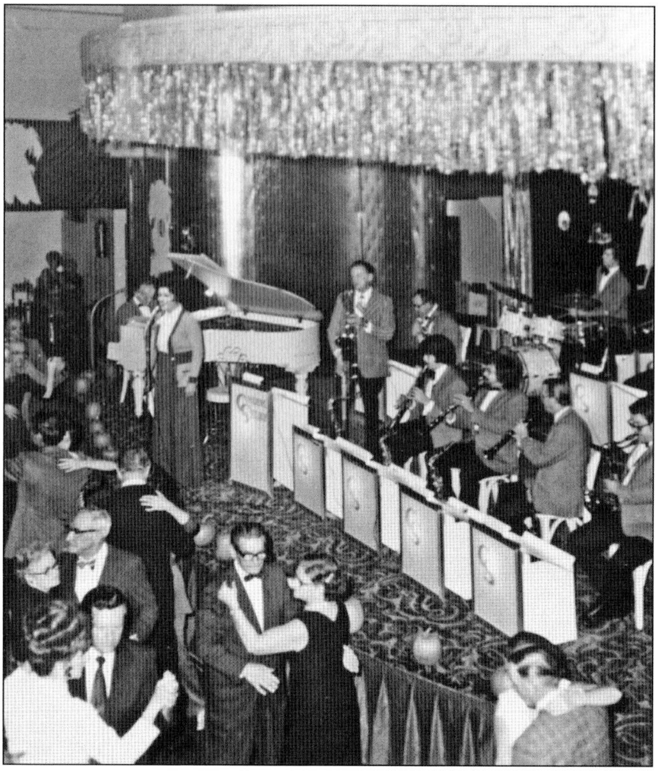

Born as Anne Youngblood in Marion, Ohio, Anne Young adopted her stage name while still in high school. Young was hired as the featured vocalist in the Chuck Selby Orchestra, the house band at the VDB in 1958. She later married Chuck Selby. After his 1979 death, Anne assumed leadership of the band a decade before starting the Anne Young Trio, which she performed with in Columbus and Florida until her passing at 83 years old, singing until seven days before her passing with a voice that showed no age in her last years. Fred and Betty Persinger, dancing in their VDB bandstand spot wearing a bow tie and black gown, respectively, will be recognized again in these pages.

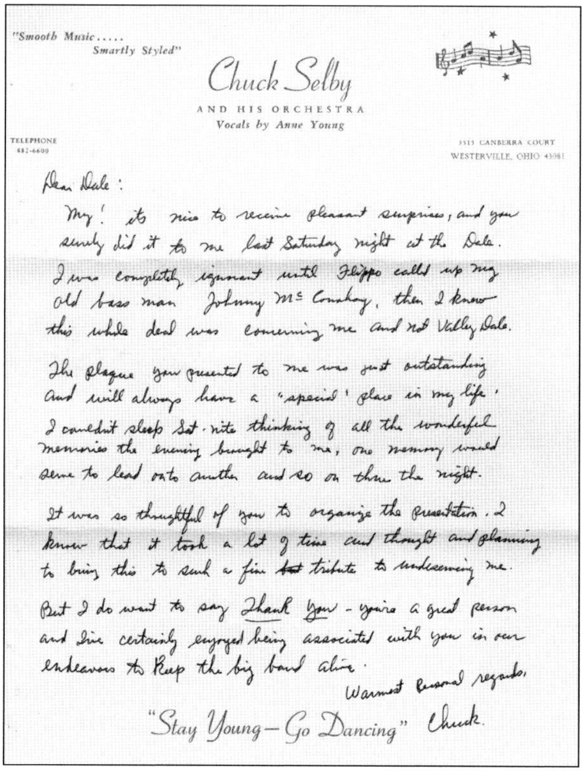

"Smooth Music.....
Smartly Styled"

Chuck Selby
AND HIS ORCHESTRA
Vocals by Anne Young

TELEPHONE
882-6600

3515 CANBERRA COURT
WESTERVILLE, OHIO 43081

Dear Dale:

My! its nice to receive pleasant surprises, and you surely did it to me last Saturday night at the Dale.

I was completely ignorant until Flippo called up my old bass man Johnny McConahay, then I knew this whole deal was concerning me and not Valley Dale.

The plaque you presented to me was just outstanding and will always have a "special" place in my life. I couldn't sleep Sat. nite thinking of all the wonderful memories the evening brought to me, one memory would serve to lead onto another and so on thru the night.

It was so thoughtful of you to organize the presentation. I know that it took a lot of time and thought and planning to bring this to such a fine ~~but~~ tribute to undeserving me.

But I do want to say Thank You - you're a great person and I've certainly enjoyed being associated with you in our endeavors to keep the big band alive.

Warmest personal regards,

"Stay Young—Go Dancing" Chuck.

In an old-fashioned battle of the bands, the Chuck Selby Orchestra battled Dale Groves's Fabulous Forties. Selby sent a heartfelt letter to Dale Groves in appreciation for a deeply memorable evening. The aging leader had logged over 40 years at the VDB. This evening was one of Chuck's last significant bandstands, and Groves, the crowd of more than 1,100, and Selby knew it. Everyone wanted to attend this unspoken farewell. (Dale Groves archives.)

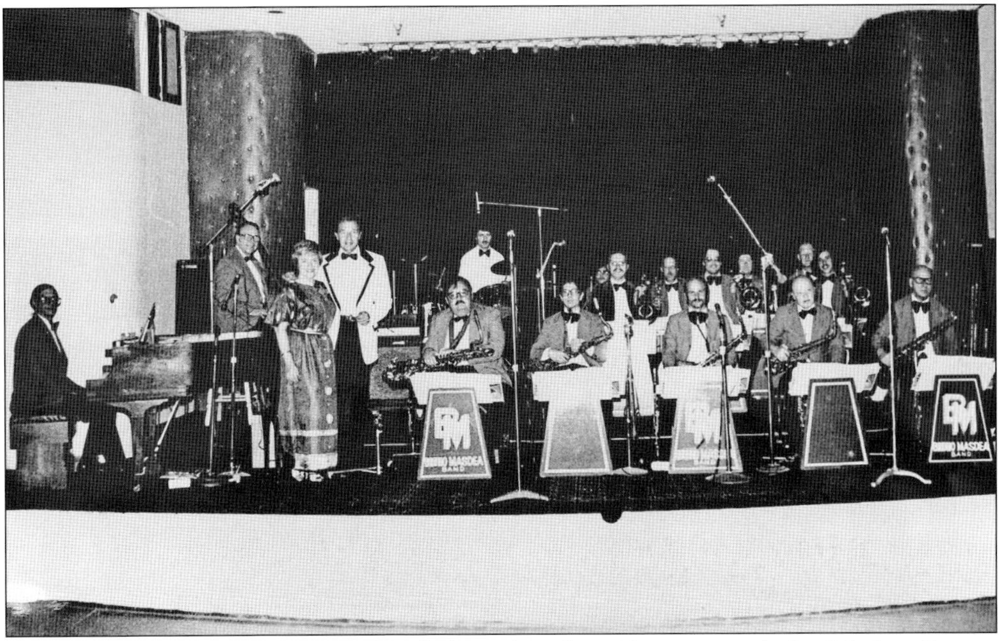

Bruno Masdea began his big dance band after a friendly 1973 parting with the Fabulous Forties. Masdea's book contained swing classics accented with fresh arrangements and contemporary 1970s hits in big band style: "It's a Sign of the Times," "After the Loving," "Love Will Keep Us Together," and "The Way We Were." Masdea treasured VDB—playing there was like communing with the spirits of past bands. There was no facility he enjoyed performing in more. This photograph shows the first time, drummer Rick Brunetto played VDB; this was his initial job with his soon-to-be father-in-law, Bruno Masdea. Masdea was honored to be inducted into the VDB wall of fame in 2011. (Bruno Masdea archives.)

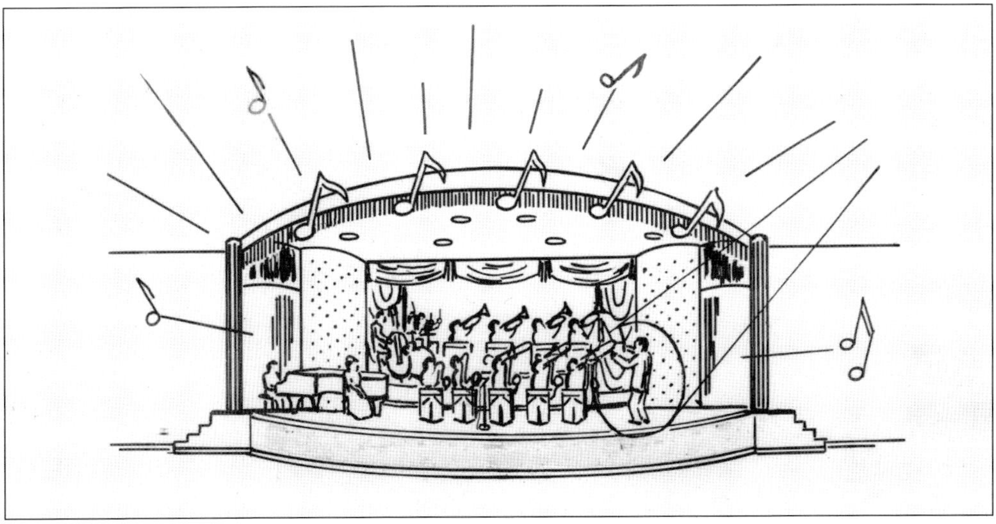

All bands had identifying logos. When Masdea introduced the Bruno Masdea Dance Band in 1973, his logo's inspiration was the Valley Dale stage. Dar Port, a graphic illustrator by day and lead saxophonist with Masdea's band by night, created this artwork. The linear ink drawing of the VDB stage, including the details of Frank Dailey's tufted leather walls and two radio booths, was seen on letterhead, posters, and T-shirts for the band. (Bruno Masdea archives.)

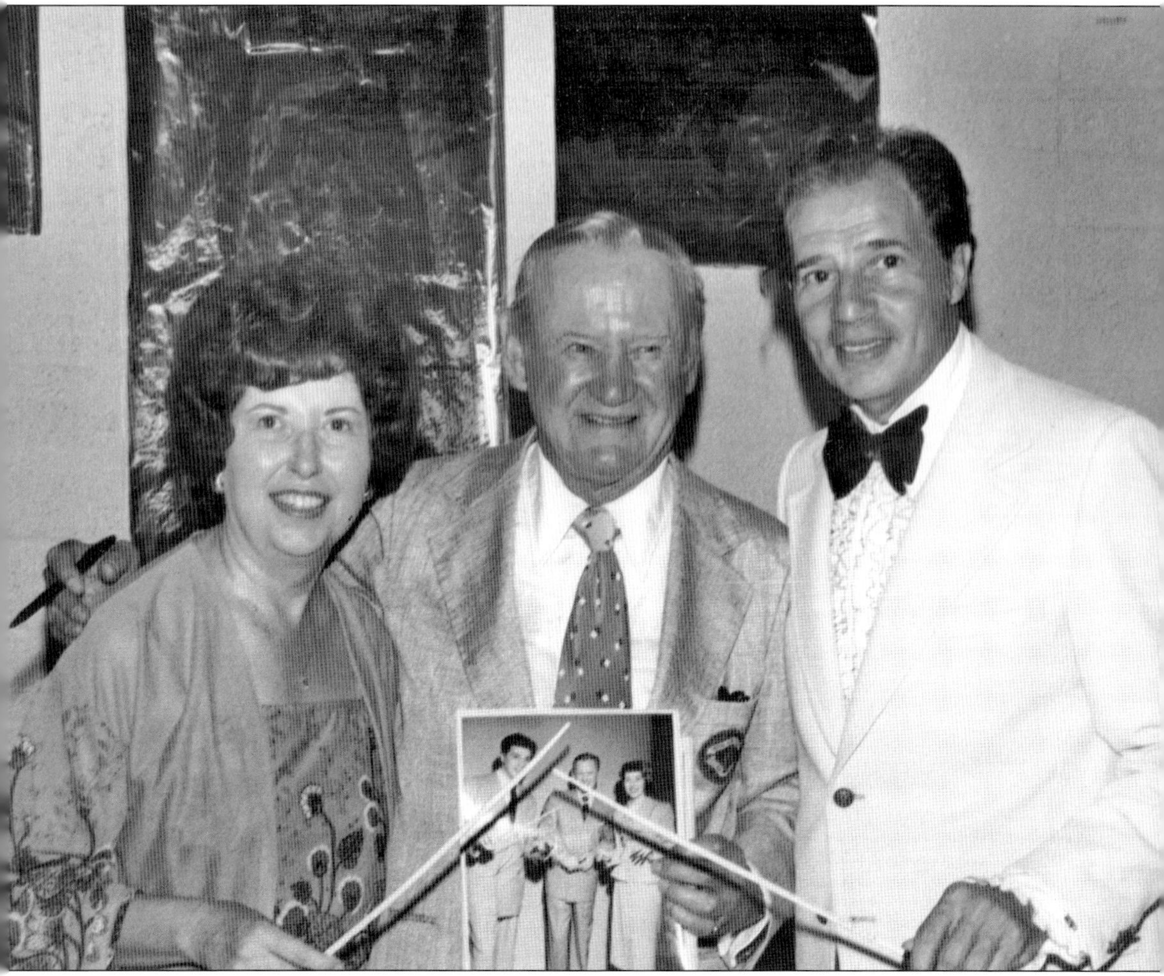

"Daddy! You gotta get the best for me" is a line from "Daddy!", a huge hit for Sammy Kaye, who was being recognized in 1979 at Ohio University, from which he graduated in 1932. Feeling the impact of the sound of his era, Sammy Kaye crept closer to the stage. The evening's bandleader gazed into his enthusiastic crowd and spotted the guest of honor, immediately breaking into Sammy Kaye's theme song. Sammy approached the stage. The band was the VDB house band, Bruno Masdea's Big Dance Band. Kaye conversed with bandleader Masdea and his wife, "Wezi," about VDB and dearest friend Lou Peppe and fondly remembered Jim Peppe, Kaye's one-time band partner. Bruno Masdea was also from Kaye's past. To "Swing and Sway, Kaye," Masdea presented Kaye with a photograph from Kaye's CBS television show depicting honeymooners Wezi and Bruno Masdea onstage with him in 1952. Above is the trio at Ohio University in 1979 holding the original 1952 photograph. (Louise "Wezi" Masdea.)

Eight

Big Bands Are Really Back in the 1980s

Weddings were taking over the weekend business at VDB. More professional events and trade shows were being held at the ballroom. Even though the big bands only played a few times a month, huge crowds would appear when dances and bands were performing. On New Year's Eve, 1979, the fire marshal and city officials converged on the ballroom to shutter it permanently, citing an array of safety issues. The ire of the dancers was lit. Letters flooded the newspapers as the rain had flooded Valley Dale decades earlier. The editorial page was saturated with only one topic for weeks and weeks: "Save the Valley Dale," its admirers wrote from their hearts, the passionate headlines were unceasing; "PLEADS for "DALE," "A part of our History," "Say it ain't so." The over-50-year VDB fans the Persingers wrote a poignant letter to the editor to Save VDB, her *Citizen-Journal* published quote: "We were there when it closed and we'll be there when it re-opens." The disruption to the ballroom dances were devastatingly unwelcome.

Valley Dale patron Joyce Fridley authored her sentiments to the newspaper for her cherished shrine: "I wish everyone could have experienced the laughter, memories, dreams and romantic moments those walls hold. Thousands of people have shared similar feelings with friends and loved ones. Now more than ever we need such a place to escape from the harsh realities of daily living—if only for a few hours. However, a group of people determined to take that away from us by closing the Dale. I hope they reconsider. If they do not reconsider we certainly will think a lot harder when we vote at the next elections." History will write an unexpected narrative for 1980s Valley Dale.

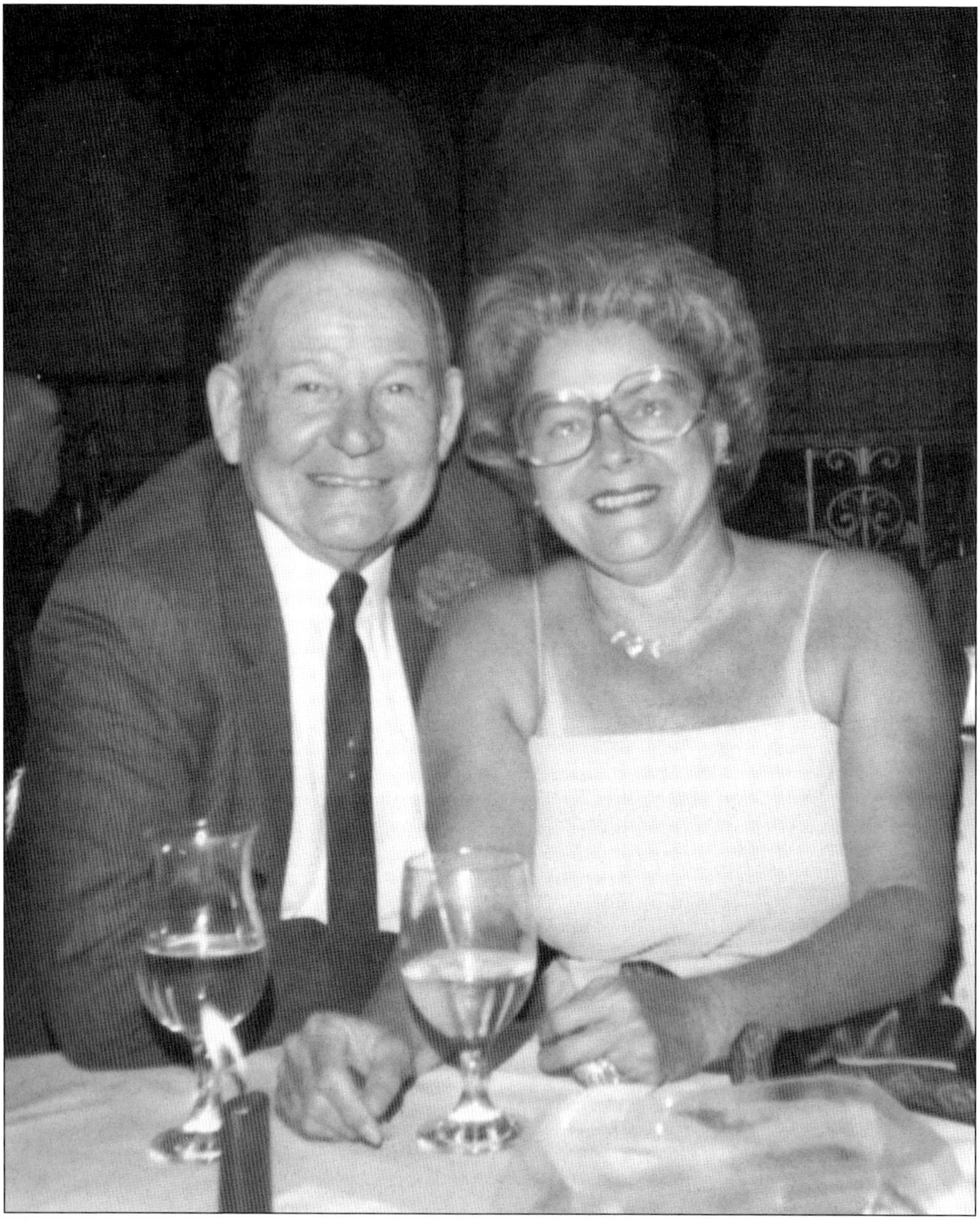

Thirty years after her original VDB photograph, Lola Mattox joined to stave off the VDB's demolition as one of the hundreds writing letters to the mayor. She wrote to the editor of the *Citizen Journal* on March 11, 1980: "There isn't any other dancefloor in Columbus to compare. . . . All we know is the New Year's Eve inspections surely was not a routine trip. Why did they pick NYE? Why were their newspaper and TV people along? Who and why is someone making it their business to close VDB?" The following is a sampling of the hundreds of letters published in the letters to the editor. Pat Eckman wrote, "Memories of the great bands come out the walls at you. Make you forget your troubles, help you remember how peaceful things were," and Willa Whipple wrote, "VDB probably touched more people in this area than the art gallery and symphony combined."

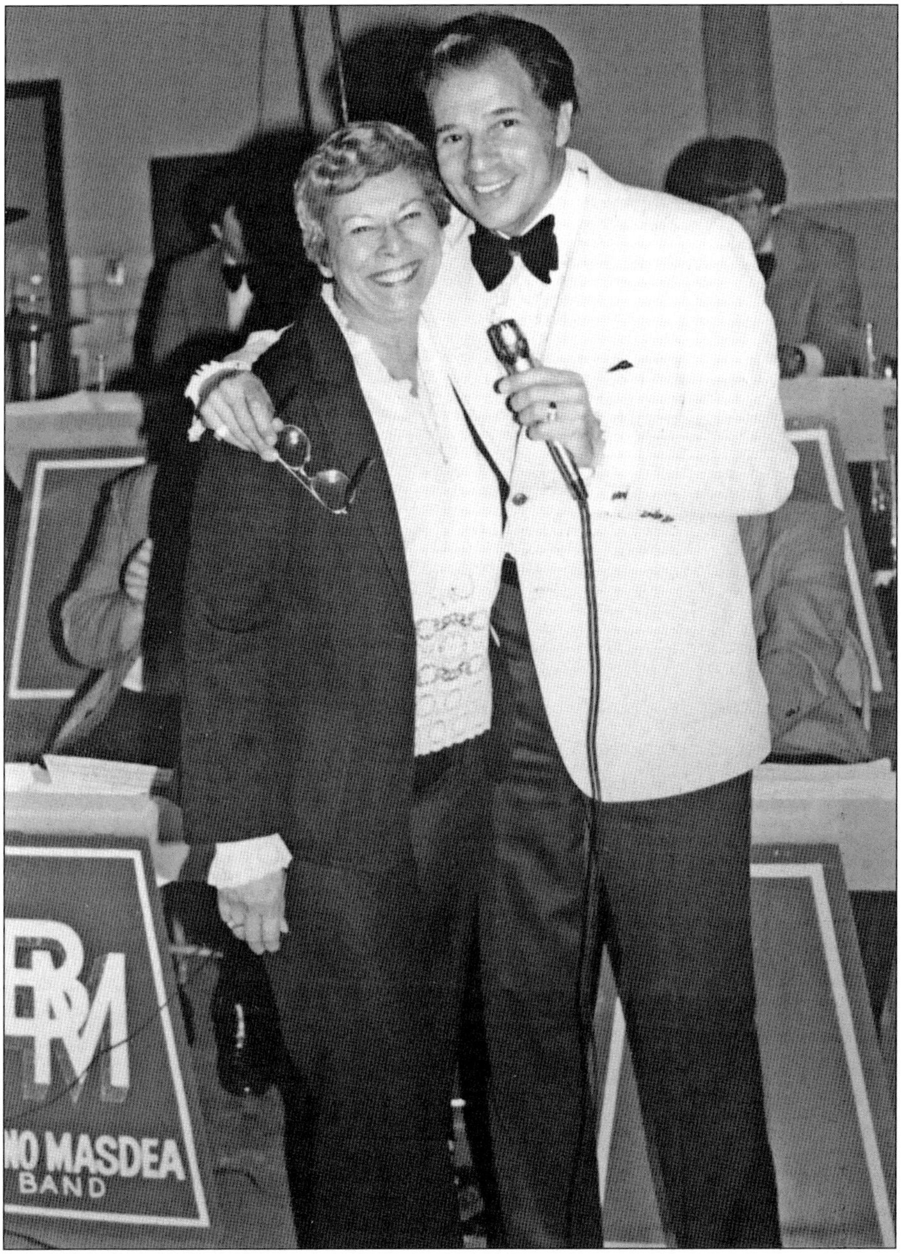

With code violations looming and safety issues unresolved, the city had decided the wrecking ball was the only way to solve the dilemma at the Valley Dale. The salvation of the VDB in 1980 was headed up by a dedicated team, including manager Mary Max Stants through her letter-writing campaign to "Save the Dale" and house bandleader Bruno Masdea through volunteer dances. All ticket proceeds were donated to the cause; Masdea and his musicians also donated their wages for the planned benefit dances. Several dances bringing over 500 attendees each were hosted at the General Beightler Armory in Worthington, Ohio. These events alerted central Ohio to the urgent situation, sparking private and corporate donations. When Mike and Kathy Peppe felt the outpouring of pure love from the community for the Valley Dale, they joined in the rescue effort by absorbing additional costs, totaling over $350,000 was spent to renovate the aging ballroom.

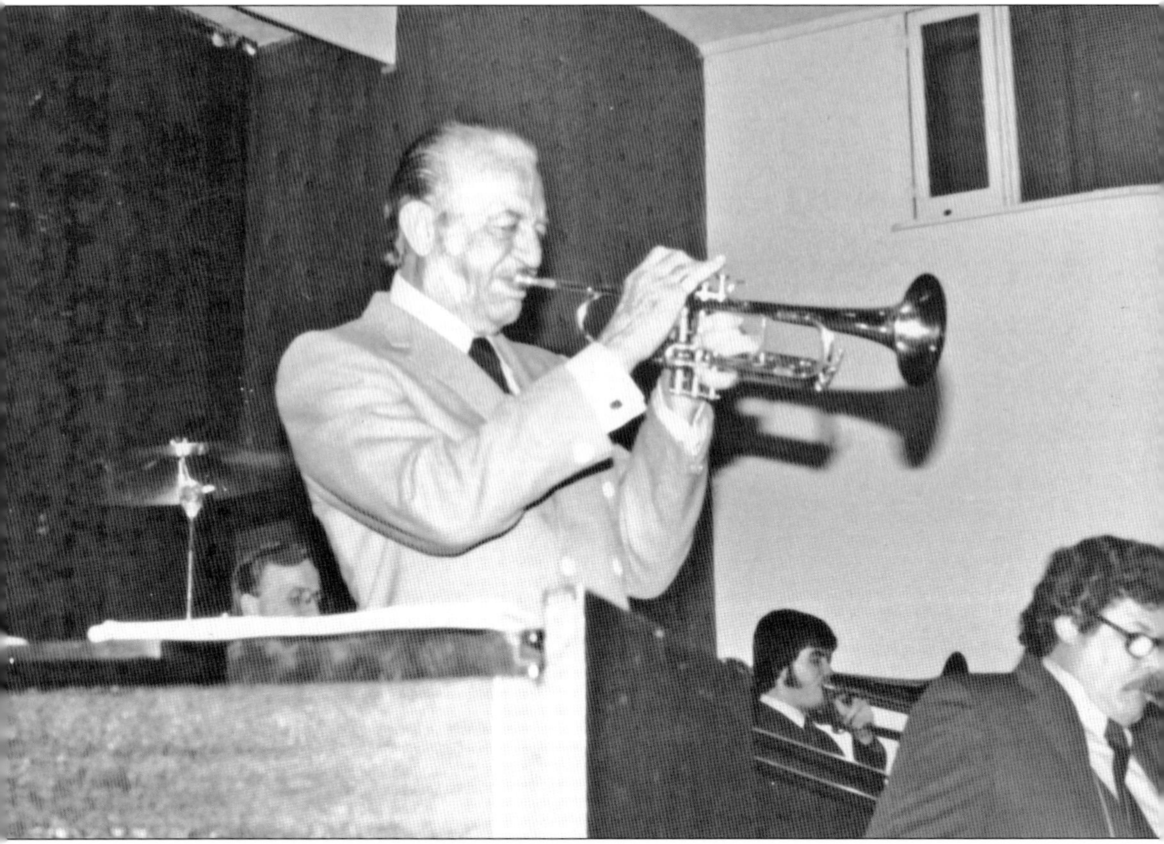

On September 17, 1981, a crowd of over 850 people were thrilled to be back at VDB. It was opening night The Valley Dale had been saved. The grand opening band was Harry James and his Orchestra. The author at 28 years old found herself dancing at what was now her favorite location. Her father lead The Bruno Masdea Big Dance Band. Her husband was the drummer with the Columbus-based Bob Allen Jazz trio; he was playing with the trio that night. While she boogied with musician Vaughn Wesiter, she felt a tap on her shoulder, she recognizes the appearing bands drummer, Les De Merle, who said. "Excuse me miss, Mr. James would like to see you backstage." Startled, she followed him, to the undersized backstage room. Sitting in the midst of standing musicians was the striking presence she recognized from album covers since childhood. As she entered, Harry James hushed the chatter with his raised arm, his crystal eyes peered straight into her wide eyes. She never thought of him as handsome until she met his stunning icy blue eyes. Limpid blue eyes, not green, is what she quickly thought. James began, "I've been watching you all evening, you know my book (music) better than I do. You know every splash, crash, hit, pop, of each chart I have played so far. How can this be? You can't even be 22 years old?" Her heart was pounding as he talked with her, she believed the collar on her crème and turquoise paisley dress was vibrating. She responded excitedly, "You are my dad's favorite musician, my dad is the current VDB house big band, he too, plays trumpet. I grew up listening to your records played by my dad. In fact my dad had a photograph taken with you at The Crystal Ballroom when you played there in the 50s." "Well," he murmured, "I believe I could call you up to lead a chart," Oh," I stammered, "I could never do that, you would have to ask my dad, he would just adore meeting you." Later in the evening he nodded to her from the dancefloor. Harry James died July 5, 1983, at age 67, exactly 40 years after his marriage to Betty Grable on July 5, 1943; she was buried on their anniversary, July 5, 1973.

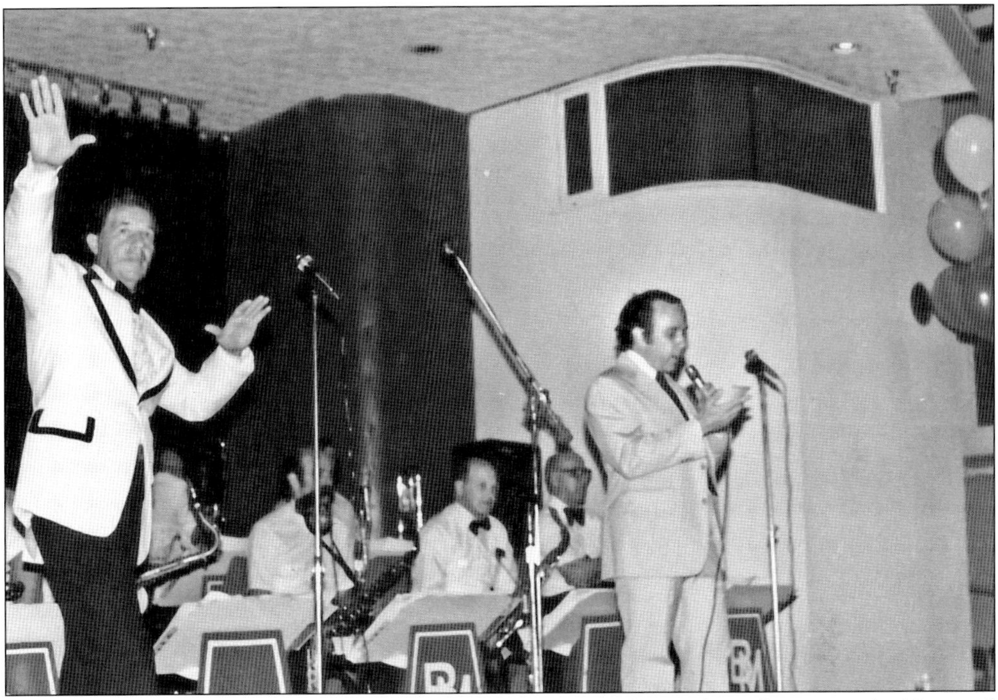

VDB owner Mike Peppe announces the addition of the Valley Dale Ballroom to the National Register of Historic Places in 1983. VDB house bandleader Bruno Masdea quiets the crowd for the thrilling announcement that Mary Max Stants and Mike and Kathy Peppe worked so tirelessly to achieve.

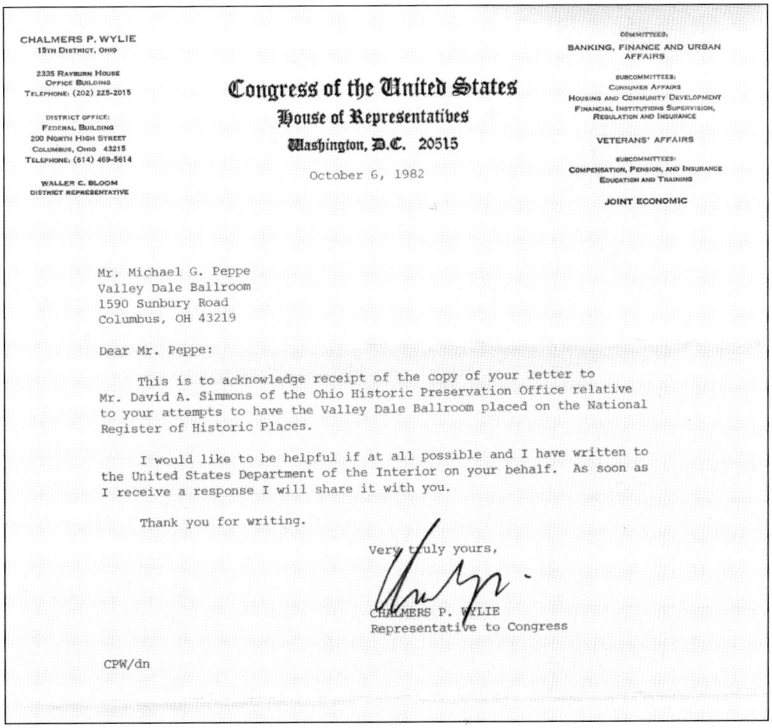

CHALMERS P. WYLIE
15TH DISTRICT, OHIO

2335 RAYBURN HOUSE
OFFICE BUILDING
TELEPHONE: (202) 225-2015

DISTRICT OFFICE:
FEDERAL BUILDING
200 NORTH HIGH STREET
COLUMBUS, OHIO 43215
TELEPHONE: (614) 469-5614

WALLER C. BLOOM
DISTRICT REPRESENTATIVE

Congress of the United States
House of Representatives
Washington, D.C. 20515

COMMITTEES:
BANKING, FINANCE AND URBAN AFFAIRS
SUBCOMMITTEES:
CONSUMER AFFAIRS
HOUSING AND COMMUNITY DEVELOPMENT
FINANCIAL INSTITUTIONS SUPERVISION, REGULATION AND INSURANCE

VETERANS' AFFAIRS
SUBCOMMITTEES:
COMPENSATION, PENSION, AND INSURANCE
EDUCATION AND TRAINING

JOINT ECONOMIC

October 6, 1982

Mr. Michael G. Peppe
Valley Dale Ballroom
1590 Sunbury Road
Columbus, OH 43219

Dear Mr. Peppe:

This is to acknowledge receipt of the copy of your letter to Mr. David A. Simmons of the Ohio Historic Preservation Office relative to your attempts to have the Valley Dale Ballroom placed on the National Register of Historic Places.

I would like to be helpful if at all possible and I have written to the United States Department of the Interior on your behalf. As soon as I receive a response I will share it with you.

Thank you for writing.

Very truly yours,

CHALMERS P. WYLIE
Representative to Congress

CPW/dn

This significant letter from Ohio congressman Chalmers P. Wylie updated the Peppes on the progress of listing the VDB in the National Register of Historic Places.

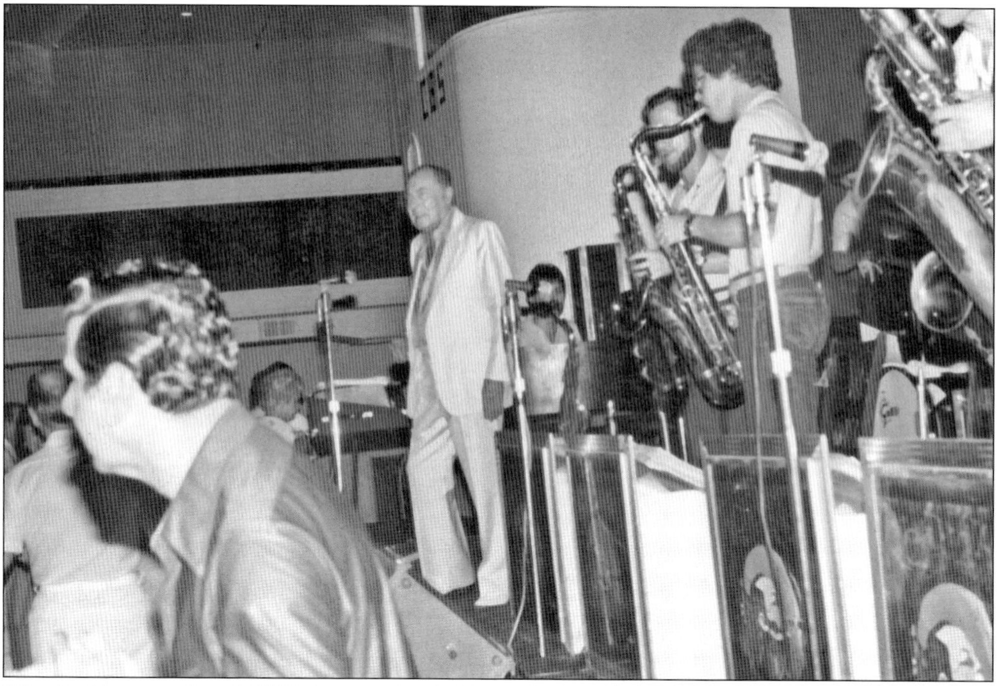

Woody Herman played VDB during the 1940s, and after the saving of VDB, he appeared each year until 1985. Big-name bands of that era returned to VDB for their final bow during the 1980s. Sadly, only a handful of the leaders returned with their bands: Les Brown, Woody Herman, Harry James, and Lionel Hampton.

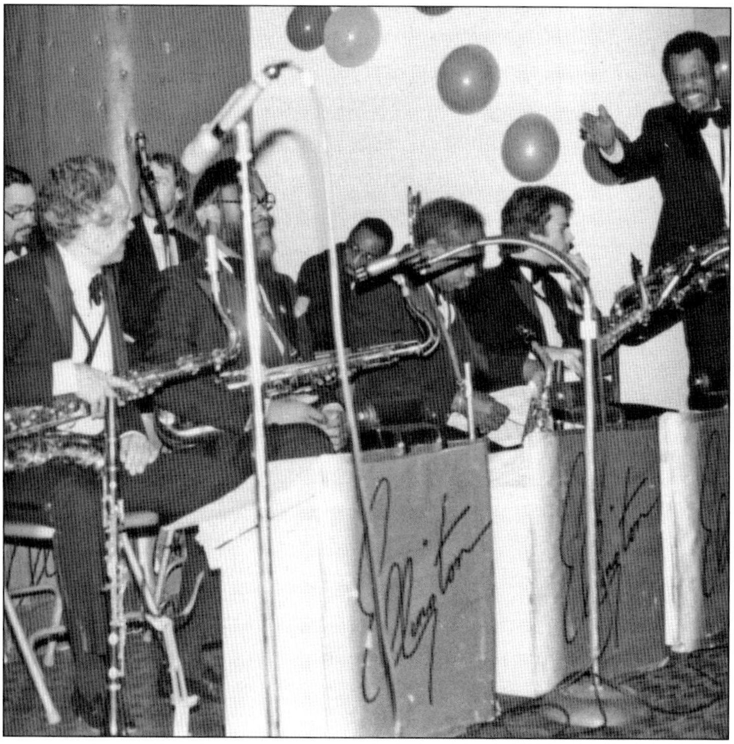

These bands' encore performances were solely brought about through the passion of the sons of the bandmasters who carried on their fathers' legacy, such as Les Brown Jr., Jack Morgan, and Mercer Ellington. Other bands continued with their sidemen holding the baton, such as the Glenn Miller, Tommy Dorsey, Ted Weems, Count Basie, Guy Lombardo, and Jimmy Dorsey Orchestras. Pictured here is Mercer Ellington, Duke's son, on July 16, 1984, leading the band on the VDB stage.

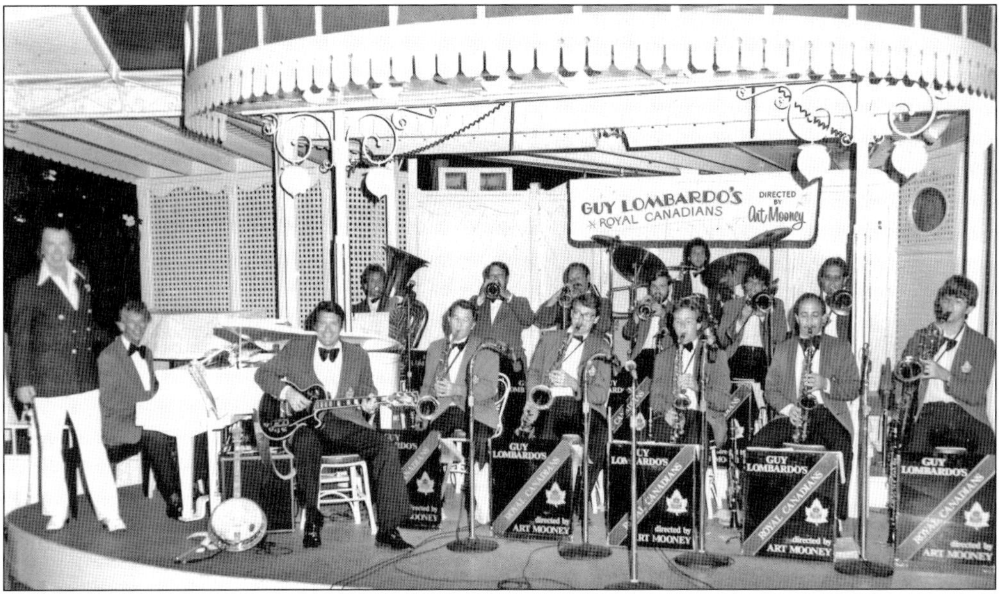

The Guy Lombardo Orchestra of 1925 broke VDB attendance records for all time and successfully carried on after the big band era, as did the showplace Valley Dale. Eight members of the 1980s musical congregation left Lombardo to settle in Columbus. One of the eight, John Vermeulen, would reignite the irreverent attitude and sound of the assemblage with the New Remnants Dance Orchestra, which played central Ohio and VDB for dances and weddings. As in the above photograph from 1983, Vermeulen and Matt Ellis were asked, mainly by then leader Art Mooney, to come back on the road for special Lombardo gigs. (John Vermeulen.)

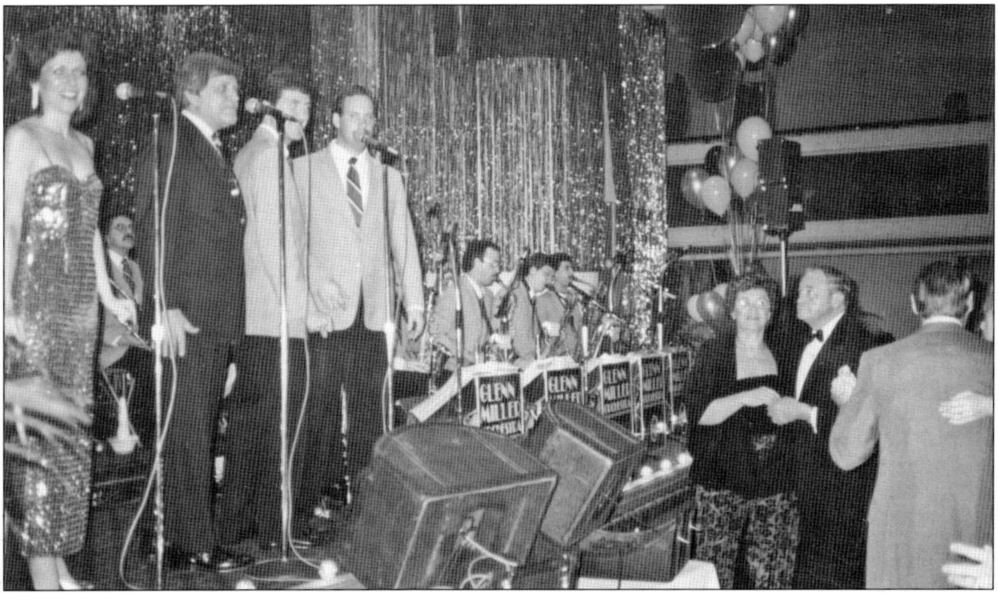

Almost 40 years after Glenn Miller's death, his orchestra was still the signature band of a generation. In the 1980s, it developed into a showier band with female vocalists drenched in sequins. The orchestra sets adopted hues of blue in tribute to Miller's "Moonlight Serenade" and "Serenade in Blue." Currently, now 80 years after Miller's death, his music is still the first of his genre to be requested at dances or weddings.

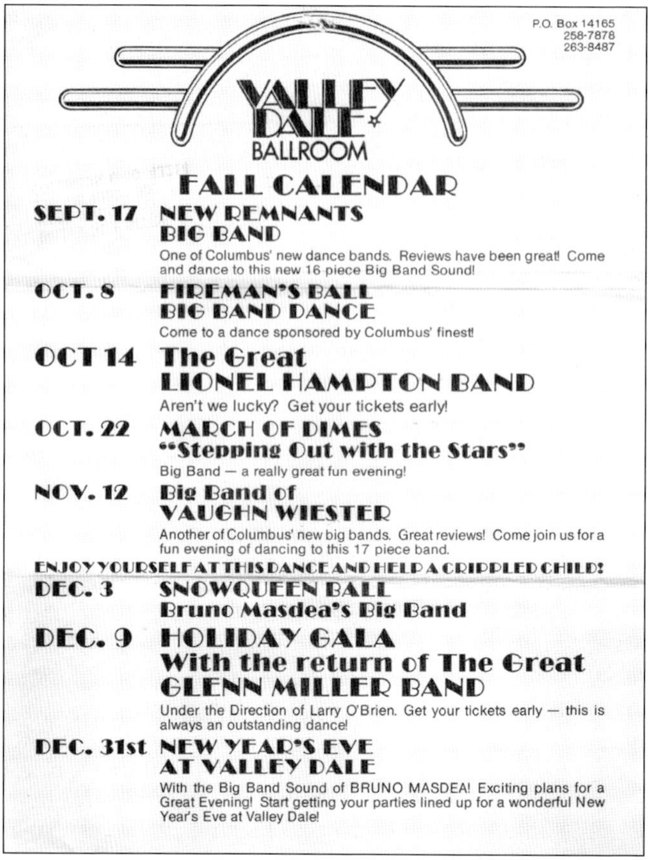
P.O. Box 14165
258-7878
263-8487

VALLEY DALE BALLROOM

FALL CALENDAR

SEPT. 17 **NEW REMNANTS BIG BAND**
One of Columbus' new dance bands. Reviews have been great! Come and dance to this new 16 piece Big Band Sound!

OCT. 8 **FIREMAN'S BALL BIG BAND DANCE**
Come to a dance sponsored by Columbus' finest!

OCT 14 **The Great LIONEL HAMPTON BAND**
Aren't we lucky? Get your tickets early!

OCT. 22 **MARCH OF DIMES "Stepping Out with the Stars"**
Big Band — a really great fun evening!

NOV. 12 **Big Band of VAUGHN WIESTER**
Another of Columbus' new big bands. Great reviews! Come join us for a fun evening of dancing to this 17 piece band.

ENJOY YOURSELF AT THIS DANCE AND HELP A CRIPPLED CHILD!

DEC. 3 **SNOWQUEEN BALL Bruno Masdea's Big Band**

DEC. 9 **HOLIDAY GALA With the return of The Great GLENN MILLER BAND**
Under the Direction of Larry O'Brien. Get your tickets early — this is always an outstanding dance!

DEC. 31st **NEW YEAR'S EVE AT VALLEY DALE**
With the Big Band Sound of BRUNO MASDEA! Exciting plans for a Great Evening! Start getting your parties lined up for a wonderful New Year's Eve at Valley Dale!

During the VDB 1980s big band rebirth, a mailer was sent to fans of the ballroom advertising quarterly events. This one for the fall of 1984 presented Lionel Hampton, Glenn Miller, New Remnants, and Vaughn Wesiter. The remaining four house events were played by Bruno Masdea.

Percussionist Lionel Hampton played VDB with Benny Goodman, Gene Krupa, and Teddy Wilson during the late 1930s in Goodman's famous quartet. Trumpeter Louis Armstrong urged Hampton to play the vibraphone, and he became one of the most prominent vibe artists over several generations. Dancing in the foreground at right are VDB manager Mary Max Stants and husband. In 1984, Hampton returned to VDB with his orchestra, providing a marvelous evening vibe.

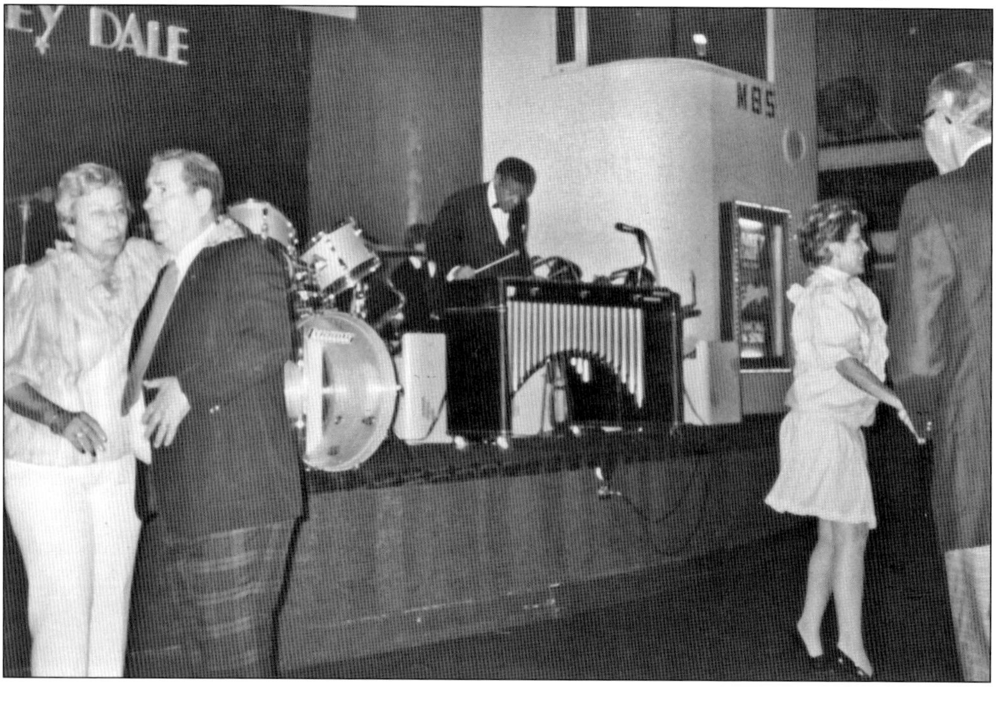

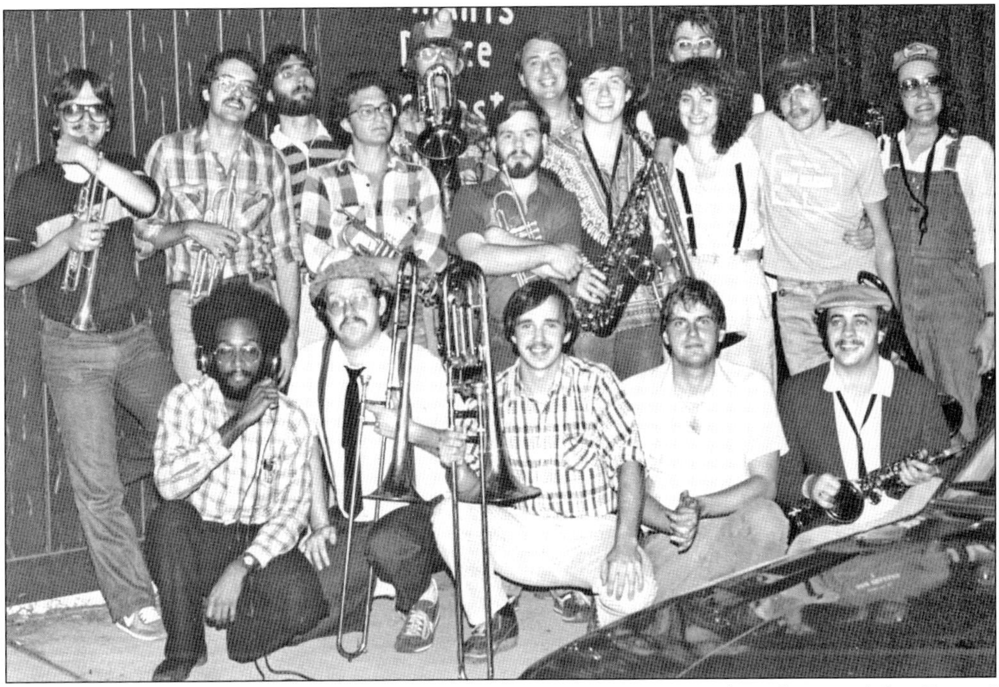

In 1982, big band was introduced to the current generation. Several graduates of the Capital University Conservatory of Music went on to play with the legendary orchestras of Glenn Miller, and others before returning home to reinvent the music. Missing the charts of their traveling bands and their college jazz band, directed by Vaughn Wesiter (of the Woody Herman Orchestra), John Vermeulen (of the Lombardo band) and Karl Ott (of the Miller band) built the New Remnants Dance Orchestra. John collected big band charts that emphasized intricate arranging or historical curiosities. He told the author: "I realized only a handful of authentic charts written for the original bands were actually published. I started to buy those. Others were in the books of traveling bands, in trunks or file cabinets, lost or with collectors. I found local big bands had a rare arrangement in their library, too. Through the kindness of others, I put together a gem of a book." When John left for grad school, Matt Ellis took over the band. (John Vermeulen.)

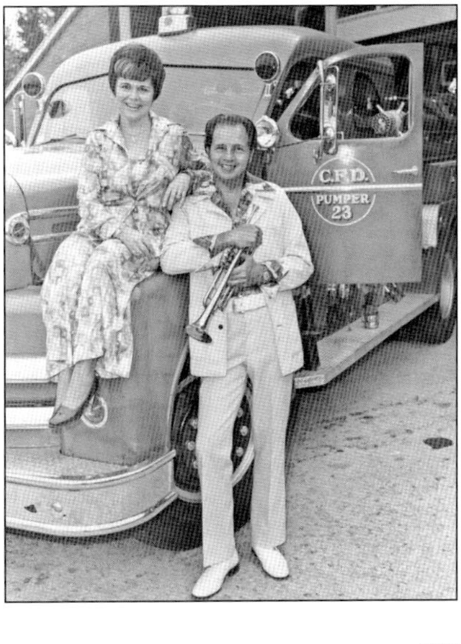

A hipper, more casual style was happening in the 1980s, for sounds, clothing, and advertising. Vocalist Lois Lynne posing in a stylish jumpsuit and Bruno Masdea strutting a white leisure suit as pictured in this promotional image for the Fireman's Ball listed on page 106. Masdea's band always cast a male and female vocal duo, a rarity for Columbus bands, but quite common during the big band era (Rocky Lattore is not pictured). (Bruno Masdea archives.)

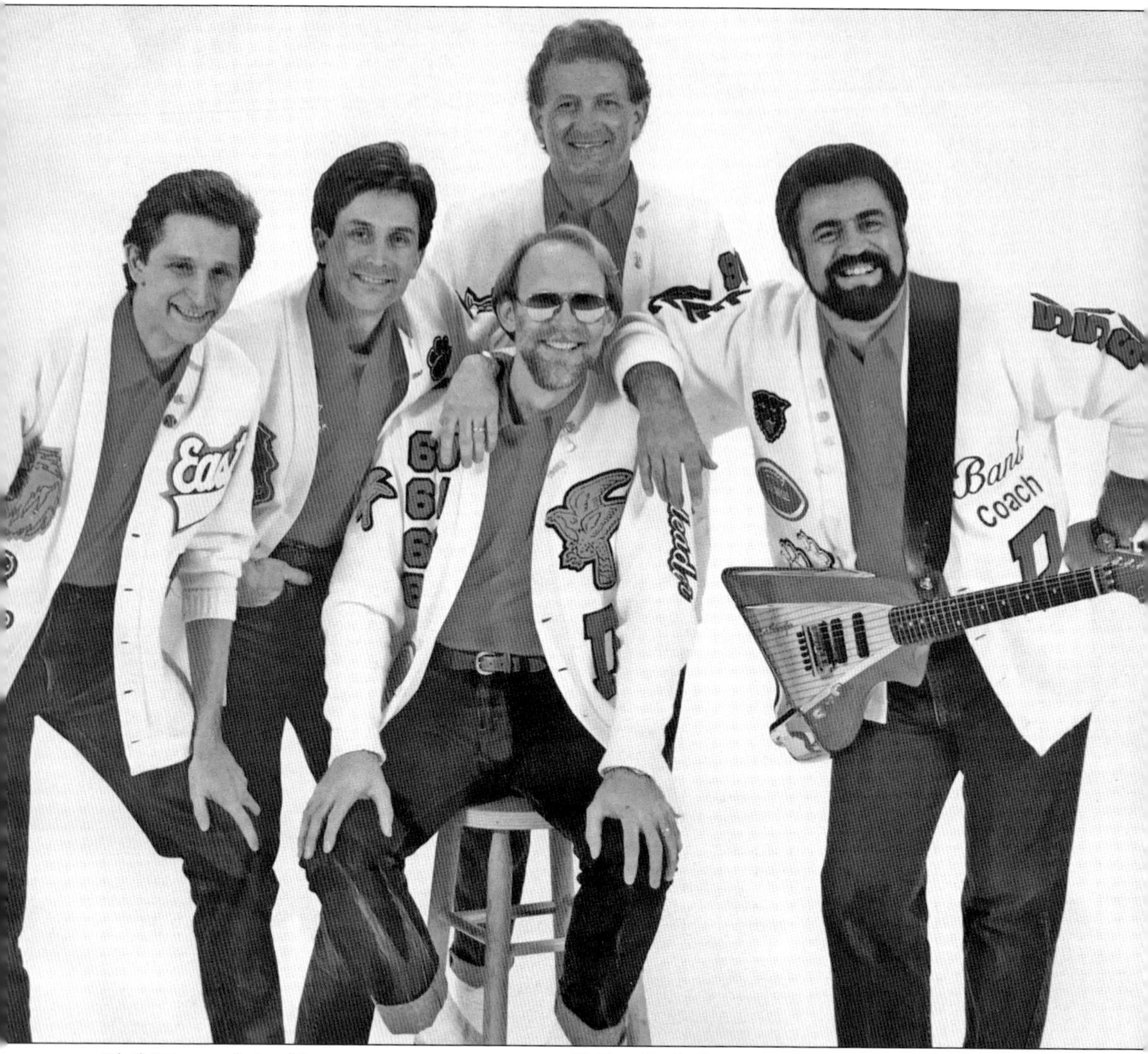

Phil Dirt and the Dozers were quite active at Valley Dale between 1983 and 1998 and beyond. Mark Frye, the leader of the band, said, "Mike Peppe was great to work with back then and always made sure we had a dressing room etc. We spent many sweltering hot summer nights there rockin' it out." Many concerts, fundraising events for charities expressly the Beat Michigan Dance and hospitals, and every social gala one could name took place multiple times per month in those days at Valley Dale, featuring Phil Dirt onstage. "It was the perfect vibe for our nostalgia act, with the radio booth and retro details of the venue's architecture. It seemed like a second home at the time! In 1985, when MTV was all the rage, we partnered with WCMH NBC 4 in the filming of a rock video [Phil Dirt and the Dozers' original song "I've Gotta Be Cooler", filmed at VDB]. . . . We are excited to see it back in full swing again with updates and improvements!" Pictured here are, from left to right, Rick Frye, Mark Frye, Steve Cabot, Howard Kandel (standing behind Cabot), and Bill Lehr. (Mark Frye.)

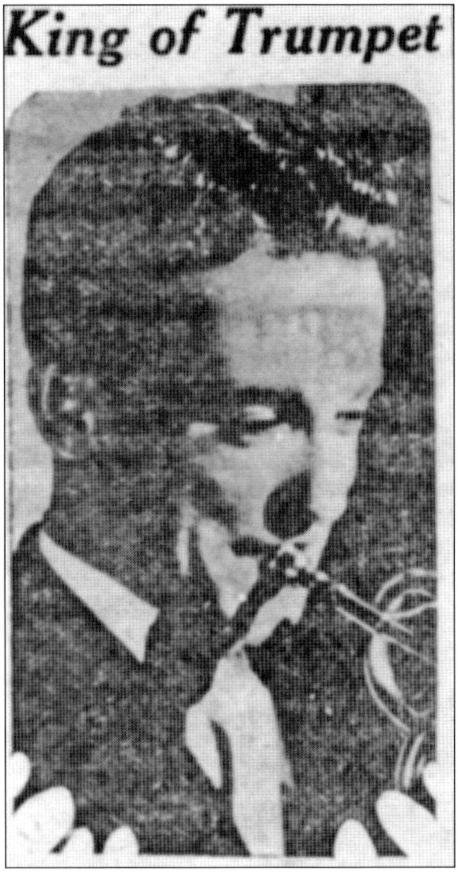

The Beat Michigan Dance has always been a huge VDB event. The first ever Beat Michigan Dance has been traced back to November 11, 1934, when it was a homecoming dance for the Ohio State University with trumpeter "Red" Nichols and his CBS orchestra. Glenn Miller, Benny Goodman, and Gene Krupa all played or recorded with Red Nichols before the 1934 VDB event.

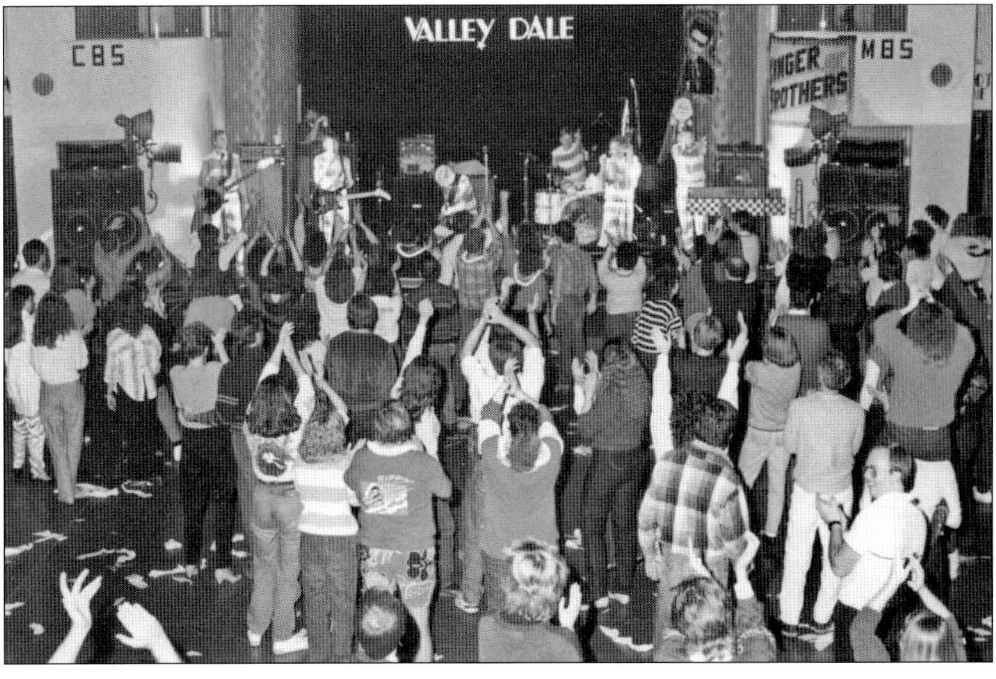

The Danger Brothers knew what fun was. Drummer Tom Smith said, "It's infectious. When we're up on stage having fun, then the crowd is having fun, too." The band played the yearly Beat Michigan Dance the Friday before every OSU-Michigan game in the 1970s. The classic rowdy Buckeye crowd would choreograph "O H I O" to "Hang on Sloopy." The Danger Brothers lineup also included Dave Hessler, guitar and saxophone; Tom Beougher, bass; Bill Bendler, organ, trumpet, and trombone; and Mike Thompson, guitar. (For a juxtaposition of teens and their decades refer to page 47.) (Tom Smith.)

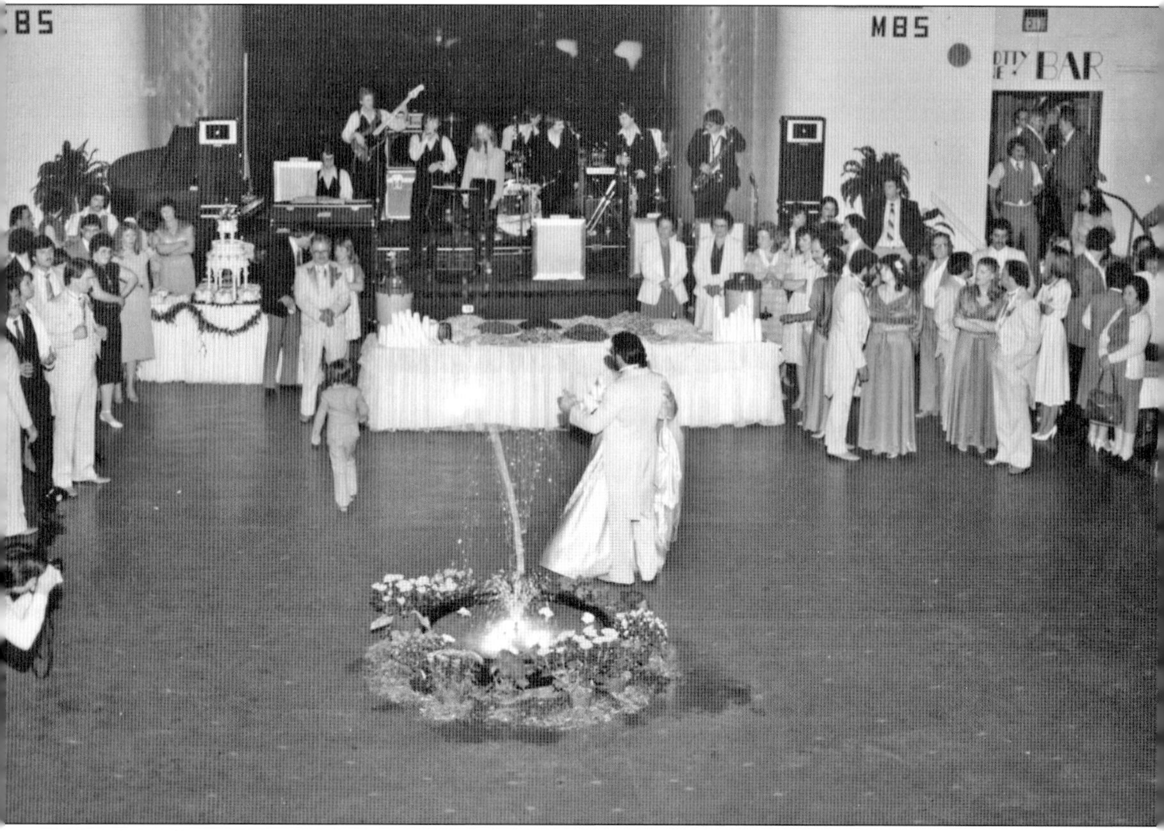

The call letters are still prominent, but the twin radio booths have become conversational pieces. On April 17, 1982, nearly thirty years after the 1953 wedding shown on page 66, the Cuas' son held his own wedding at VDB. Noticeably, the music stand fronts with big band logos, chapters of sheet music, and multiple brass sections have been replaced by standing musicians displaying choreographed moves while covering contemporary rock sounds. The band is Energy, featuring Bobby and Larry Everhart, the son and nephew of the admired medical doctor and recognized VDB band leader Doc Everhart. (Michael Cua.)

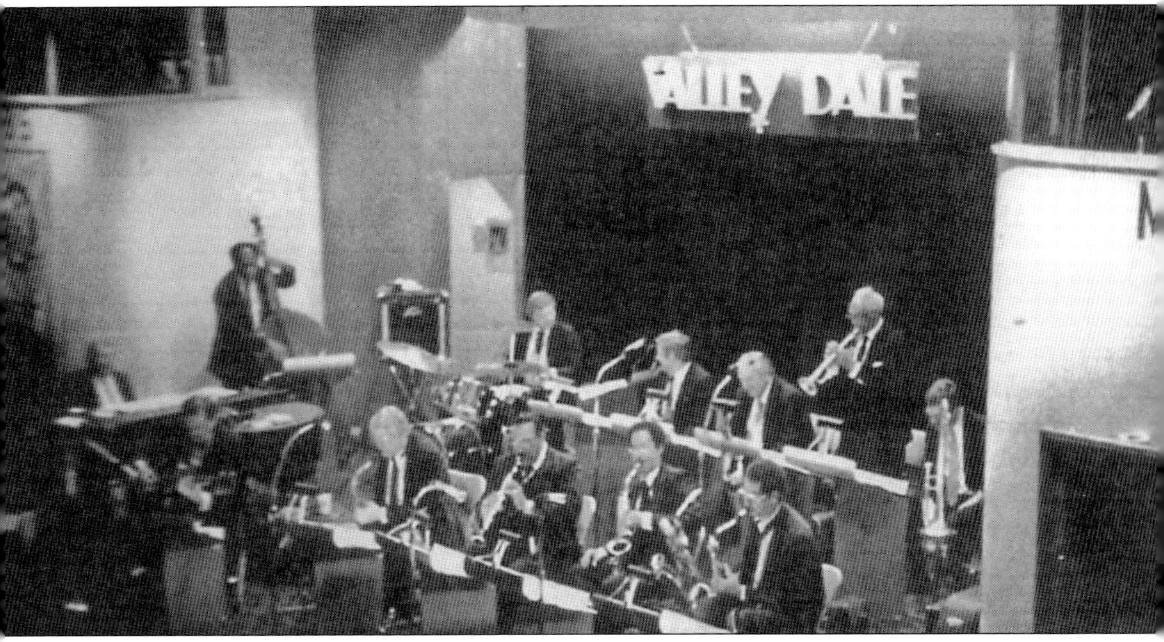

The 1992 Roop Brothers Backyard Bash honored an original VDB musician, Ray Roop, and consisted of an all-day jam session at Valley Dale. In the middle of the set of Columbus A-lister "Chuz" Alfred, a lovely woman inquired if her husband could sit in for one tune. An elegant older gentleman clutching an instrument case climbed on stage, turning for a slight nod to the musicians or perhaps to savor the band's presence. Chuz invited a tune, and 86-year-old George James responded, " 'Satin Doll' in B flat!" James hadn't toured since his 1977 retirement, but the finely aged alto sax man played like a seasoned 43-year-old. The dais was mobbed as spectators cheered his solos and begged for more. While the final notes blew, thunderous applause and whistles filled the air. George's wife helped him off his afternoon pedestal, and they gently sauntered to their table. George lovingly bestowed a smile and wave to his marveling subjects while Chuz exclaimed "George James!" Chuz wonders now if James "was reminiscing [about] his time in 1931 with Louis Armstrong. . . . He made our day the day George James came out to play." The image above is the final return of The McKinney Cotton Pickers led by local musician Chuz Alfred, far left sax section. McKCP played VDB, returning countless times, they were one of the very first to play VDB in 1925 and researched to be the last of the original bands to play as pictured in their final VDB performance in 1986. (Chuz Alfred.)

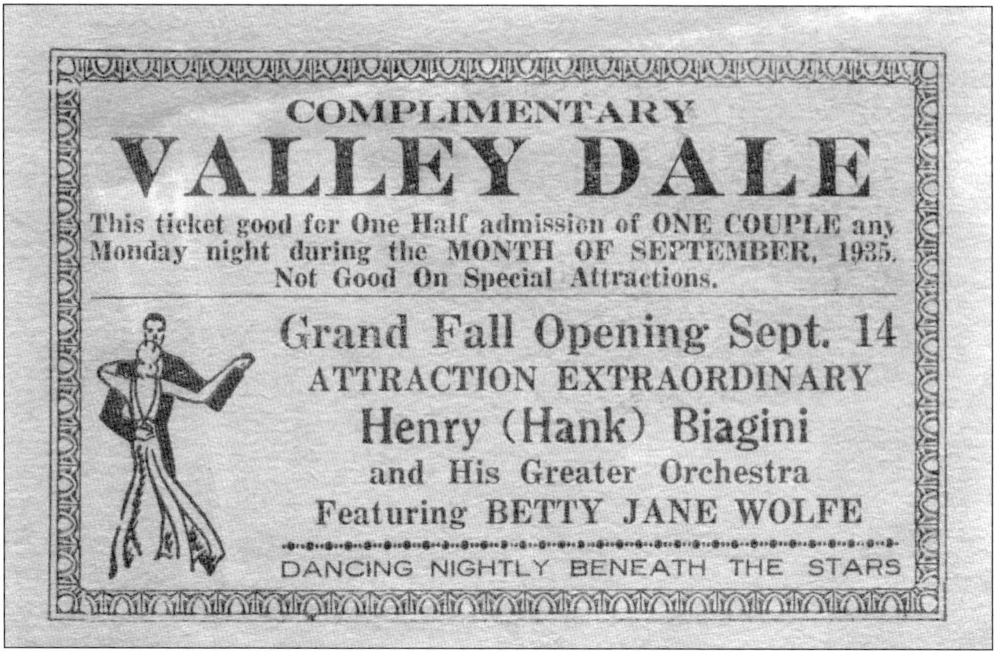

This VDB ruby red toned admittance ticket is for a 1935 concert by Hank Biagini, the one-time Casa Loma bandleader who left to begin his own band. The couple presented below had been dancing at the VDB three years before the ticketed concert. (Danger Brothers–Tom Smith.)

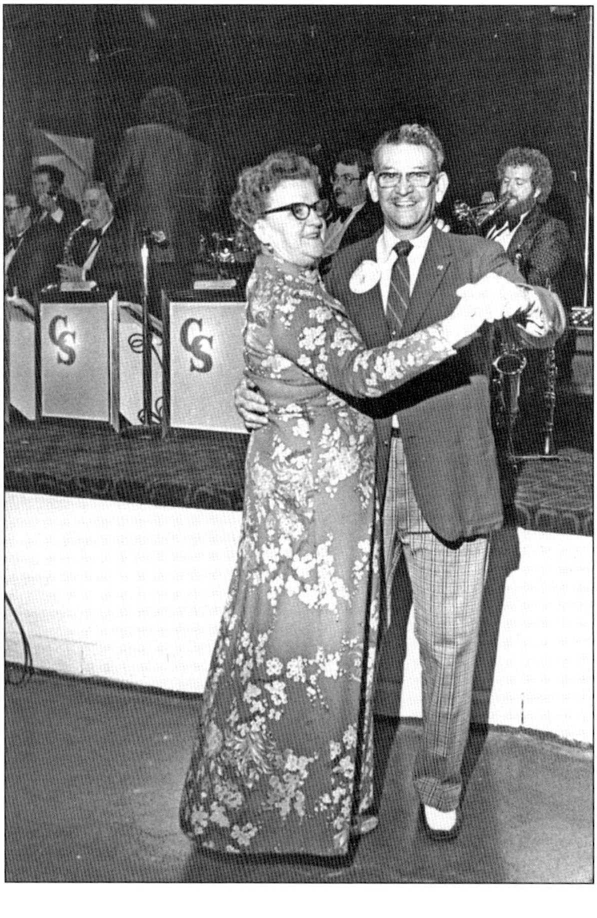

After the VDB was saved from the 1980 obliteration, a 1981 May Day dance doubled as one of the previews before the grand reopening. Fred and Betty Persinger, joyful fans of the VDB since 1932, waltzed to music this night from the Chuck Selby Orchestra. On this occasion, the band was led by Selby's wife, Anne Young, who took over her husband's legacy after his passing two years earlier. (*Columbus Dispatch*.)

Nine

Come to Holiday Inn, then Party Like It's 1999

During the 1990s through 2014, the Finta organization captured unusual events for VDB under their 25-year event management, there were fewer public events and an abundance of lavish private and corporate affairs, one included zoo animals. Cirque-esque-artistry for The Red Ball requested the central chandelier to be removed once a year to execute the evenings' acrobatic exotics.

A keyboard player booked the ballroom for a private afternoon affair with an understanding the piano would be in tune. Billy Preston had read about Valley Dale and wished to play the hall, if only for himself. The Impressive Mr. Preston, known to many as the fifth Beatle, was enthralled with the ballroom and its sound.

Hip-hop's 50 Cent enjoyed being a guest and performing at VDB for a private birthday party with guests P Diddy and J-Lo. MTV filmed an episode of Making the Band in VDB. Buster Douglas reclaimed his WBC and WBA belt holding his 1990 boxing match belt ceremony at VDB. March 10, 1990. Frankie Valli Returned for the second time in 1992 for a 50th birthday party. 2003 brought Marty Finta's captivation with the Dale's history creating events paying homage to the ballroom's original era.

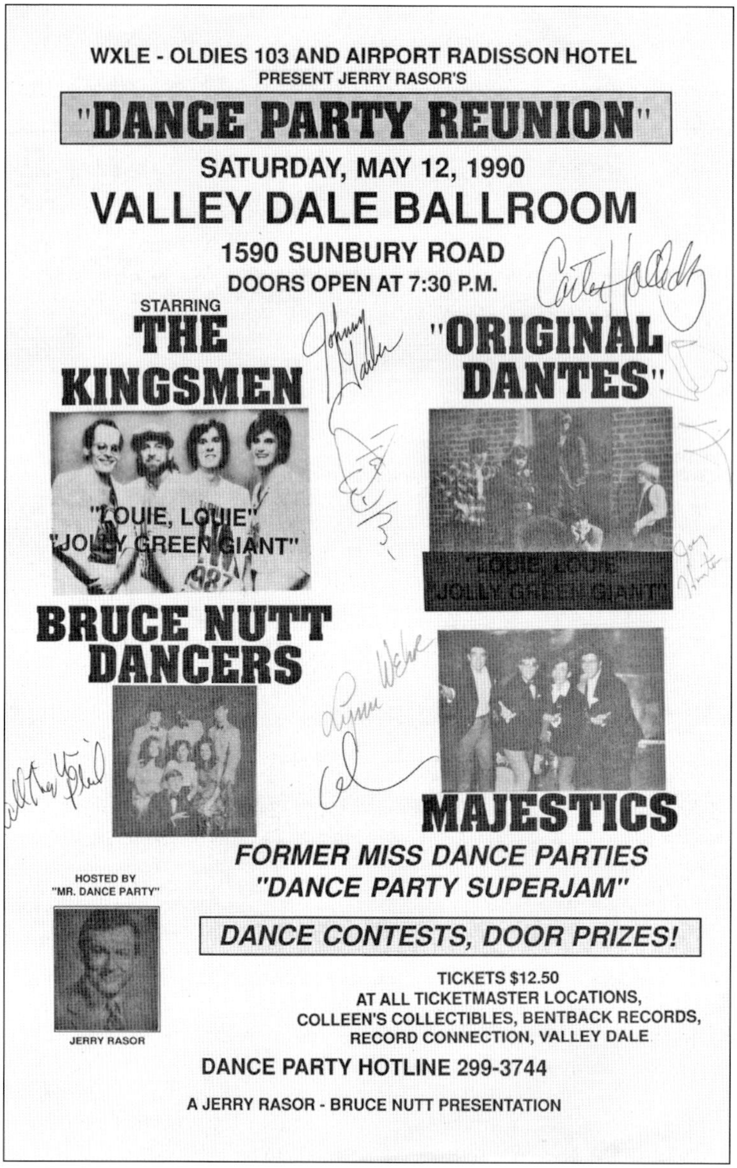

Dec 1, 1986, Michael Kapson and his father, Henry, of Nospak Inc. (Kapson backward), took over operations from VDB owner, Peppe. Kapson planned to keep the return of national big band's to VDB also adding the hottest contemporary artists, by attempting to bring in the 18 to 25 age group. It was pushing twenty-five years since the rock bands raided the home of the big bands, the rock bands now too had earned their VDB reunion celebrations. Nospack Inc.'s opening group was 1970s local band PURE JAM, whose member's included Bentley Austin with brothers, Craig and Eric, Glen Dalton and Joe Mellencamp, the roadie for this band was Joe's little brother John Cougar Mellencamp, this experience composed John's desire for playing. Kapson's impressive pop circuit coup was Natalie Cole, premiering her blazing hit album Everlasting. Kapson leased the VDB for less than one year, Mike Peppe took back day to day operations, until he hired his new facilities manager in 1987, Bentley Austin of Pure Jam who stayed through 1991. Natalie Cole is listed on the VDB Wall of fame. The poster presents Jerry Rasor and the return of the 1960s and 1970s rock bands to VDB during the 1990s. (Lynn Wehr.)

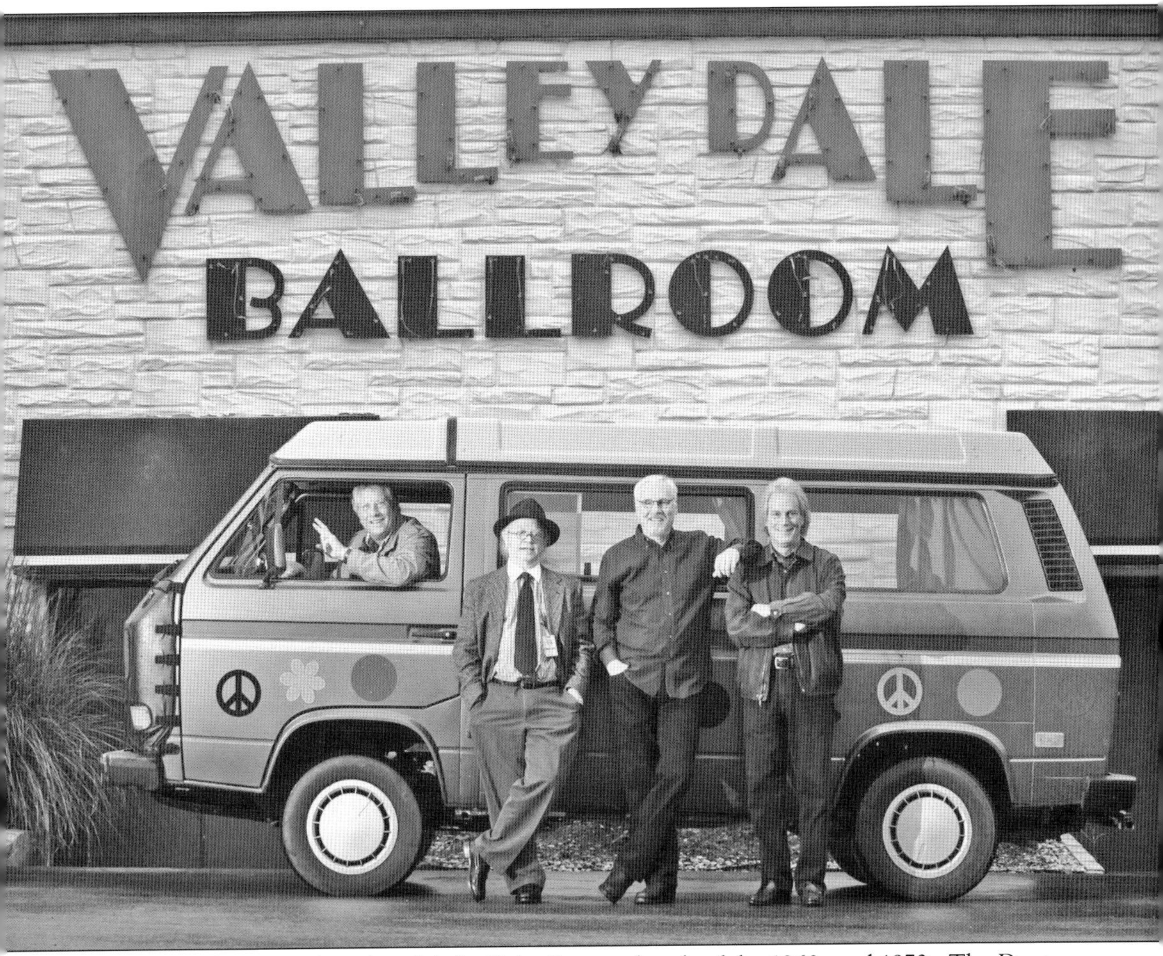

The big bands returned, and so did the Baby Boomer bands of the 1960s and 1970s. The Dantes are promoting a reunion concert in 2011. Lynn Wehr drives a 1985 VW Westfalia Vanagan with, from left to right, Barry Hayden, Jeff Johnson, and the Fifth Order's Jim Hilditch posing outside the van. "Dance Party" reunion sock-hops were held at VDB, and Jerry Rasor always requested that the Dantes share the bill. In 1991, Rasor passed at 61 years of age, but the reunion dances continued until September 2017. Johnathan Smith recalls, "I had almost as much fun as I did in 1965 at Valley Dale. 1,000 people showed up and 950 danced." Randy Emrich reminisces as the brother, his dad making him accompany his older sister on Sunday to VDB as a chaperone, when The Dantes' impact and rock music first grabbed his soul. (*Columbus Dispatch.*)

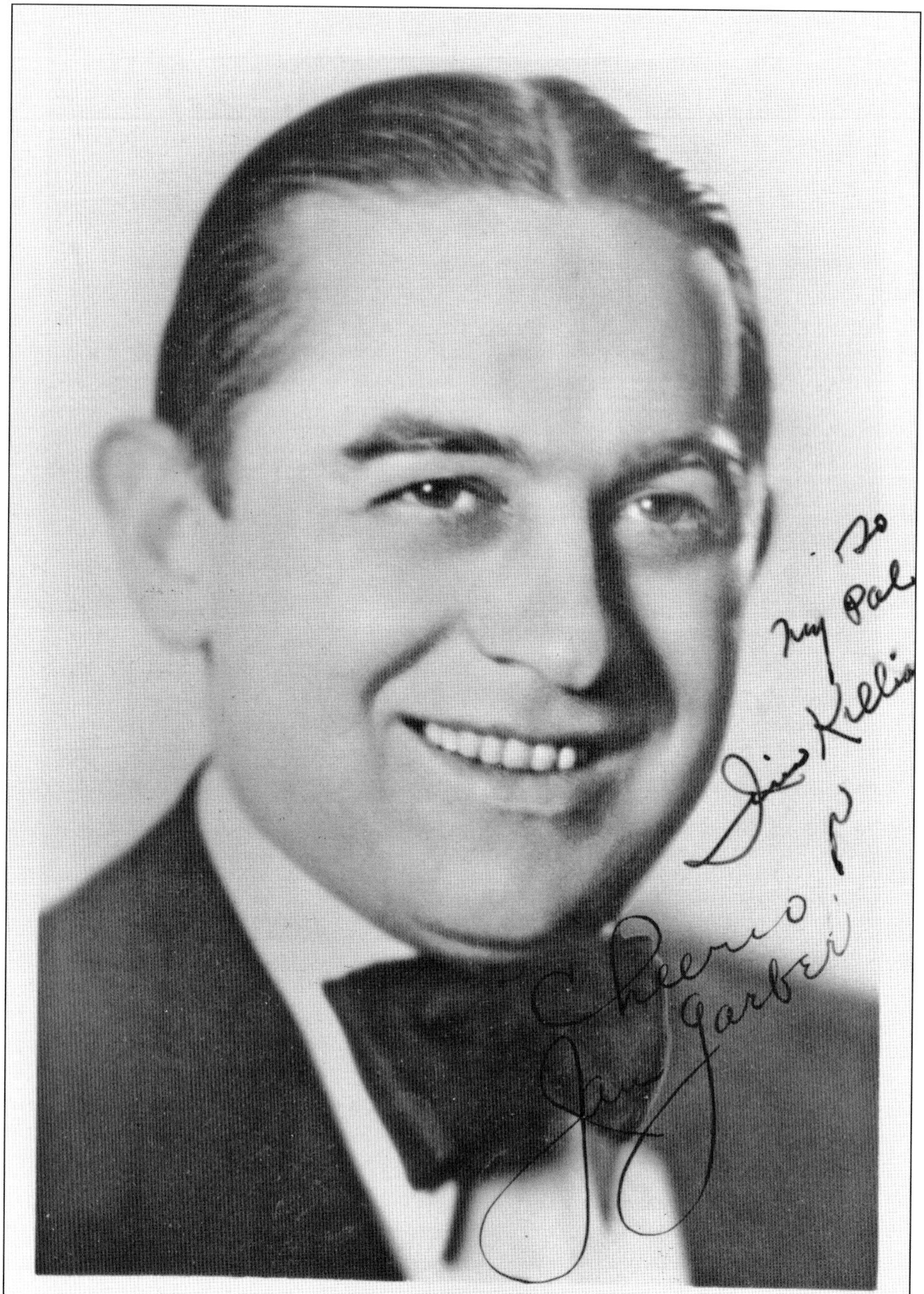

Traditions, tunes, and tinsel envelop Marty Finta's childhood recollections of Christmas. Thanksgiving marked the family's seasonal kickoff ritual, when they would enjoy watching *Holiday Inn*, followed by a sing-a-long of Finta's signature Christmas melody, "Jumpin' Jiminy Christmas," a schmaltzy salute to December 25 by bandleader Jan Garber. Some 50 years later, the Fintas, now managing VDB, were decorating one Christmas when Marty casually gazed at his handsome wall of fame and abruptly realized his childhood buddy Garber's portrait was featured. This prompted Finta to develop the VDB Holiday Show Series. Garber's photograph is autographed to then manager Jim Killilea.

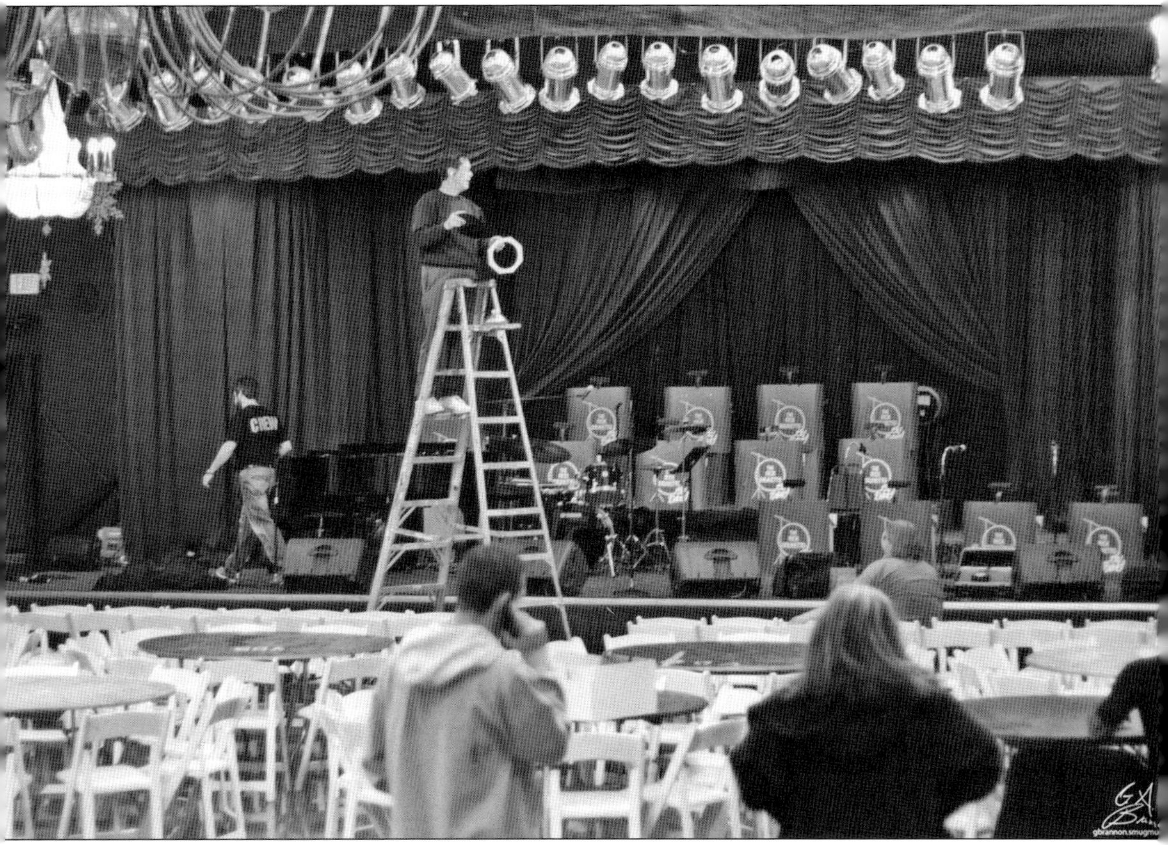

Over the 25-year Finta proprietorship at VDB, Marty Finta, an avid student of the big band age, sought an event for VDB that would be an homage to the 1942 movie *Holiday Inn*. Finta contacted Rick and Landa Masdea Brunetto to invent, develop, and execute his Holiday Show Series. Rick Brunetto created the musical arrangements, including composing stirring overtures and monumental finales for each holiday performance. Masdea Brunetto wrote and directed the theatrical scripts. The productions included actors for an in-the-round theater featuring the Rick Brunetto Big Band and began on Mother's Day, 2011; the series captured most holidays through Christmas 2013. The Holiday Show Series had components making it fresh and unique, something unseen in Columbus since dinner theater or Kenley Players: a big band tinged with orchestral undertones, an emcee, vocalists, dancers with chorus lines, moving drama, and wry comedy. At left is Adam Brunell; Bill Hoffman is on the ladder. Lights, camera, downbeat!

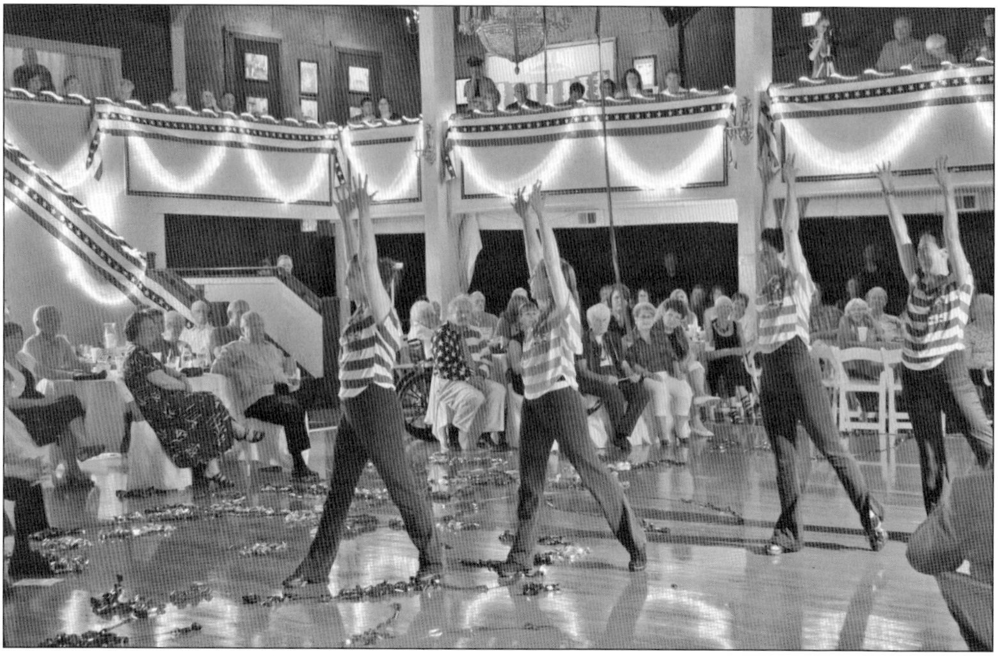

What Fourth of July would be complete without "fireworks?" The Swing Columbus Dancers create a floor show spectacular to Rick Brunetto's arrangement of Katy Perry's song. This is also a clear view of the upper balcony showing the cavalcade of VDB performers. (Graham Brannon Photography.)

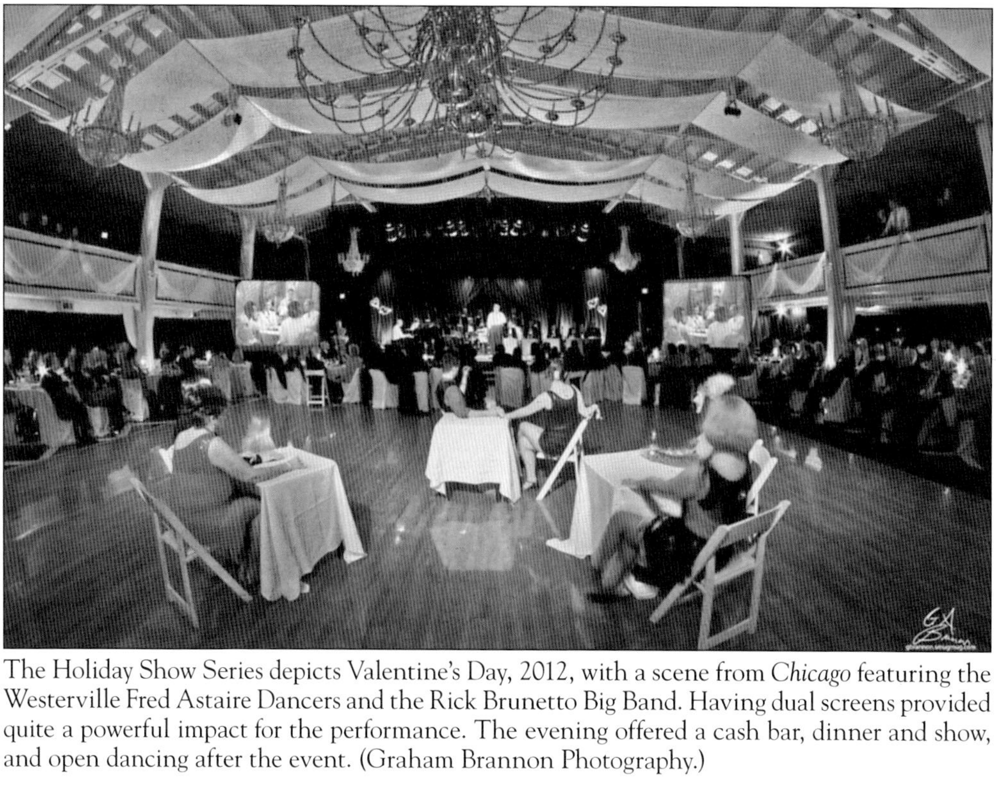

The Holiday Show Series depicts Valentine's Day, 2012, with a scene from *Chicago* featuring the Westerville Fred Astaire Dancers and the Rick Brunetto Big Band. Having dual screens provided quite a powerful impact for the performance. The evening offered a cash bar, dinner and show, and open dancing after the event. (Graham Brannon Photography.)

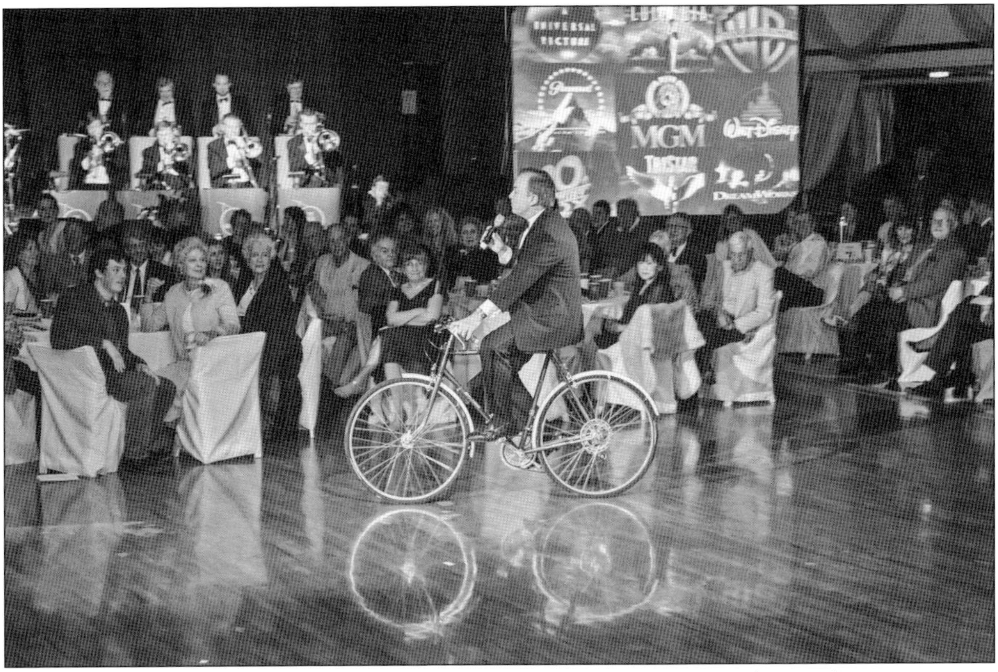

Celebrating Mother's Day in 2013 was as simple as taking mom to a dinner show presenting movies with scores of movie themes arranged by Rick Brunetto. Vocalist Chuck Gillespie glided with ease on a bicycle over the iconic dancefloor as he reenacted the blissful signature song from *Butch Cassidy and the Sundance Kid*, Hal David and Burt Bacharach's "Raindrops Keep Falling on My Head." (Graham Brannon Photography.)

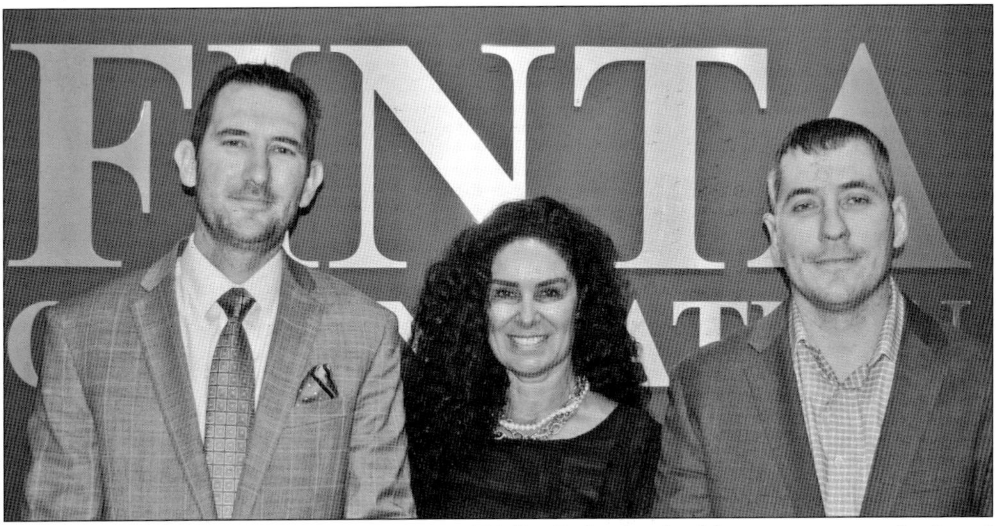

For a quarter of a century, the Fintas managed Valley Dale, the third longest tenure in the famed ballroom's history behind Jim Killilea's almost 70 years and Lou Peppe's 53 years. Early on. Marty Finta IV promoted concerts in the hall. After the Fintas extensively renovated the ballroom, dressing it to the nines, Dana Finta changed the business model to a multipurpose special events venue. The Fintas produced many events at the ballroom, including national concerts, shows, corporate and social events, weddings, proms, fundraisers, boxing matches, dances, themed parties, reunions, and more.

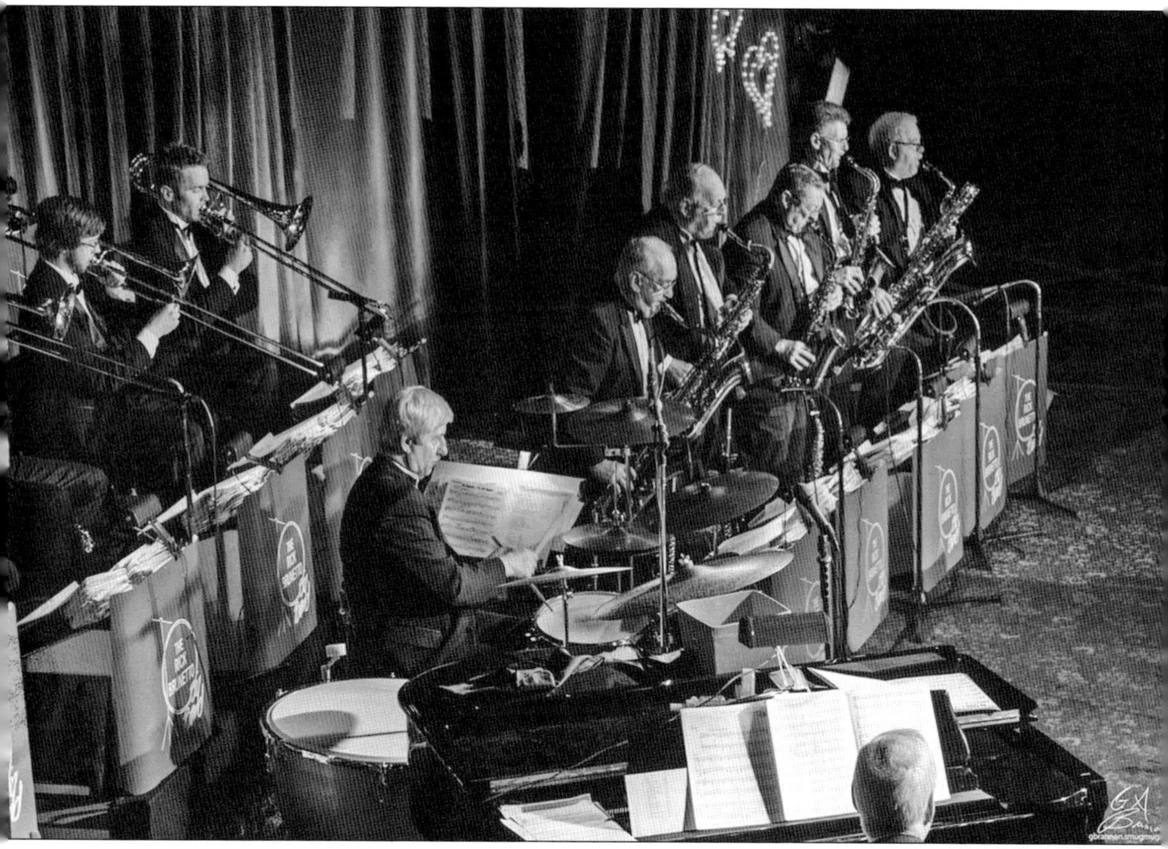

Piqua, Ohio, native Rick Brunetto revealed, "By far the Valley Dale has been our favorite performing venue. When on that stage you can feel the presence of all the great big bands that have played throughout its history. It is truly a spiritual experience. As a big band playing at the Valley Dale I have always seen this as a badge of honor." Brunetto, son-in-law of Bruno Masdea, began playing VDB in the 1980s for New Year's Eve. He also participated in battles of the bands with Masdea in 2001 and 2002. Brunetto's band was inducted in the VDB hall of fame in 2012, when it was the starring band of the Holiday Show Series until 2014. Brunetto's band has played to date 30 years of Thursday nights in a local club. Another Columbus orchestra sharing over 20 years of weekly club gigs is Vaughn Weister's (formerly with Woody Herman) Famous Jazz Orchestra. These are two sentinel bands preserving the art of bandleaders, sidemen, soloists, writers, and arrangers presented weekly in Columbus, igniting newer generations to be impassioned by this music now some 90 years since its inception.

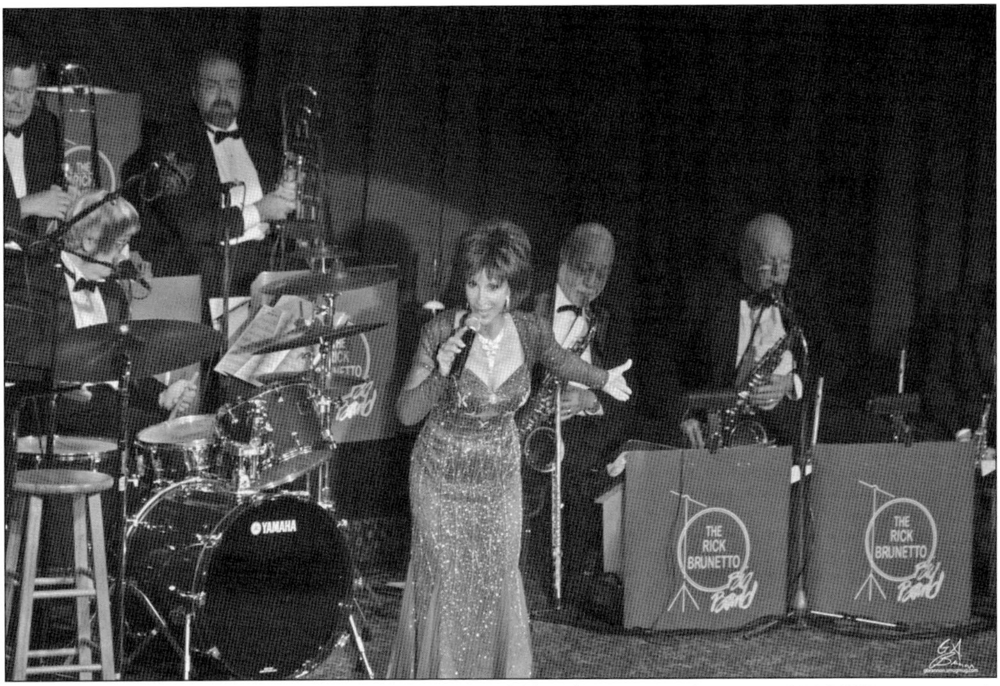

Deana Martin takes center stage, giving an incredible Christmas gift to over 800 VDB guests with her melodic voice and unbelievable sense of comedic timing. After each VDB show, the artist signed autographs and posed for photographs, quite gracious until the last guest left. (Graham Brannon Photography.)

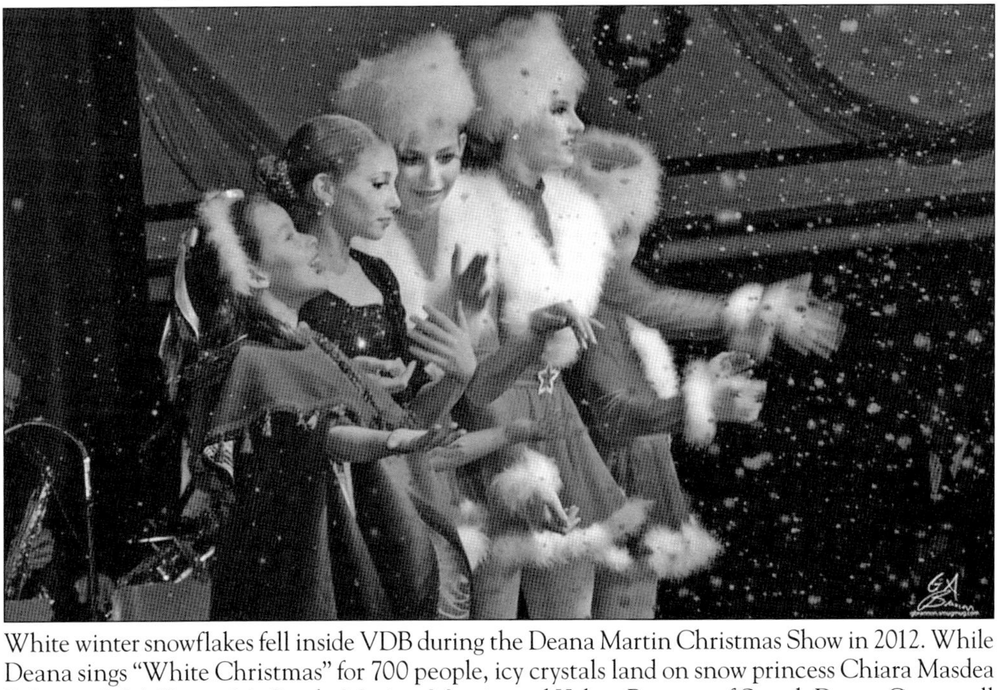
White winter snowflakes fell inside VDB during the Deana Martin Christmas Show in 2012. While Deana sings "White Christmas" for 700 people, icy crystals land on snow princess Chiara Masdea Baker with McKenzie McGrath, Marissa Morris, and Kelsey Ranney of Straub Dance Center, all dressed in ruby velvet costumes trimmed in white fur. (Graham Brannon Photography.)

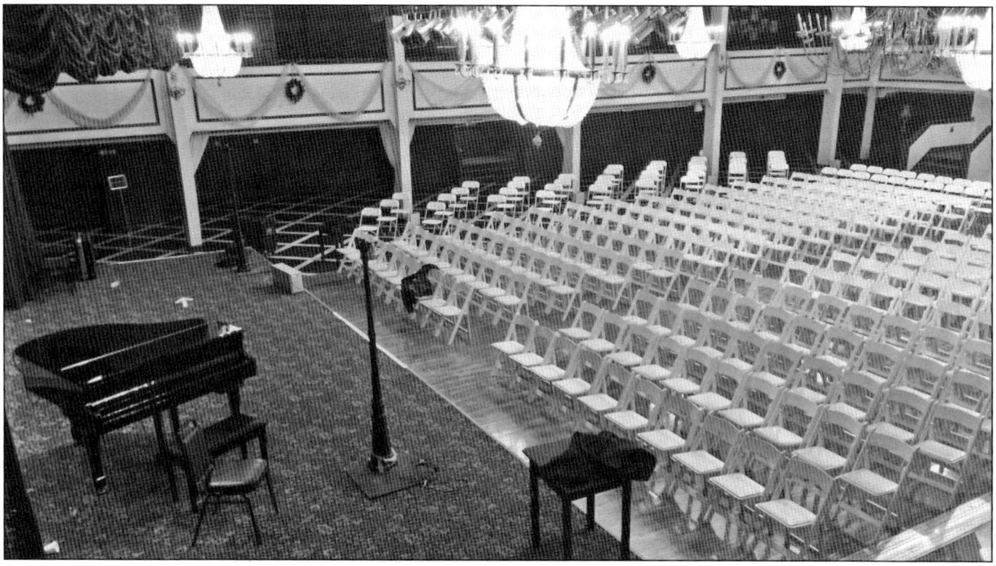

After the decline and return of big bands, VDB shared its stage with other genres and generations. On the quiet snowy night of December 12, 2013, the author invited her high school friends to VDB to relive moments of one of the great folk-rock duos of their generation. "VDB was as much a part of our teenage years as Simon and Garfunkel were," musician, Walter Adamkosky began, "and now they were going to converge in one marvelous evening. The intimacy of the venue made it seem more like an evening with Art Garfunkel than a concert. The performance further enhanced the comfortable mood, as Art, who asked not to be photographed, punctuated the audience's favorites with background stories and personal anecdotes." (Graham Brannon Photography.)

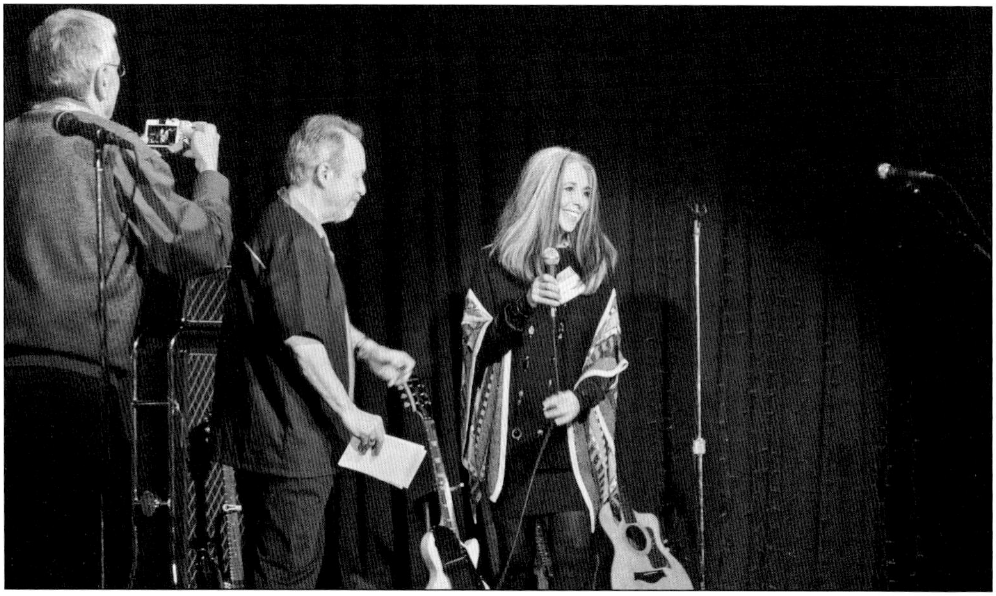

Although the author has participated in hundreds of VDB events since 1971, her perfect night was her 2014 VDB event, hosting 900 guests for the 50th anniversary of the Beatles on *The Ed Sullivan Show*. Proceeds benefited the Alzheimer's Association, stating, "one's precious memories should always be preserved." From left to right are Mike Adams, Chuck Gillespie, and Landa Masdea Brunetto. (Graham Brannon Photography.)

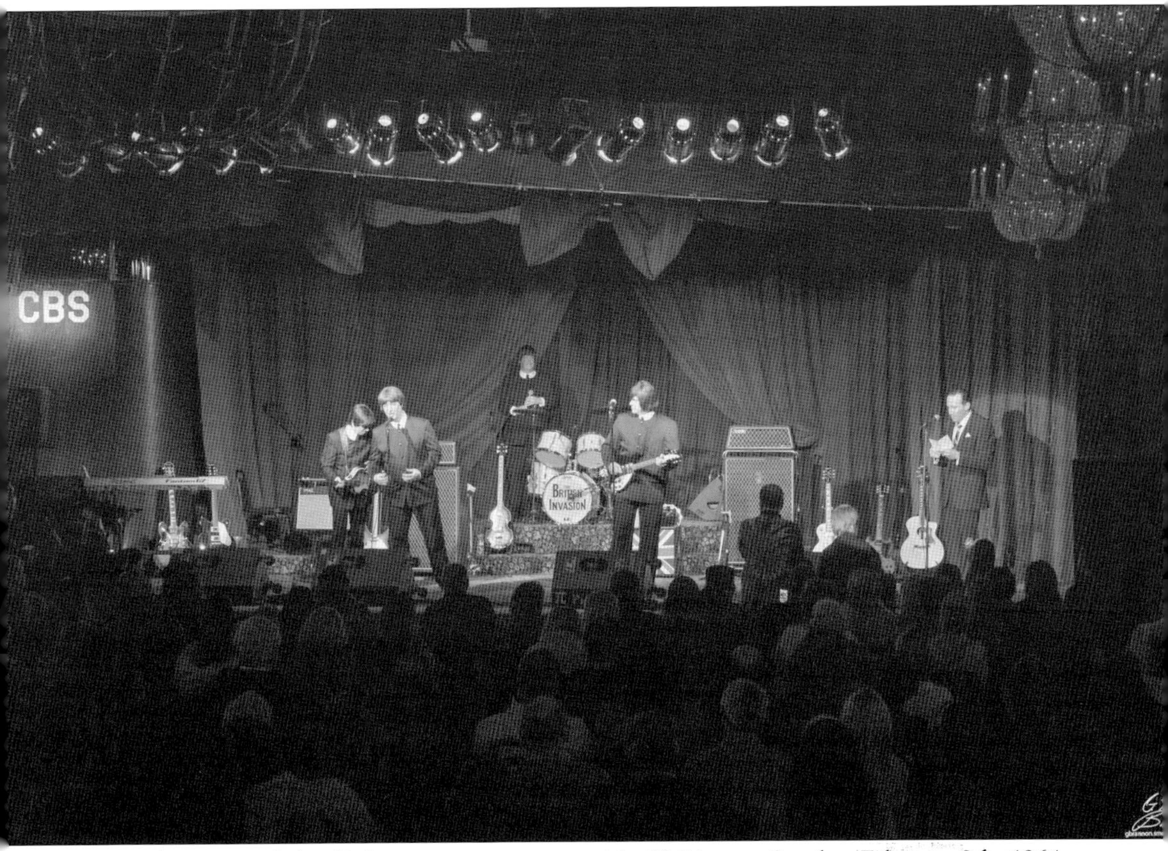

The author opened the 50th anniversary event with: "8:04 p.m., Sunday, February 9th, 1964, the moment that changed young girls' hearts, teenage boys' hair, and left parents' comfort levels severely shaken. That single moment transformed each one of a generation, forever." The ultimate 50-years-in-the-making party commemorating the Beatles on The Ed Sullivan Show began with former WCOL radio DJs of the day inside the iconic radio booths, spinning Top 40 hits from January 1 through February 8, 1964: music before the Beatles. At precisely 8:00 p.m., the actual 1964 television show was replayed on dual 10-foot screens. Immediately following the black-and-white film, a reenactment occurred, with actor Ken Erney as Ed Sullivan and Columbus-based Mersey-beat band the British Invasion playing Beatles tunes from 1964 through 1966. Radio and television commercials from February 1964 were presented all evening. The event also saluted WCOL who introduced the Beatles to their teen listeners. The City of Columbus sent emeritus council woman, Fran Ryan to present proclamations for the 1960s D.J. Bob Harrington, Mike Adams, Terry Wilson and Neal Martin (Shapiro). The British Invasion was made up of Tony Burlingame, Robb Anagnostis, Paul Minsterman, and Mike Clark (Evan Baisden is not pictured). (Graham Brannon Photography.)

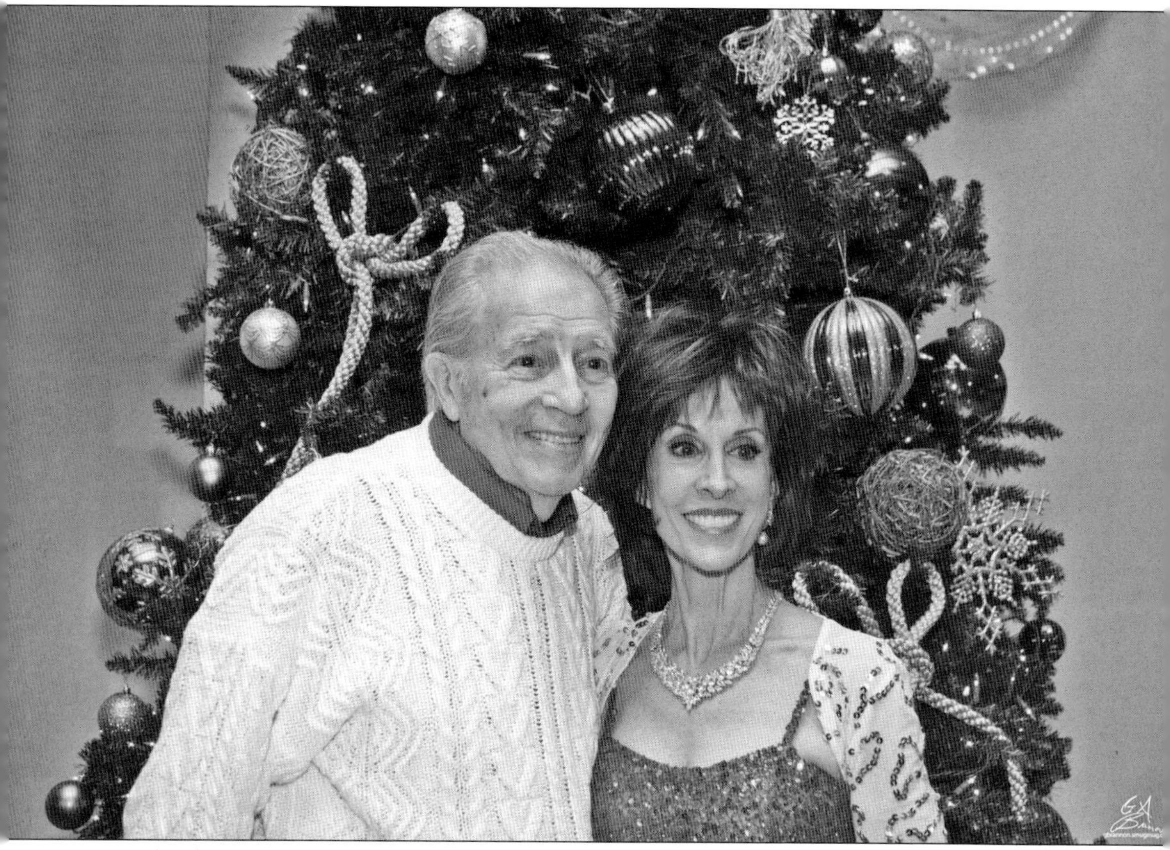

Joe Blundo, writing in the *Columbus Dispatch* about the passing of Bruno Masdea, stated: "'There was someone in heaven helping me with that,' singer Deana Martin whispered after flawlessly performing 'What Are You Doing New Year's Eve?' unrehearsed with the Rick Brunetto Big Band at a 2016 New Year's Eve performance. The someone was VDB bandleader Bruno Masdea, and the song was Bruno's favorite for his favorite night of the year. Deana visited Columbus multiple times, performing with Rick, Bruno's son-in-law and one of her musical arrangers, and Rick's band for the VDB Holiday Show Series from 2011 to 2013. She became close to Bruno after meeting him in 2010. Their first chat was about his favorite song, which she had recorded for her album. Each year on his birthday, she telephoned to sing him that song. Deana confided to the author how much she adored Bruno and how he was so much like her own father, commenting, "I feel like I have a dad again." Bruno reciprocated her admiration. As a bandleader, New Year's Eve was his preferred night to play, especially at VDB. Early in the afternoon of December 31, 2016, Deana called Bruno to singing to him his song on his day; a few hours later, the elegant 88-year-old musician passed from this earth. (Graham Brannon Photography.)

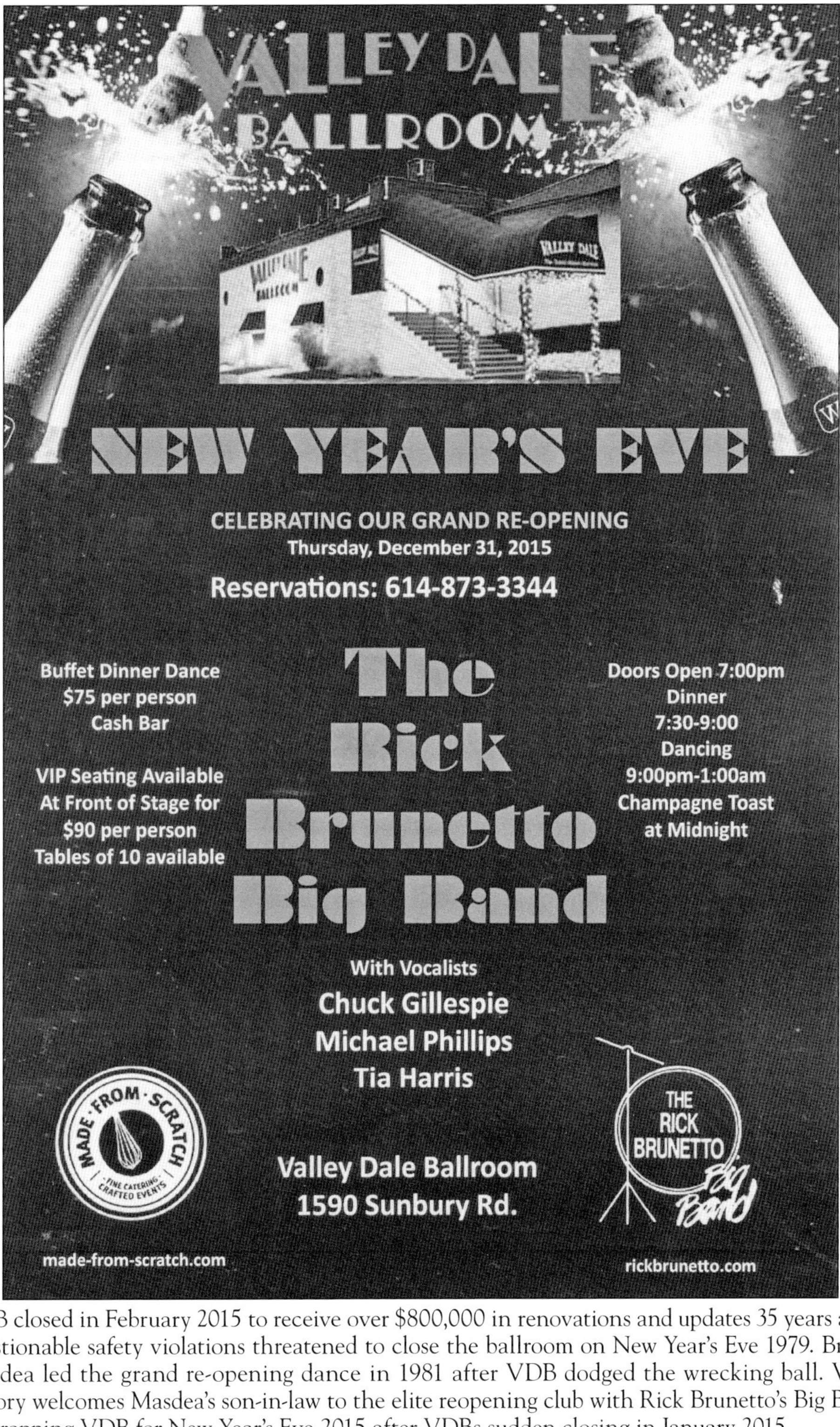

VDB closed in February 2015 to receive over $800,000 in renovations and updates 35 years after questionable safety violations threatened to close the ballroom on New Year's Eve 1979. Bruno Masdea led the grand re-opening dance in 1981 after VDB dodged the wrecking ball. VDB history welcomes Masdea's son-in-law to the elite reopening club with Rick Brunetto's Big Band unwrapping VDB for New Year's Eve 2015 after VDBs sudden closing in January 2015.

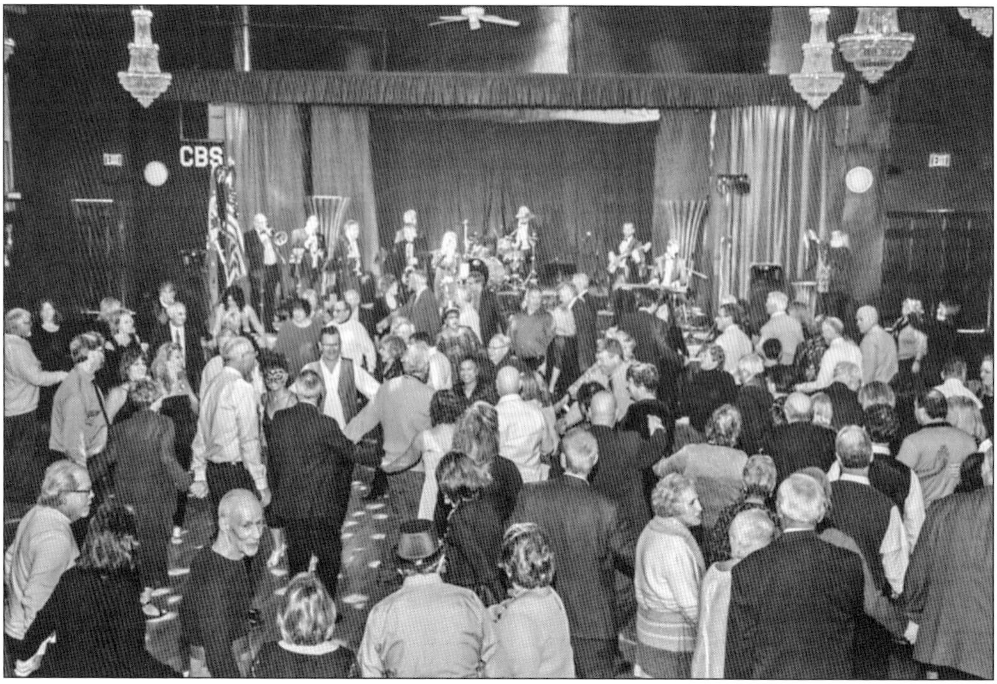

The year 2017 started the fresh "Ballroom Breakout" VDB concert series. The folk-rock-blues duchess Lucinda Williams helped to restore current music to VDB with her 1,000-person gate. Eddie Polina led one of Columbus's premier good-time party bands; formed in 1969, his band has played countless VDB events, most recently New Year's Eve 2017, shown in this image. (Larry Pishitelli Photography.)

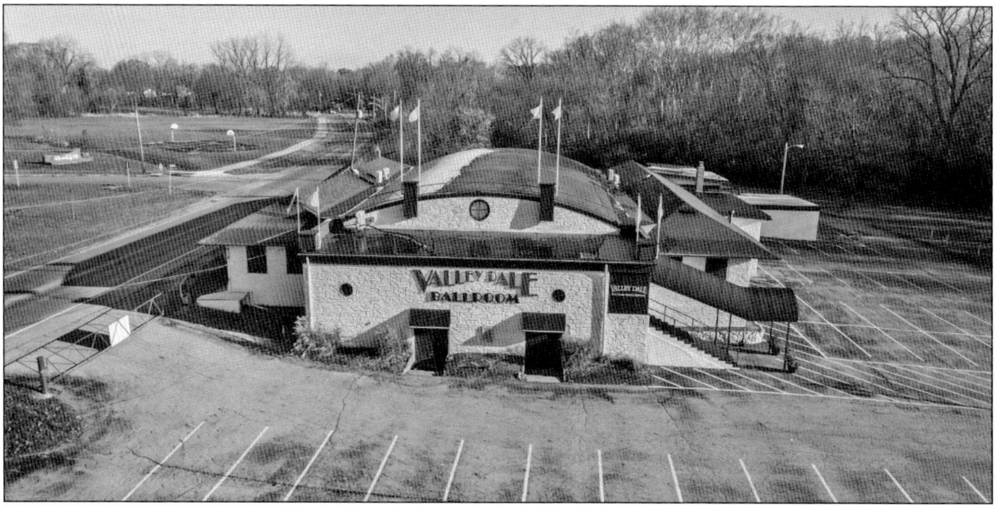

In 2018, the Valley Dale Ballroom history is kept safe by owners Mike and Kathy Peppe, and daily management is under Larry Clark's Made From Scratch Catering. The VDB is honored to celebrate its place on the National Register of Historic Places since 1983, remaining one of the crown jewels of Columbus, Ohio. VDB is seen from above in 2018. "Our Grand Dame" is painted glistening white—her signage is forest green with the ballroom letters in lipstick red. The admired shrine invites everyone reading this chronicle to tour this outstanding tribute to a bygone era and, in more than a few ways, a future era. (Larry Pishitelli Photography.)

AFTERWORD

A Family Affair

The Peppe family has been involved for most of the 100 years since Valley Dale opened. Nearly all of the big band leaders gave me signed photographs, some of which are blown up and displayed on the Valley Dale balcony. One of my fondest memories was when I was in college at Ohio State in the late 1960s. My dad called me and asked if I had ever heard of Frankie Valli and the Four Seasons. "Of course," I replied. Dad then asked if I would like to pay them and I jumped at the chance to actually meet Frankie Valli. He had asked to be paid in cash so that he could pay his band members. Valli was warm and friendly.

As the American music scene changed, the Dale changed. In the 1980s, I bought the Dale from my dad, and after an extensive renovation, including a complete sprinkler fire suppression system, we reopened with the Harry James big band. We promoted rock 'n' roll, reggae, country, R&B, and blues and secured TV and radio promotions.

Our hottest ticket each year was our Secret Santa–WTVN Beat Michigan Dance Party, my favorite event. The OSU band performed a modified script Ohio around the dancefloor, and the entire building pulsed with the music and crowds marching along. As the popularity of Valley Dale continued to rise, my wife, Kathy, and I found it difficult to manage the Dale with our full-time careers. I tried leasing the Dale to others, with mixed results.

Most recently, in 2016–2017, another expensive renovation has been accomplished, including new roofing and sanitary sewer service. My dad, Lou, and uncle Jim would be amazed and proud that Valley Dale Ballroom is one of the very few remaining ballrooms in America, surviving and thriving for its next 100 years.

—Mike Peppe

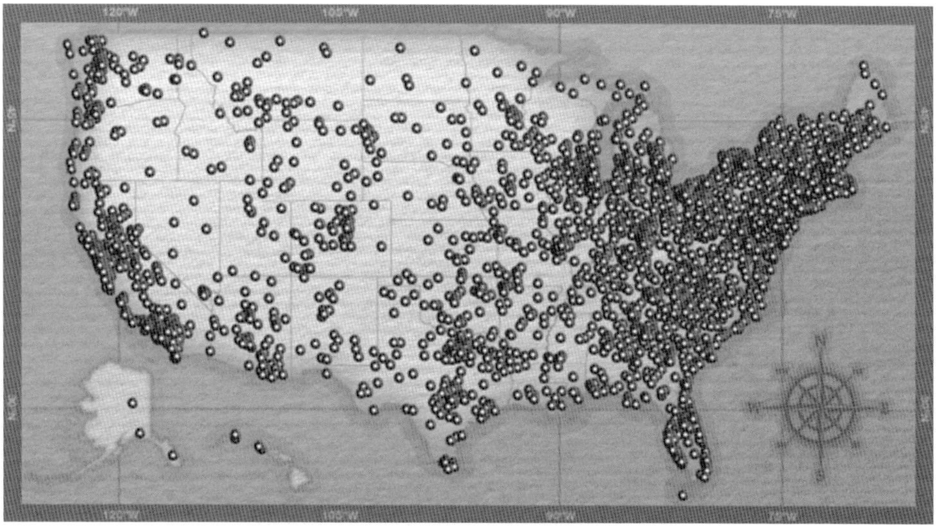